HOLT SCIENCE & TECHNOLOGY

Human Body Systems and Health

HOLT, RINEHART AND WINSTON

A Harcourt Education Company

Orlando • **Austin** • New York • San Diego • Toronto • London

Acknowledgments

Contributing Authors

Katy Z. Allen
Science Writer
Wayland, Massachusetts

Linda Ruth Berg, Ph.D.
Adjunct Professor
Natural Sciences
St. Petersburg College
St. Petersburg, Florida

Mark F. Taylor, Ph.D.
Associate Professor of Biology
Biology Department
Baylor University
Waco, Texas

Inclusion Specialist

Ellen McPeek Glisan
Special Needs Consultant
San Antonio, Texas

Safety Reviewer

Jack Gerlovich, Ph.D.
Associate Professor
School of Education
Drake University
Des Moines, Iowa

Academic Reviewers

William E. Dunscombe
Chairman
Biology Department
Union County College
Cranford, New Jersey

William Grisham, Ph.D.
Lecturer
Psychology Department
University of California, Los Angeles
Los Angeles, California

Ping H. Johnson, M.D., Ph.D., CHES
Assistant Professor of Health Education
Department of Health, Physical Education and Sport Science
Kennesaw State University
Kennesaw, Georgia

Linda Jones
Program Manager
Texas Department of Public Health
Austin, Texas

Eva Oberdoerster, Ph.D.
Lecturer
Department of Biology
Southern Methodist University
Dallas, Texas

Laurie Santos, Ph.D.
Assistant Professor
Department of Psychology
Yale University
New Haven, Connecticut

Teacher Reviewers

Diedre S. Adams
Physical Science Instructor
West Vigo Middle School
West Terre Haute, Indiana

Debra S. Kogelman, MAed.
Science Teacher
University of Chicago Laboratory Schools
Chicago, Illinois

Augie Maldonado
Science Teacher
Grisham Middle School
Round Rock, Texas

Jean Pletchette
Health Educator
Winterset Community Schools
Winterset, Iowa

Elizabeth Rustad
Science Teacher
Higley School District
Gilbert, Arizona

Helen P. Schiller
Instructional Coach
The School District of Greenville County
Greenville, South Carolina

Florence Vaughan
Science Teacher
University of Chicago Laboratory Schools
Chicago, Illinois

Lab Development

Diana Scheidle Bartos
Research Associate
School of Mines
Golden, Colorado

Carl Benson
General Science Teacher
Plains High School
Plains, Montana

Charlotte Blassingame
Technology Coordinator
White Station Middle School
Memphis, Tennessee

Marsha Carver
Science Teacher and Department Chair
McLean County High School
Calhoun, Kentucky

Kenneth E. Creese
Science Teacher
White Mountain Junior High School
Rock Springs, Wyoming

Linda Culp
Science Teacher and Department Chair
Thorndale High School
Thorndale, Texas

James Deaver
Science Teacher and Department Chair
West Point High School
West Point, Nebraska

Frank McKinney, Ph.D.
Professor of Geology
Appalachian State University
Boone, North Carolina

ISBN 0-03-025537-6

3 4 5 6 7 048 08 07 06 05 04

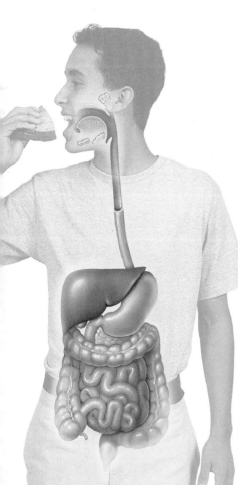

Human Body Systems and Health

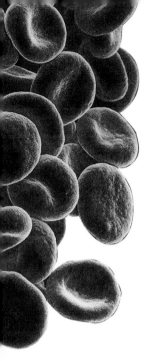
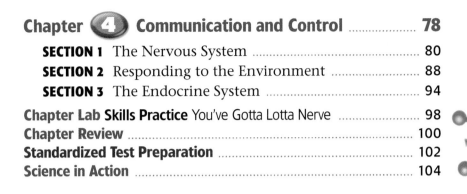

Labs and Activities

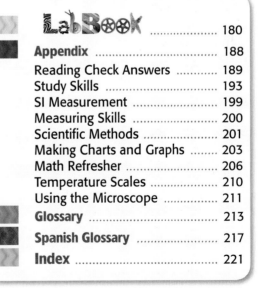

How to Use Your Textbook

Your Roadmap for Success with Holt Science and Technology

Reading Warm-Up

A Reading Warm-Up at the beginning of every section provides you with the section's objectives and key terms. The objectives tell you what you'll need to know after you finish reading the section.

Key terms are listed for each section. Learn the definitions of these terms because you will most likely be tested on them. Each key term is highlighted in the text and is defined at point of use and in the margin. You can also use the glossary to locate definitions quickly.

STUDY TIP Reread the objectives and the definitions to the key terms when studying for a test to be sure you know the material.

Get Organized

A Reading Strategy at the beginning of every section provides tips to help you organize and remember the information covered in the section. Keep a science notebook so that you are ready to take notes when your teacher reviews the material in class. Keep your assignments in this notebook so that you can review them when studying for the chapter test.

SECTION 1

Body Organization

Imagine jumping into a lake. At first, your body feels very cold. You may even shiver. But eventually you get used to the cold water. How?

Your body gets used to cold water because of homeostasis (HOH mee OH STAY sis). **Homeostasis** is the maintenance of a stable internal environment in the body. When you jump into a lake, homeostasis helps your body adapt to the cold water.

Cells, Tissues, and Organs

Maintaining homeostasis is not easy. Your internal environment is always changing. Your cells need nutrients and oxygen to survive. Your cells need wastes removed. If homeostasis is disrupted, cells may not get the materials they need. So, cells may be damaged or may die.

Your cells must do many jobs to maintain homeostasis. Fortunately, each of your cells does not have to do all of those jobs. Just as each person on a soccer team has a role during a game, each cell in your body has a job in maintaining homeostasis. Your cells are organized into groups. A group of similar cells working together forms a **tissue**. Your body has four main kinds of tissue. The four kinds of tissue are shown in **Figure 1**.

READING WARM-UP

Objectives
- Describe how tissues, organs, and organ systems are related.
- List 12 organ systems.
- Identify how organ systems work together to maintain homeostasis.

Terms to Learn

homeostasis   organ
tissue

READING STRATEGY

Reading Organizer As you read this section, make a concept map by using the terms above.

homeostasis the maintenance of a constant internal state in a changing environment

tissue a group of similar cells that perform a common function

Figure 1   Four Kinds of Tissue

Epithelial tissue covers and protects underlying tissue. When you look at the surface of your skin, you see epithelial tissue. The cells form a continuous sheet.

Nervous tissue sends electrical signals through the body. It is found in the brain, nerves, and sense organs.

580   Chapter 22   Body Organization and Structure

Be Resourceful—Use the Web

SCiLINKS.

Internet Connect boxes in your textbook take you to resources that you can use for science projects, reports, and research papers. Go to scilinks.org, and type in the SciLinks code to get information on a topic.

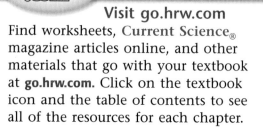

go.hrw.com

Visit go.hrw.com Find worksheets, Current Science® magazine articles online, and other materials that go with your textbook at **go.hrw.com.** Click on the textbook icon and the table of contents to see all of the resources for each chapter.

Figure 2 Organization of the Stomach

The stomach is an organ. The four kinds of tissue work together so that the stomach can carry out digestion.

Nervous tissue in the stomach partly controls the production of acids that aid in the digestion of food. Nervous tissue signals when the stomach is full.

Epithelial tissue lines the stomach.

Blood and another connective tissue called collagen are found in the wall of the stomach.

Layers of muscle tissue break up stomach contents.

Tissues Form Organs

One kind of tissue alone cannot do all of the things that several kinds of tissue working together can do. Two or more tissues working together form an **organ.** Your stomach, shown in **Figure 2,** uses all four kinds of tissue to carry out digestion.

organ a collection of tissues that carry out a specialized function of the body

Organs Form Systems

Your stomach does a lot to help you digest your food. But the stomach doesn't do it all. Your stomach works with other organs, such as the small and large intestines, to digest your food. Organs that work together make up an *organ system.*

Reading Check How is the stomach part of an organ system? *(See the Appendix for answers to Reading Checks.)*

Muscle tissue is made of cells that contract and relax to produce movement

Connective tissue

Nervous System Your nervous system receives and sends electrical messages throughout your body.

Digestive System Your digestive system breaks down the food you eat into nutrients that your body can absorb.

Lymphatic System The lymphatic system returns leaked fluids to blood vessels and helps get rid of bacteria and viruses.

Endocrine System Your glands send out chemical messages. Ovaries and testes are part of this system.

SECTION Review

Summary

- A group of cells that work together is a tissue. Tissues form organs. Organs that work together form organ systems.
- There are four kinds of tissue in the human body.
- There are 12 major organ systems in the human body.
- Organ systems work together to help the body maintain homeostasis.

Using Key Terms

1. Use the following terms in the same sentence: *homeostasis, tissue,* and *organ.*

Understanding Key Ideas

2. Which of the following statements describes how tissues, organs, and organ systems are related?
   a. Organs form tissues, which form organ systems.
   b. Organ systems form organs, which form tissues.
   c. Tissues form organs, which form organ systems.
   d. None of the above

3. List the 12 organ systems.

Math Skills

4. The human skeleton has 206 bones. The human skull has 22 bones. What percentage of human bones are skull bones?

Critical Thinking

5. **Applying Concepts** Tanya went to a restaurant and ate a hamburger. Describe how Tanya used five organ systems to eat and digest her hamburger.

6. **Predicting Consequences** Predict what might happen if the human body did not have specialized cells, tissues, organs, and organ systems to maintain homeostasis.

SciLINKS. Developed and maintained by the National Science Teachers Association

For a variety of links related to this chapter, go to www.scilinks.org

Topic: Tissues and Organs; Body Systems
SciLinks code: HSM1530; HSM0184

583

Use the Illustrations and Photos

Art shows complex ideas and processes. Learn to analyze the art so that you better understand the material you read in the text.

Tables and graphs display important information in an organized way to help you see relationships.

A picture is worth a thousand words. Look at the photographs to see relevant examples of science concepts that you are reading about.

Answer the Section Reviews

Section Reviews test your knowledge of the main points of the section. Critical Thinking items challenge you to think about the material in greater depth and to find connections that you infer from the text.

STUDY TIP When you can't answer a question, reread the section. The answer is usually there.

Do Your Homework

Your teacher may assign worksheets to help you understand and remember the material in the chapter.

STUDY TIP Don't try to answer the questions without reading the text and reviewing your class notes. A little preparation up front will make your homework assignments a lot easier. Answering the items in the Chapter Review will help prepare you for the chapter test.

Holt Online Learning

Visit Holt Online Learning
If your teacher gives you a special password to log onto the Holt Online Learning site, you'll find your complete textbook on the Web. In addition, you'll find some great learning tools and practice quizzes. You'll be able to see how well you know the material from your textbook.

CNN Student News

Visit CNN Student News
You'll find up-to-date events in science at cnnstudentnews.com.

SAFETY FIRST!

Exploring, inventing, and investigating are essential to the study of science. However, these activities can also be dangerous. To make sure that your experiments and explorations are safe, you must be aware of a variety of safety guidelines. You have probably heard of the saying, "It is better to be safe than sorry." This is particularly true in a science classroom where experiments and explorations are being performed. Being uninformed and careless can result in serious injuries. Don't take chances with your own safety or with anyone else's.

The following pages describe important guidelines for staying safe in the science classroom. Your teacher may also have safety guidelines and tips that are specific to your classroom and laboratory. Take the time to be safe.

Safety Rules!

Start Out Right

Always get your teacher's permission before attempting any laboratory exploration. Read the procedures carefully, and pay particular attention to safety information and caution statements. If you are unsure about what a safety symbol means, look it up or ask your teacher. You cannot be too careful when it comes to safety. If an accident does occur, inform your teacher immediately regardless of how minor you think the accident is.

Safety Symbols

All of the experiments and investigations in this book and their related worksheets include important safety symbols to alert you to particular safety concerns. Become familiar with these symbols so that when you see them, you will know what they mean and what to do. It is important that you read this entire safety section to learn about specific dangers in the laboratory.

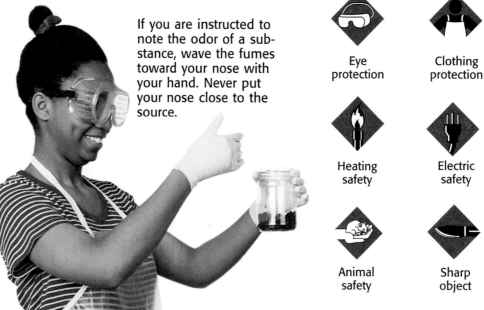

If you are instructed to note the odor of a substance, wave the fumes toward your nose with your hand. Never put your nose close to the source.

Eye protection

Clothing protection

Hand safety

Heating safety

Electric safety

Chemical safety

Animal safety

Sharp object

Plant safety

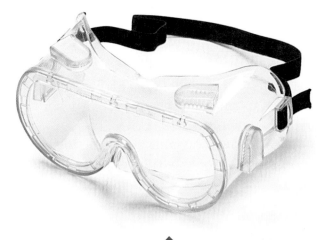

Eye Safety

Wear safety goggles when working around chemicals, acids, bases, or any type of flame or heating device. Wear safety goggles any time there is even the slightest chance that harm could come to your eyes. If any substance gets into your eyes, notify your teacher immediately and flush your eyes with running water for at least 15 minutes. Treat any unknown chemical as if it were a dangerous chemical. Never look directly into the sun. Doing so could cause permanent blindness.

Avoid wearing contact lenses in a laboratory situation. Even if you are wearing safety goggles, chemicals can get between the contact lenses and your eyes. If your doctor requires that you wear contact lenses instead of glasses, wear eye-cup safety goggles in the lab.

Safety Equipment

Know the locations of the nearest fire alarms and any other safety equipment, such as fire blankets and eyewash fountains, as identified by your teacher, and know the procedures for using the equipment.

Neatness

Keep your work area free of all unnecessary books and papers. Tie back long hair, and secure loose sleeves or other loose articles of clothing, such as ties and bows. Remove dangling jewelry. Don't wear open-toed shoes or sandals in the laboratory. Never eat, drink, or apply cosmetics in a laboratory setting. Food, drink, and cosmetics can easily become contaminated with dangerous materials.

Certain hair products (such as aerosol hair spray) are flammable and should not be worn while working near an open flame. Avoid wearing hair spray or hair gel on lab days.

Sharp/Pointed Objects

Use knives and other sharp instruments with extreme care. Never cut objects while holding them in your hands. Place objects on a suitable work surface for cutting.

Be extra careful when using any glassware. When adding a heavy object to a graduated cylinder, tilt the cylinder so the object slides slowly to the bottom.

Heat

Wear safety goggles when using a heating device or a flame. Whenever possible, use an electric hot plate as a heat source instead of using an open flame. When heating materials in a test tube, always angle the test tube away from yourself and others. To avoid burns, wear heat-resistant gloves whenever instructed to do so.

Electricity

Be careful with electrical cords. When using a microscope with a lamp, do not place the cord where it could trip someone. Do not let cords hang over a table edge in a way that could cause equipment to fall if the cord is accidentally pulled. Do not use equipment with damaged cords. Be sure that your hands are dry and that the electrical equipment is in the "off" position before plugging it in. Turn off and unplug electrical equipment when you are finished.

Chemicals

Wear safety goggles when handling any potentially dangerous chemicals, acids, or bases. If a chemical is unknown, handle it as you would a dangerous chemical. Wear an apron and protective gloves when you work with acids or bases or whenever you are told to do so. If a spill gets on your skin or clothing, rinse it off immediately with water for at least 5 minutes while calling to your teacher.

Never mix chemicals unless your teacher tells you to do so. Never taste, touch, or smell chemicals unless you are specifically directed to do so. Before working with a flammable liquid or gas, check for the presence of any source of flame, spark, or heat.

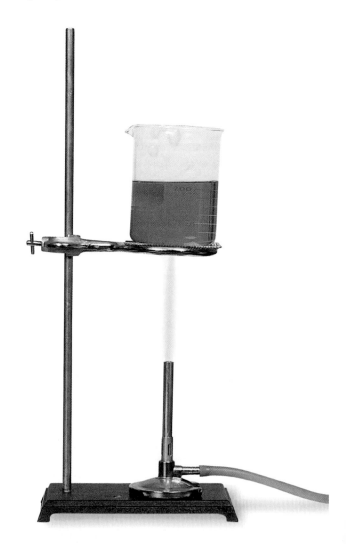

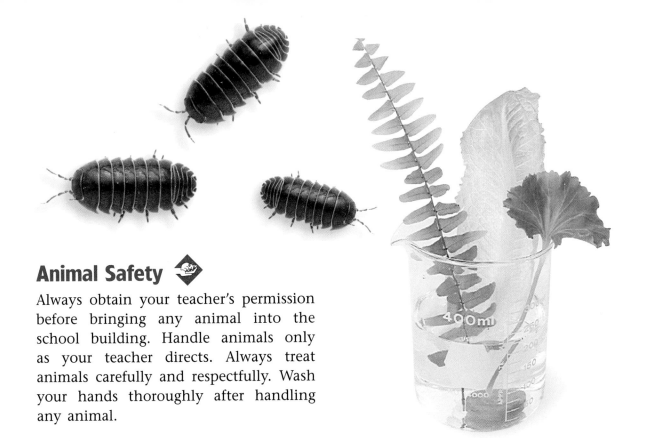

Animal Safety

Always obtain your teacher's permission before bringing any animal into the school building. Handle animals only as your teacher directs. Always treat animals carefully and respectfully. Wash your hands thoroughly after handling any animal.

Plant Safety

Do not eat any part of a plant or plant seed used in the laboratory. Wash your hands thoroughly after handling any part of a plant. When in nature, do not pick any wild plants unless your teacher instructs you to do so.

Glassware

Examine all glassware before use. Be sure that glassware is clean and free of chips and cracks. Report damaged glassware to your teacher. Glass containers used for heating should be made of heat-resistant glass.

1

Body Organization and Structure

About the

Lance Armstrong has won the Tour de France several times. These victories are especially remarkable because he was diagnosed with cancer in 1996. But with medicine and hard work, he grew strong enough to win one of the toughest events in all of sports.

PRE-READING ACTIVITY

FOLDNOTES 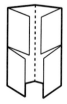 **Four-Corner Fold**
Before you read the chapter, create the FoldNote entitled "Four-Corner Fold" described in the **Study Skills** section of the Appendix. Label the flaps of the four-corner fold with "The skeletal system," "The muscular system," and "The integumentary system." Write what you know about each topic under the appropriate flap. As you read the chapter, add other information that you learn.

START-UP ACTIVITY

Too Cold for Comfort

Your nervous system sends you messages about your body. For example, if someone steps on your toe, your nervous system sends you a message. The pain you feel is a message that tells you to move your toe to safety. Try this exercise to watch your nervous system in action.

Procedure

1. Hold **a few pieces of ice** in one hand. Allow the melting water to drip into a **dish.** Hold the ice until the cold is uncomfortable. Then, release the ice into the dish.

2. Compare the hand that held the ice with your other hand. Describe the changes you see.

Analysis

1. What message did you receive from your nervous system while you held the ice?

2. How quickly did the cold hand return to normal?

3. What organ systems do you think helped restore your hand to normal?

4. Think of a time when your nervous system sent you a message, such as an uncomfortable feeling of heat, cold, or pain. How did your body react?

Body Organization

Imagine jumping into a lake. At first, your body feels very cold. You may even shiver. But eventually you get used to the cold water. How?

Your body gets used to cold water because of homeostasis (HOH mee OH STAY sis). **Homeostasis** is the maintenance of a stable internal environment in the body. When you jump into a lake, homeostasis helps your body adapt to the cold water.

Cells, Tissues, and Organs

Maintaining homeostasis is not easy. Your internal environment is always changing. Your cells need nutrients and oxygen to survive. Your cells need wastes removed. If homeostasis is disrupted, cells may not get the materials they need. So, cells may be damaged or may die.

Your cells must do many jobs to maintain homeostasis. Fortunately, each of your cells does not have to do all of those jobs. Just as each person on a soccer team has a role during a game, each cell in your body has a job in maintaining homeostasis. Your cells are organized into groups. A group of similar cells working together forms a **tissue.** Your body has four main kinds of tissue. The four kinds of tissue are shown in **Figure 1.**

homeostasis the maintenance of a constant internal state in a changing environment

tissue a group of similar cells that perform a common function

---

Figure 1   Four Kinds of Tissue

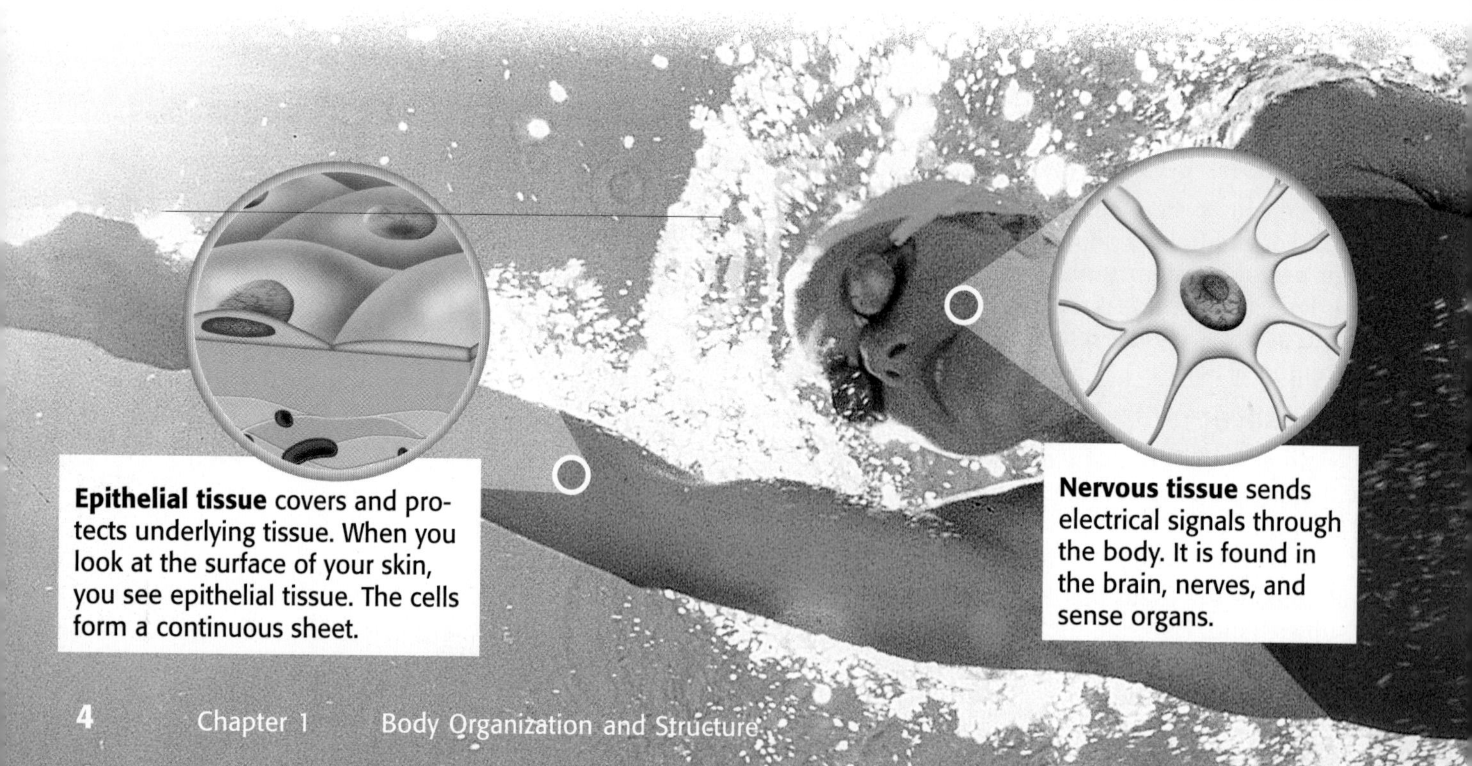

Epithelial tissue covers and protects underlying tissue. When you look at the surface of your skin, you see epithelial tissue. The cells form a continuous sheet.

Nervous tissue sends electrical signals through the body. It is found in the brain, nerves, and sense organs.

Figure 2 Organization of the Stomach

The stomach is an organ. The four kinds of tissue work together so that the stomach can carry out digestion.

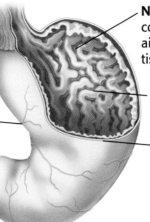

Nervous tissue in the stomach partly controls the production of acids that aid in the digestion of food. Nervous tissue signals when the stomach is full.

Epithelial tissue lines the stomach.

Blood and another **connective tissue** called *collagen* are found in the wall of the stomach.

Layers of **muscle tissue** break up stomach contents.

Tissues Form Organs

One kind of tissue alone cannot do all of the things that several kinds of tissue working together can do. Two or more tissues working together form an **organ.** Your stomach, shown in **Figure 2,** uses all four kinds of tissue to carry out digestion.

organ a collection of tissues that carry out a specialized function of the body

Organs Form Systems

Your stomach does a lot to help you digest your food. But the stomach doesn't do it all. Your stomach works with other organs, such as the small and large intestines, to digest your food. Organs that work together make up an *organ system.*

✓ Reading Check How is the stomach part of an organ system? *(See the Appendix for answers to Reading Checks.)*

Muscle tissue is made of cells that contract and relax to produce movement.

Connective tissue joins, supports, protects, insulates, nourishes, and cushions organs. It also keeps organs from falling apart.

Working Together

Organ systems work together to maintain homeostasis. Your body has 12 major organ systems, as shown in **Figure 3**. The circulatory and cardiovascular systems are shown together. The cardiovascular system includes your heart and blood vessels. Additionally, these organs are part of the circulatory system, which also includes blood. Together, these two systems deliver the materials your cells need to survive. This is just one example of how organ systems work together to keep you healthy.

✓ **Reading Check** Give an example of how organ systems work together in the body.

Figure 3 **Organ Systems**

 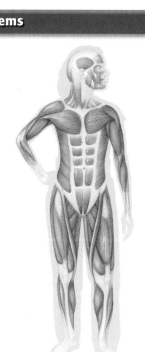 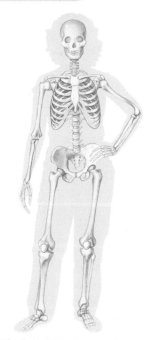 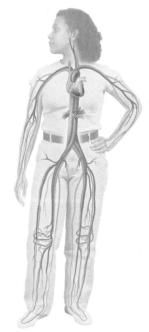

Integumentary System Your skin, hair, and nails protect the tissue that lies beneath them.

Muscular System Your muscular system works with the skeletal system to help you move.

Skeletal System Your bones provide a frame to support and protect your body parts.

Cardiovascular and Circulatory Systems Your heart pumps blood through all of your blood vessels.

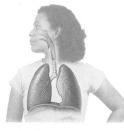 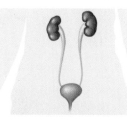  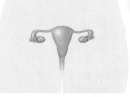

Respiratory System Your lungs absorb oxygen and release carbon dioxide.

Urinary System Your urinary system removes wastes from the blood and regulates your body's fluids.

Male Reproductive System The male reproductive system produces and delivers sperm.

Female Reproductive System The female reproductive system produces eggs and nourishes and protects the fetus.

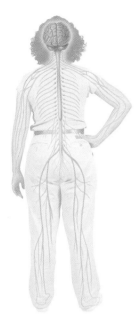

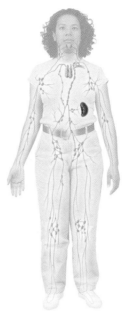

Nervous System Your nervous system receives and sends electrical messages throughout your body.

Digestive System Your digestive system breaks down the food you eat into nutrients that your body can absorb.

Lymphatic System The lymphatic system returns leaked fluids to blood vessels and helps get rid of bacteria and viruses.

Endocrine System Your glands send out chemical messages. Ovaries and testes are part of this system.

SECTION Review

Summary

- A group of cells that work together is a tissue. Tissues form organs. Organs that work together form organ systems.

- There are four kinds of tissue in the human body.

- There are 12 major organ systems in the human body.

- Organ systems work together to help the body maintain homeostasis.

Using Key Terms

1. Use the following terms in the same sentence: *homeostasis*, *tissue*, and *organ*.

Understanding Key Ideas

2. Which of the following statements describes how tissues, organs, and organ systems are related?
   a. Organs form tissues, which form organ systems.
   b. Organ systems form organs, which form tissues.
   c. Tissues form organs, which form organ systems.
   d. None of the above

3. List the 12 organ systems.

Math Skills

4. The human skeleton has 206 bones. The human skull has 22 bones. What percentage of human bones are skull bones?

Critical Thinking

5. **Applying Concepts** Tanya went to a restaurant and ate a hamburger. Describe how Tanya used five organ systems to eat and digest her hamburger.

6. **Predicting Consequences** Predict what might happen if the human body did not have specialized cells, tissues, organs, and organ systems to maintain homeostasis.

SCLINKS®

NSTA
Developed and maintained by the National Science Teachers Association

For a variety of links related to this chapter, go to www.scilinks.org

Topic: Tissues and Organs; Body Systems
SciLinks code: HSM1530; HSM0184

The Skeletal System

When you hear the word skeleton, *you may think of the remains of something that has died. But your skeleton is not dead. It is very much alive.*

You may think your bones are dry and brittle. But they are alive and active. Bones, cartilage, and the connective tissue that holds bones together make up your **skeletal system.**

Bones

The average adult human skeleton has 206 bones. Bones help support and protect parts of your body. They work with your muscles so you can move. Bones also help your body maintain homeostasis by storing minerals and making blood cells. **Figure 1** shows the functions of your skeleton.

READING WARM-UP

Objectives
- Identify the major organs of the skeletal system.
- Describe four functions of bones.
- Describe three joints.
- List three injuries and two diseases that affect bones and joints.

Terms to Learn
skeletal system
joint

READING STRATEGY

Reading Organizer As you read this section, create an outline of the section. Use the headings from the section in your outline.

skeletal system the organ system whose primary function is to support and protect the body and to allow the body to move

Figure 1 The Skeleton

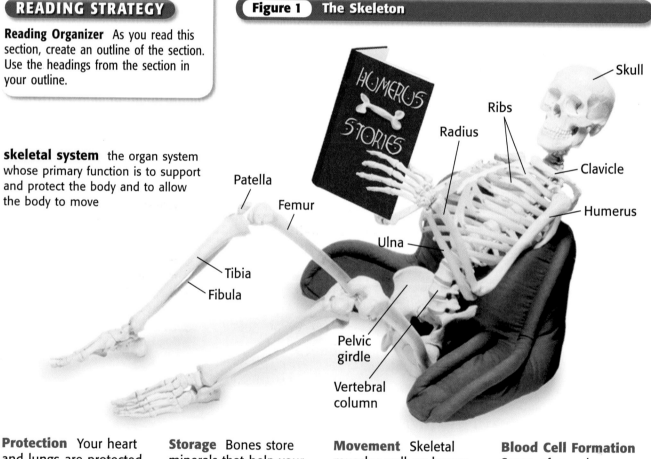

Skull
Ribs
Radius
Clavicle
Humerus
Patella
Femur
Ulna
Tibia
Fibula
Pelvic girdle
Vertebral column

Protection Your heart and lungs are protected by ribs, your spinal cord is protected by vertebrae, and your brain is protected by the skull.

Storage Bones store minerals that help your nerves and muscles function properly. Long bones store fat that can be used for energy.

Movement Skeletal muscles pull on bones to produce movement. Without bones, you would not be able to sit, stand, walk, or run.

Blood Cell Formation Some of your bones are filled with a special material that makes blood cells. This material is called *marrow.*

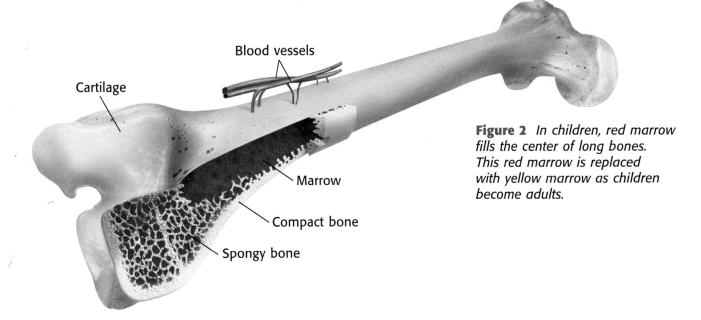

Cartilage

Blood vessels

Marrow

Compact bone

Spongy bone

Figure 2 *In children, red marrow fills the center of long bones. This red marrow is replaced with yellow marrow as children become adults.*

Bone Structure

A bone may seem lifeless. But a bone is a living organ made of several different tissues. Bone is made of connective tissue and minerals. These minerals are deposited by living cells called *osteoblasts* (AHS tee oh BLASTS).

If you look inside a bone, you will notice two kinds of bone tissue. If the bone tissue does not have any visible open spaces, it is called *compact bone*. Compact bone is rigid and dense. Tiny canals within compact bone contain small blood vessels. Bone tissue that has many open spaces is called *spongy bone*. Spongy bone provides most of the strength and support for a bone.

Bones contain a soft tissue called *marrow*. There are two types of marrow. Red marrow produces both red and white blood cells. Yellow marrow, found in the central cavity of long bones, stores fat. **Figure 2** shows a cross section of a long bone, the femur.

Bone Growth

Did you know that most of your skeleton used to be soft and rubbery? Most bones start out as a flexible tissue called *cartilage*. When you were born, you didn't have much true bone. But as you grew, most of the cartilage was replaced by bone. During childhood, most bones still have growth plates of cartilage. These growth plates provide a place for bones to continue to grow.

Feel the end of your nose. Or bend the top of your ear. These areas are two places where cartilage is never replaced by bone. These areas stay flexible.

✓ **Reading Check** How do bones grow? (*See the Appendix for answers to Reading Checks.*)

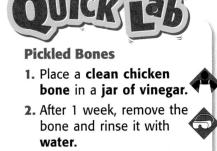

Pickled Bones

1. Place a **clean chicken bone** in a **jar of vinegar.**
2. After 1 week, remove the bone and rinse it with **water.**
3. Describe the changes that you can see or feel.
4. How has the bone's strength changed?
5. What did the vinegar remove?

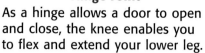

Gliding Joint

Gliding joints allow bones in the hand and wrist to glide over one another and give some flexibility to the area.

Ball-and-Socket Joint

As a video-game joystick lets you move your character all around, the shoulder lets your arm move freely in all directions.

Hinge Joint

As a hinge allows a door to open and close, the knee enables you to flex and extend your lower leg.

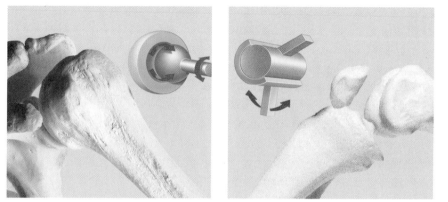

Joints

A place where two or more bones meet is called a **joint.** Your joints allow your body to move when your muscles contract. Some joints, such as fixed joints, allow little or no movement. Many of the joints in the skull are fixed joints. Other joints, such as your shoulder, allow a lot of movement. Joints can be classified based on how the bones in a joint move. For example, your shoulder is a ball-and-socket joint. Three joints are shown in **Figure 3.**

Joints are held together by *ligaments* (LIG uh muhnts). Ligaments are strong elastic bands of connective tissue. They connect the bones in a joint. Also, cartilage covers the ends of many bones. Cartilage helps cushion the area in a joint where bones meet.

joint a place where two or more bones meet

✓ **Reading Check** Describe the basic structure of joints.

CONNECTION TO Environmental Science

WRITING SKILL **Bones from the Ocean** Sometimes, a bone or joint may become so damaged that it needs to be repaired or replaced with surgery. Often, replacement parts are made from a metal, such as titanium. However, some scientists have discovered that coral skeletons from coral reefs in the ocean can be used to replace human bone. Research bone surgery. Identify why doctors use metals such as titanium. Then, identify the advantages that coral may offer. Write a report discussing your findings.

Skeletal System Injuries and Diseases

Sometimes, parts of the skeletal system are injured. As shown in **Figure 4,** bones may be fractured, or broken. Joints can also be injured. A dislocated joint is a joint in which one or more bones have been moved out of place. Another joint injury, called a *sprain*, happens if a ligament is stretched too far or torn.

There are also diseases of the skeletal system. *Osteoporosis* (AHS tee OH puh ROH sis) is a disease that causes bones to become less dense. Bones become weak and break more easily. Age and poor eating habits can make it more likely for people to develop osteoporosis. Other bone diseases affect the marrow or make bones soft. A disease that affects the joints is called *arthritis* (ahr THRIET is). Arthritis is painful. Joints may swell or stiffen. As they get older, some people are more likely to have some types of arthritis.

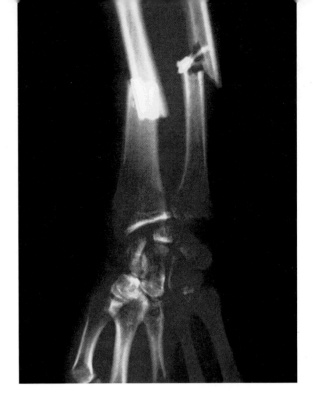

Figure 4 *This X ray shows that the two bones of the forearm have been fractured, or broken.*

SECTION Review

Summary

- The skeletal system includes bones, cartilage, and the connective tissue that connects bones.
- Bones protect the body, store minerals, allow movement, and make blood cells.
- Joints are places where two or more bones meet.
- Skeletal system injuries include fractures, dislocations, and sprains. Skeletal system diseases include osteoporosis and arthritis.

Using Key Terms

1. In your own words, write a definition for the term *skeletal system.*

Understanding Key Ideas

2. Which of the following is NOT an organ of the skeletal system?
   a. bone
   b. cartilage
   c. muscle
   d. None of the above

3. Describe four functions of bones.

4. What are three joints?

5. Describe two diseases that affect the skeletal system.

Math Skills

6. A broken bone usually heals in about six weeks. A mild sprain takes one-third as long to heal. In days, about how long does it take a mild sprain to heal?

Critical Thinking

7. **Identifying Relationships** Red bone marrow produces blood cells. Children have red bone marrow in their long bones, while adults have yellow bone marrow, which stores fat. Why might adults and children have different kinds of marrow?

8. **Predicting Consequences** What might happen if children's bones didn't have growth plates of cartilage?

SCiLINKS®

NSTA
Developed and maintained by the
National Science Teachers Association

For a variety of links related to this chapter, go to www.scilinks.org

Topic: Skeletal System
SciLinks code: HSM1399

11

The Muscular System

Have you ever tried to sit still, without moving any muscles at all, for one minute? It's impossible! Somewhere in your body, muscles are always working.

Your heart is a muscle. Muscles make you breathe. And muscles hold you upright. If all of your muscles rested at the same time, you would collapse. The **muscular system** is made up of the muscles that let you move.

Kinds of Muscle

Figure 1 shows the three kinds of muscle in your body. *Smooth muscle* is found in the digestive tract and in the walls of blood vessels. *Cardiac muscle* is found only in your heart. *Skeletal muscle* is attached to your bones for movement. Skeletal muscle also helps protect your inner organs.

Muscle action can be voluntary or involuntary. Muscle action that is under your control is *voluntary*. Muscle action that is not under your control is *involuntary*. Smooth muscle and cardiac muscle are involuntary muscles. Skeletal muscles can be both voluntary and involuntary muscles. For example, you can blink your eyes anytime you want to. But your eyes will also blink automatically.

Figure 1 Three Kinds of Muscle

Skeletal muscle enables bones to move.

Smooth muscle moves food through the digestive system.

Cardiac muscle pumps blood around the body.

Figure 2 **A Pair of Muscles in the Arm**

Skeletal muscles, such as the biceps and triceps muscles, work in pairs. When the biceps muscle contracts, the arm bends. When the triceps muscle contracts, the arm straightens.

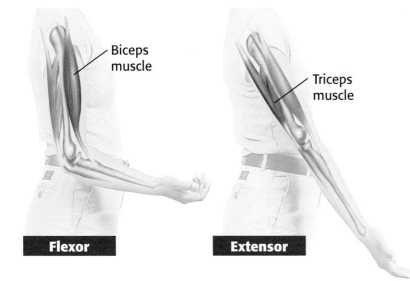

Biceps muscle

Triceps muscle

Flexor

Extensor

muscular system the organ system whose primary function is movement and flexibility

Movement

Skeletal muscles can make hundreds of movements. You can see many of these movements by watching a dancer, a swimmer, or even someone smiling or frowning. When you want to move, signals travel from your brain to your skeletal muscle cells. The muscle cells then contract, or get shorter.

Muscles Attach to Bones

Strands of tough connective tissue connect your skeletal muscles to your bones. These strands are called *tendons*. When a muscle that connects two bones gets shorter, the bones are pulled closer to each other. For example, tendons attach the biceps muscle to a bone in your shoulder and to a bone in your forearm. When the biceps muscle contracts, your forearm bends toward your shoulder.

Muscles Work in Pairs

Your skeletal muscles often work in pairs. Usually, one muscle in the pair bends part of the body. The other muscle straightens part of the body. A muscle that bends part of your body is called a *flexor* (FLEKS uhr). A muscle that straightens part of your body is an *extensor* (ek STEN suhr). As shown in **Figure 2,** the biceps muscle of the arm is a flexor. The triceps muscle of the arm is an extensor.

✓ **Reading Check** Describe how muscles work in pairs. (*See the Appendix for answers to Reading Checks.*)

SCHOOL to HOME

Power in Pairs
Ask a parent to sit in a chair and place a hand palm up under the edge of a table. Tell your parent to apply gentle upward pressure. Feel the front and back of your parent's upper arm. Next, ask your parent to push down on top of the table. Feel your parent's arm again. What did you notice about the muscles in your parent's arm when he or she was pressing up? pushing down?

Figure 3 *This girl is strengthening her heart and improving her endurance by doing aerobic exercise. This boy is doing resistance exercise to build strong muscles.*

Use It or Lose It

What happens when someone wears a cast for a broken arm? Skeletal muscles around the broken bone become smaller and weaker. The muscles weaken because they are not exercised. Exercised muscles are stronger and larger. Strong muscles can help other organs, too. For example, contracting muscles squeeze blood vessels. This action increases blood flow without needing more work from the heart.

Certain exercises can give muscles more strength and endurance. More endurance lets muscles work longer without getting tired. Two kinds of exercise can increase muscle strength and endurance. They are resistance exercise and aerobic exercise. You can see an example of each kind in **Figure 3.**

Resistance Exercise

Resistance exercise is a great way to strengthen skeletal muscles. During resistance exercise, people work against the resistance, or weight, of an object. Some resistance exercises, such as curl-ups, use your own weight for resistance.

Aerobic Exercise

Steady, moderately intense activity is called *aerobic exercise*. Jogging, cycling, skating, swimming, and walking are aerobic exercises. This kind of exercise can increase muscle strength. However, aerobic exercise mostly strengthens the heart and increases endurance.

CONNECTION TO Chemistry

Muscle Function Body chemistry is very important for healthy muscle function. Spasms or cramps happen if too much sweating, poor diet, or illness causes a chemical imbalance in muscles. Identify three chemicals that the body needs for muscles to work properly. Make a poster explaining how people can make sure that they have enough of each chemical.

ACTIVITY

Muscle Injury

Any exercise program should be started slowly. Starting slowly means you are less likely to get hurt. You should also warm up for exercise. A *strain* is an injury in which a muscle or tendon is overstretched or torn. Strains often happen because a muscle has not been warmed up. Strains also happen when muscles are worked too hard.

People who exercise too much can hurt their tendons. The body can't repair an injured tendon before the next exercise session. So, the tendon becomes inflamed. This condition is called *tendinitis*. Often, a long rest is needed for the injured tendon to heal.

Some people try to make their muscles stronger by taking drugs. These drugs are called *anabolic steroids* (A nuh BAH lik STER oidz). They can cause long-term health problems. Anabolic steroids can damage the heart, liver, and kidneys. They can also cause high blood pressure. If taken before the skeleton is mature, anabolic steroids can cause bones to stop growing.

Reading Check What are the risks of using anabolic steroids?

Runner's Time

Jan has decided to enter a 5 km road race. She now runs 5 km in 30 min. She would like to decrease her time by 15% before the race. What will her time be when she reaches her goal?

SECTION Review

Summary

- The three kinds of muscle tissue are smooth muscle, cardiac muscle, and skeletal muscle.
- Skeletal muscles work in pairs. Skeletal muscles contract to move bones.
- Resistance exercise improves muscle strength. Aerobic exercise improves heart strength and muscle endurance.
- Strains are injuries that affect muscles and tendons. Tendinitis affects tendons.

Using Key Terms

1. In your own words, write a definition for the term *muscular system*.

Understanding Key Ideas

2. Muscles
   a. work in pairs.
   b. move bones by relaxing.
   c. get smaller when exercised.
   d. All of the above

3. Describe three kinds of muscle.

4. List two kinds of exercise. Give an example of each.

5. Describe two muscular system injuries.

Math Skills

6. If Trey can do one curl-up every 2.5 s, about how long will it take him to do 35 curl-ups?

Critical Thinking

7. **Applying Concepts** Describe some of the muscle action needed to pick up a book. Include flexors and extensors in your description.

8. **Predicting Consequences** If aerobic exercise improves heart strength, what likely happens to heart rate as the heart gets stronger? Explain your answer.

Developed and maintained by the National Science Teachers Association

For a variety of links related to this chapter, go to www.scilinks.org

Topic: Muscular System
SciLinks code: HSM1008

SECTION 4

The Integumentary System

What part of your body has to be partly dead to keep you alive? Here are some clues: It comes in many colors, it is the largest organ in the body, and it is showing right now!

Did you guess your skin? If you did, you guessed correctly. Your skin, hair, and nails make up your **integumentary system** (in TEG yoo MEN tuhr ee SIS tuhm). The integumentary system covers your body and helps you maintain homeostasis.

READING WARM-UP

Objectives

- List four functions of skin.
- Describe the two layers of skin.
- Describe the structure and function of hair and nails.
- Describe two kinds of damage that can affect skin.

Terms to Learn

integumentary system
epidermis
dermis

READING STRATEGY

Paired Summarizing Read this section silently. In pairs, take turns summarizing the material. Stop to discuss ideas that seem confusing.

Functions of Skin

Why do you need skin? Here are four good reasons:

- Skin protects you by keeping water in your body and foreign particles out of your body.
- Skin keeps you in touch with the outside world. Nerve endings in your skin let you feel things around you.
- Skin helps regulate your body temperature. Small organs in the skin called *sweat glands* make sweat. Sweat is a salty liquid that flows to the surface of the skin. As sweat evaporates, the skin cools.
- Skin helps get rid of wastes. Several kinds of waste chemicals can be removed in sweat.

As shown in **Figure 1,** skin comes in many colors. Skin color is determined by a chemical called *melanin.* If a lot of melanin is present, skin is very dark. If little melanin is present, skin is very light. Melanin absorbs ultraviolet light from the sun. So, melanin reduces damage that can lead to skin cancer. However, all skin, even dark skin, is vulnerable to cancer. Skin should be protected from sunlight whenever possible.

integumentary system the organ system that forms a protective covering on the outside of the body

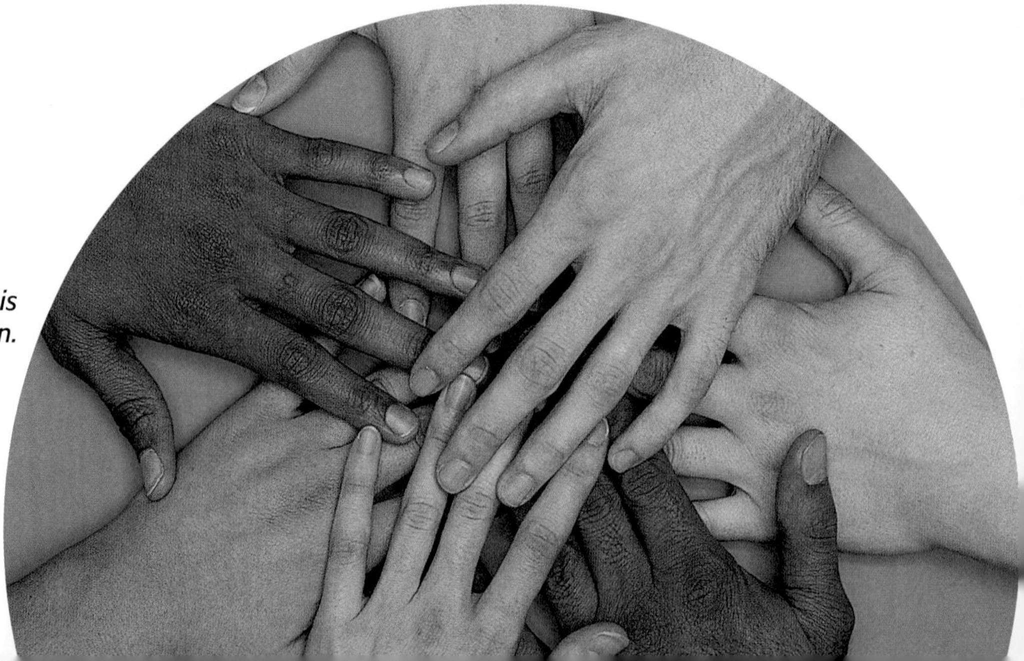

Figure 1 *Variety in skin color is caused by the pigment melanin. The amount of melanin varies from person to person.*

Figure 2 **Structures of the Skin**

Beneath the surface, your skin is a complex organ made of blood vessels, nerves, glands, and muscles.

Blood vessels transport substances and help regulate body temperature.

Nerve fibers carry messages to and from the brain.

Hair follicles in the dermis make hair.

Muscle fibers attached to a hair follicle can contract and cause the hair to stand up.

Oil glands release oil that keeps hair flexible and waterproofs the epidermis.

Sweat glands release sweat to cool the body. Sweating is also a way to remove waste materials from the body.

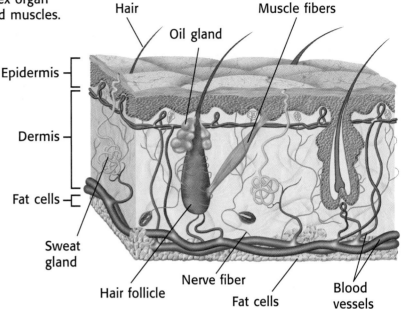

Layers of Skin

Skin is the largest organ of your body. In fact, the skin of an adult covers an area of about 2 m^2! However, there is more to skin than meets the eye. Skin has two main layers: the epidermis (EP uh DUHR mis) and the dermis. The **epidermis** is the outermost layer of skin. You see the epidermis when you look at your skin. The thicker layer of skin that lies beneath the epidermis is the **dermis.**

epidermis the surface layer of cells on a plant or animal

dermis the layer of skin below the epidermis

Epidermis

The epidermis is made of epithelial tissue. Even though the epidermis has many layers of cells, it is as thick as only two sheets of paper over most of the body. It is thicker on the palms of your hands and on the soles of your feet. Most cells in the epidermis are dead. These cells are filled with a protein called *keratin*. Keratin helps make the skin tough.

Dermis

The dermis lies beneath the epidermis. The dermis has many fibers made of a protein called *collagen*. These fibers provide strength. They also let skin bend without tearing. The dermis contains many small structures, as shown in **Figure 2.**

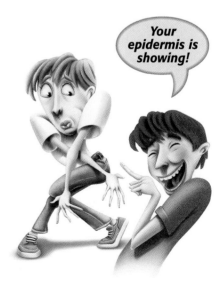

Your epidermis is showing!

✓ *Reading Check* Describe the dermis. How does it differ from the epidermis? (*See the Appendix for answers to Reading Checks.*)

Hair

Figure 3 *A hair is made up of layers of dead, tightly packed, keratin-filled cells. In nails, new cells are produced in the nail root, just beneath the lunula. The new cells push older cells toward the outer edge of the nail.*

Lunula
Nail body
Free edge

Hair and Nails

Hair and nails are important parts of the integumentary system. Like skin, hair and nails are made of living and dead cells. **Figure 3** shows hair and nails.

A hair forms at the bottom of a tiny sac called a *hair follicle*. The hair grows as new cells are added at the hair follicle. Older cells get pushed upward. The only living cells in a hair are in the hair follicle. Like skin, hair gets its color from melanin.

Hair helps protect skin from ultraviolet light. Hair also keeps particles, such as dust and insects, out of your eyes and nose. In most mammals, hair helps regulate body temperature. A tiny muscle attached to the hair follicle contracts. If the follicle contains a hair, the hair stands up. The lifted hairs work like a sweater. They trap warm air around the body.

A nail grows from living cells in the *nail root* at the base of the nail. As new cells form, the nail grows longer. Nails protect the tips of your fingers and toes. So, your fingers and toes can be soft and sensitive for a keen sense of touch.

✔ **Reading Check** Describe how nails grow.

CONNECTION TO
Social Studies

WRITING SKILL **Using Hair** Many traditional cultures use animal hair to make products, such as rugs and blankets. Identify a culture that uses animal hair. In your **science journal,** write a report describing how the culture uses animal hair.

Skin Injuries

Skin is often damaged. Fortunately, your skin can repair itself, as shown in **Figure 4.** Some damage to skin is very serious. Damage to the genetic material in skin cells can cause skin cancer. Skin may also be affected by hormones that cause oil glands in skin to make too much oil. This oil combines with dead skin cells and bacteria to clog hair follicles. The result is acne. Proper cleansing can help but often cannot prevent this problem.

Figure 4 **How Skin Heals**

❶ A blood clot forms over a cut to stop bleeding and to keep bacteria from entering the wound. Bacteria-fighting cells then come to the area to kill bacteria.

❷ Damaged cells are replaced through cell division. Eventually, all that is left on the surface is a scar.

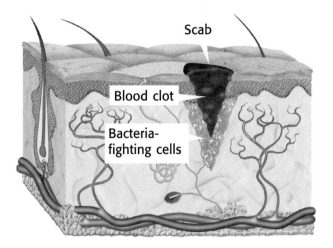

Scab

Blood clot

Bacteria-fighting cells

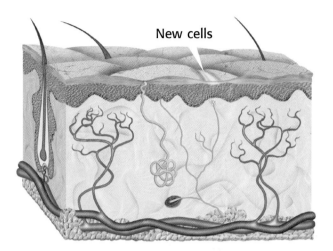

New cells

SECTION Review

Summary

● Skin keeps water in the body, keeps foreign particles out of the body, lets people feel things around them, regulates temperature, and removes wastes.

● The two layers of skin are the epidermis and the dermis.

● Hair grows from hair follicles. Nails grow from nail roots.

● Skin may develop skin cancer. Acne may develop if skin produces too much oil.

Using Key Terms

1. In your own words, write a definition for each of the following terms: *integumentary system*, *epidermis*, and *dermis*.

Understanding Key Ideas

2. Which of the following is NOT a function of skin?
   a. to regulate body temperature
   b. to keep water in the body
   c. to move your body
   d. to get rid of wastes

3. Describe the two layers of skin.

4. How do hair and nails develop?

5. Describe how a cut heals.

Math Skills

6. On average, hair grows 0.3 mm per day. How many millimeters does hair grow in 30 days? in a year?

Critical Thinking

7. **Making Inferences** Why do you feel pain when you pull on your hair or nails, but not when you cut them?

8. **Analyzing Ideas** The epidermis on the palms of your hands and on the soles of your feet is thicker than it is anywhere else on your body. Why might this skin need to be thicker?

SCi LINKS®

NSTA
Developed and maintained by the
National Science Teachers Association

For a variety of links related to this chapter, go to www.scilinks.org

Topic: Integumentary System
SciLinks code: HSM0803

Skills Practice Lab

Measure nail growth over time.

Draw a graph of nail growth.

MATERIALS

- graph paper (optional)
- metric ruler
- permanent marker

SAFETY

Seeing Is Believing

Like your hair and skin, fingernails are part of your body's integumentary system. Nails, shown in the figure below, are a modification of the outer layer of the skin. Nails grow from the nail bed and will grow continuously throughout your life. In this activity, you will measure the rate at which fingernails grow.

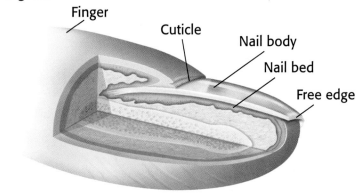

Finger
Cuticle
Nail body
Nail bed
Free edge

Procedure

1 Use a permanent marker to mark the center of the nail bed on your right index finger, as shown in the figure below. **Caution:** Do not get ink on your clothing.

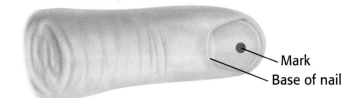

Mark
Base of nail

2 Measure from the mark to the base of your nail. Record the measurement, and label the measurement "Day 1."

3 Repeat steps 1 and 2 for your left index finger.

4 Let your fingernails grow for 2 days. Normal daily activity will not wash away the mark completely, but you may need to freshen the mark.

5 Measure the distance from the mark on your nail to the base of your nail. Record this distance, and label the measurement "Day 3."

6 Continue measuring and recording the growth of your nails every other day for 2 weeks. Refresh the mark as necessary. You may continue to file or trim your nails as usual throughout the course of the lab.

7 After you have completed your measurements, use them to create a graph similar to the graph below.

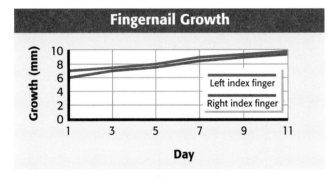

Fingernail Growth

Analyze the Results

1 **Describing Events** Did the nail on one hand grow faster than the nail on the other hand?

2 **Examining Data** Did your nails grow at a constant rate, or did your nails grow more quickly at certain times?

Draw Conclusions

3 **Making Predictions** If one nail grew more quickly than the other nail, what might explain the difference in growth?

4 **Analyzing Graphs** Compare your graph with the graphs of your classmates. Do you notice any differences in the graphs based on gender or physical characteristics, such as height? If so, describe the difference.

Applying Your Data

Do additional research to find out how nails are important to you. Also, identify how nails can be used to indicate a person's health or nutrition. Based on what you learn, describe how your nail growth indicates your health or nutrition.

USING KEY TERMS

Complete each of the following sentences by choosing the correct term from the word bank.

homeostasis   organ
joint   skeletal system
tissue   muscular system
epidermis   dermis
integumentary system

1 A(n) ___ is a place where two or more bones meet.

2 ___ is the maintenance of a stable internal environment.

3 The outermost layer of skin is the ___.

4 The organ system that includes skin, hair, and nails is the ___.

5 A(n) ___ is made up of two or more tissues working together.

6 The ___ supports and protects the body, stores minerals, and allows movement.

UNDERSTANDING KEY IDEAS

Multiple Choice

7 Which of the following lists shows the way in which the body is organized?

a. cells, organs, organ systems, tissues
b. tissues, cells, organs, organ systems
c. cells, tissues, organs, organ systems
d. cells, tissues, organ systems, organs

8 Which muscle tissue can be both voluntary and involuntary?

a. smooth muscle
b. cardiac muscle
c. skeletal muscle
d. All of the above

9 The integumentary system

a. helps regulate body temperature.
b. helps the body move.
c. stores minerals.
d. None of the above

10 Muscles

a. work in pairs.
b. can be voluntary or involuntary.
c. become stronger if exercised.
d. All of the above

Short Answer

11 How do muscles move bones?

12 Describe the skeletal system, and list four functions of bones.

13 Give an example of how organ systems work together.

14 List three injuries and two diseases that affect the skeletal system.

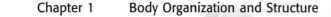

15 Compare aerobic exercise and resistance exercise.

16 What are two kinds of damage that may affect skin?

CRITICAL THINKING

17 **Concept Mapping** Use the following terms to create a concept map: *tissues, muscle tissue, connective tissue, cells, organ systems, organs, epithelial tissue,* and *nervous tissue.*

18 **Making Comparisons** Compare the shapes of the bones of the human skull with the shapes of the bones of the human leg. How do the shapes differ? Why are the shapes important?

19 **Making Inferences** Compare your elbows and fingertips in terms of the texture and sensitivity of the skin on these parts of your body. Why might the skin on these body parts differ?

20 **Making Inferences** Imagine that you are building a robot. Your robot will have a skeleton similar to a human skeleton. If the robot needs to be able to move a limb in all directions, what kind of joint would be needed? Explain your answer.

21 **Analyzing Ideas** Human bones are dense and are often filled with marrow. But many bones of birds are hollow. Why might birds have hollow bones?

22 **Identifying Relationships** Why might some muscles fail to work properly if a bone is broken?

INTERPRETING GRAPHICS

Use the cross section of skin below to answer the questions that follow.

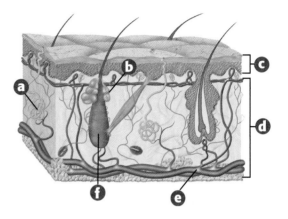

23 What is d called? What substance is most abundant in this layer?

24 What is the name and function of a?

25 What is the name and function of b?

26 Which letter corresponds to the part of the skin that is made up of epithelial tissue that contains dead cells?

27 Which letter corresponds to the part of the skin from which hair grows? What is this part called?

Standardized Test Preparation

Read the passages below. Then, answer the questions that follow each passage.

Passage 1 Sometimes, doctors perform a <u>skin graft</u> to transfer some of a person's healthy skin to an area where skin has been damaged. Doctors perform skin grafts because skin is often the best "bandage" for a wound. Like cloth or plastic bandages, skin protects the wound. Skin allows the wound to breathe. Unlike cloth or plastic bandages, skin can regenerate itself as it covers a wound. But sometimes a person's skin is so severely damaged (by burns, for example) that the person doesn't have enough skin to spare.

1. Based on the passage, what can skin do that manufactured bandages can't do?
  - **A** Skin can protect a wound.
  - **B** Skin can stop more skin from being damaged.
  - **C** Skin can regenerate itself.
  - **D** Skin can prevent burns.

2. In the passage, what does the term *skin graft* most likely mean?
  - **F** a piece of skin transplanted from one part of the body to another
  - **G** a piece of skin made of plastic
  - **H** a piece of damaged skin that has been removed from the body
  - **I** burned skin

3. Based on the passage, why might a severe burn victim not receive a skin graft?
  - **A** Manufactured bandages are better.
  - **B** He or she doesn't have enough healthy skin.
  - **C** There isn't enough damaged skin to repair.
  - **D** Skin is the best bandage for a wound.

Passage 2 Making sure that your body maintains homeostasis is not an easy task. The task is difficult because your internal environment is always changing. Your body must do many different jobs to maintain homeostasis. Each cell in your body has a specific job in maintaining homeostasis. Your cells are organized into groups. A group of similar cells working together forms a tissue. Your body has four main kinds of tissue—epithelial tissue, connective tissue, muscle tissue, and nervous tissue. These tissues work together to form organs, which help maintain homeostasis.

1. Based on the passage, which of the following statements about tissues is true?
  - **A** Tissues do not help maintain homeostasis.
  - **B** Tissues form organ systems.
  - **C** Tissues are changing because the body's internal environment is always changing.
  - **D** There are four kinds of tissue.

2. According to the passage, which of the following statements about homeostasis is true?
  - **F** It is easy for the body to maintain homeostasis.
  - **G** The body must do different jobs to maintain homeostasis.
  - **H** Your internal environment rarely changes.
  - **I** Organs and organ systems do not help maintain homeostasis.

3. Which of the following statements about cells is false?
  - **A** Cells are organized into different groups.
  - **B** Cells form tissues.
  - **C** Cells work together.
  - **D** Cells don't maintain homeostasis.

The line graph below shows hair growth over time. Use the graph to answer the questions that follow.

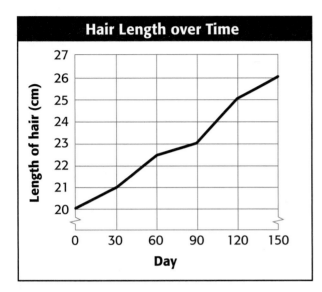

1. How long was the hair on day 60?

  A 20.0 cm

  B 21.0 cm

  C 22.5 cm

  D 23.0 cm

2. On which day was hair length 23 cm?

  F day 60

  G day 90

  H day 120

  I day 150

3. From day 0 to day 150, what is the average amount that hair grows every 30 days?

  A 0.5 cm

  B 1.2 cm

  C 1.5 cm

  D 2.0 cm

4. Based on the average amount of hair growth per 30-day period, how long would it take the hair to grow another 3.6 cm?

  F 30 days

  G 60 days

  H 90 days

  I 120 days

Read each question below, and choose the best answer.

1. About 40% of a person's mass is muscle tissue. If Max has a mass of 40 kg, about how much muscle tissue does he have?

  A 16 kg

  B 20 kg

  C 24 kg

  D 30 kg

2. When running, an adult inhales about 72 L of air per minute. That amount is 12 times the amount that an adult needs while resting. How much air does an adult inhale while resting?

  F 6 L/min

  G 12 L/min

  H 60 L/min

  I 64 L/min

3. Maggie likes to do bench presses, a resistance exercise. She bench presses 10 kg. If Maggie added 2 kg every 2 weeks, how long would it take her to reach 20 kg?

  A 4 weeks

  B 5 weeks

  C 10 weeks

  D 12 weeks

4. A box of 25 bandages costs $4.00. A roll of tape costs $1.50. Troy needs 125 bandages and 3 rolls of tape for a first-aid kit. Which of the following equations shows the cost of first-aid supplies, x?

  F $x = (125 \times 4.00) + (3 \times 1.50)$

  G $x = (25 \times 4.00) + (3 \times 1.50)$

  H $x = [(25 \times 4.00) \div 125] + (3 \times 1.50)$

  I $x = [(125 \div 25) \times 4.00] + (3 \times 1.50)$

5. Stephen wants to run a 10 K race. Right now, he can run 5 K. What is the percentage increase from 5 K to 10 K?

  A 50%

  B 100%

  C 200%

  D 500%

Science in Action

Weird Science

Engineered Skin

Your skin is your first line of defense against the outside world. Your skin keeps you safe from dehydration and infection, helps regulate body temperature, and helps remove some wastes. But what happens if a large portion of skin is damaged? Skin may not be able to function properly. For someone who has a serious burn, a doctor often uses skin from an undamaged part of the person's body to repair the damaged skin. But some burn victims don't have enough undamaged skin to spare. Doctors have discovered ways to engineer skin that can be used in place of human skin.

Math ACTIVITY

A doctor repaired 0.35 m² of an adult patient's skin with engineered skin. If an adult has about 2 m² of skin, what percentage of the patient's skin was repaired?

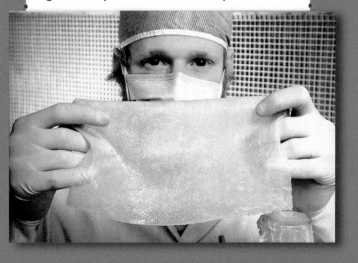

Science, Technology, and Society

Beating the Odds

Sometimes, people are born without limbs or lose limbs in accidents. Many of these people have prostheses (prahs THEE SEEZ), or human-made replacements for the body parts. Until recently, many of these prostheses made it more difficult for many people to participate in physical activities, such as sports. But new designs have led to lighter, more comfortable prostheses that move the way that a human limb does. These new designs have allowed athletes with physical disabilities to compete at higher levels.

Social Studies ACTIVITY

Research the use of prostheses throughout history. Create a timeline showing major advances in prosthesis use and design.

Zahra Beheshti

Physical Therapist A physical therapist is a licensed professional who helps people recover from injuries by using hands-on treatment instead of medicines. Dr. Zahra Beheshti is a physical therapist at the Princeton Physical Therapy Center in New Jersey. She often helps athletes who suffer from sports injuries.

After an injury, a person may go through a process called *rehabilitation* to regain the use of the injured body part. The most common mistake made by athletes is that they play sports before completely recovering from injuries. Dr. Beheshti explains, "Going back to their usual pre-injury routine could result in another injury."

Dr. Beheshti also teaches patients about preventing future sports injuries. "Most injuries happen when an individual engages in strenuous activities without a proper warm-up or cool-down period." Being a physical therapist is rewarding work. Dr. Beheshti says, "I get a lot of satisfaction when treating patients and see them regain their function and independence and return to their normal life."

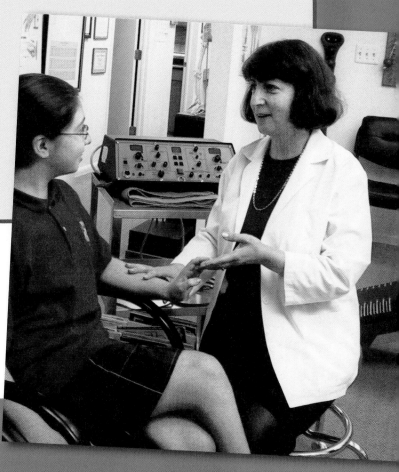

Language Arts ACTiViTY

WRITING SKILL Interview a physical therapist who works in or near your community. Write a newspaper article about your interview.

To learn more about these Science in Action topics, visit go.hrw.com and type in the keyword **HL5BD1F.**

**Check out Current Science®
articles related to this chapter
by visiting go.hrw.com. Just
type in the keyword HL5CS22.**

Circulation and Respiration

About the PHOTO

Your circulatory system is made up of the heart, blood vessels, and blood. This picture is a colored scanning electron micrograph of red and white blood cells and cell fragments called *platelets.* Red blood cells are disk shaped, white blood cells are rounded, and platelets are the small green fragments. There are millions of blood cells in a drop of blood. Blood cells are so important that your body makes about 200 billion red blood cells every day.

PRE-READING ACTiViTY

FOLDNOTES **Four-Corner Fold**
Before you read the chapter, create the FoldNote entitled "Four-Corner Fold" described in the **Study Skills** section of the Appendix. Label the flaps of the four-corner fold with the section titles "Cardiovascular system," "Blood," Lymphatic system," and "Respiratory system." Write what you know about each topic under the appropriate flap. As you read the chapter, add other information that you learn.

START-UP ACTIVITY

Exercise Your Heart

How does your heart respond to exercise? You can see this reaction by measuring your pulse.

Procedure

1. Take your pulse while remaining still. (Take your pulse by placing your fingers on the inside of your wrist just below your thumb.)

2. Using a **watch with a second hand,** count the number of heart beats in 15 s. Then, multiply this number by 4 to calculate the number of beats in 1 minute.

3. Do some moderate physical activity, such as jumping jacks or jogging in place, for 30 s.

4. Stop and calculate your heart rate again.
   Caution: Do not perform this exercise if you have difficulty breathing, if you have high blood pressure or asthma, or if you get dizzy easily.

5. Rest for 5 min.

6. Take your pulse again.

Analysis

1. How did exercise affect your heart rate? Why do you think this happened?

2. How does your heart rate affect the rate at which red blood cells travel throughout your body?

3. Did your heart rate return to normal (or almost normal) after you rested? Why or why not?

The Cardiovascular System

When you hear the word heart, *what do you think of first? Many people think of romance. Some people think of courage. But the heart is much more than a symbol of love or bravery. Your heart is an amazing pump.*

The heart is an organ that is part of your circulatory system. The *circulatory system* includes your heart; your blood; your veins, capillaries, and arteries; and your lymphatic system.

Your Cardiovascular System

Your heart creates pressure every time it beats. This pressure moves blood to every cell in your body through your cardiovascular system (KAR dee OH VAS kyoo luhr SIS tuhm). The **cardiovascular system** consists of the heart and the three types of blood vessels that carry blood throughout your body. The word *cardio* means "heart," and *vascular* means "blood vessel." The blood vessels—arteries, capillaries, and veins—carry blood pumped by the heart. **Figure 1** shows the major arteries and veins.

✓ *Reading Check* **What are the four main parts of the cardiovascular system?** (*See the Appendix for answers to Reading Checks.*)

cardiovascular system a collection of organs that transport blood throughout the body

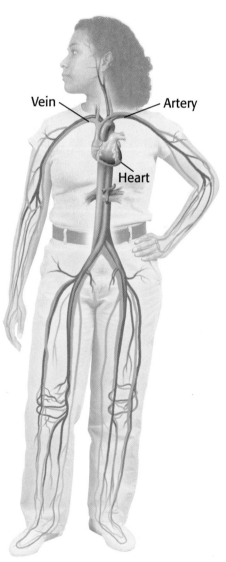

Vein — Artery

Heart

Figure 1 *The cardiovascular system carries blood to every cell in your body.*

The Heart

Your *heart* is an organ made mostly of cardiac muscle tissue. It is about the size of your fist and is almost in the center of your chest cavity. Like hearts of all mammals, your heart has a left side and a right side that are separated by a thick wall. The right side of the heart pumps oxygen-poor blood to the lungs. The left side pumps oxygen-rich blood to the body. As you can see in **Figure 2,** each side has an upper chamber and a lower chamber. Each upper chamber is called an *atrium* (plural, *atria*). Each lower chamber is called a *ventricle*.

Flaplike structures called *valves* are located between the atria and ventricles and in places where large arteries are attached to the heart. As blood moves through the heart, these valves close to prevent blood from going backward. The "lub-dub, lub-dub" sound of a beating heart is caused by the valves closing. **Figure 3** shows the flow of blood through the heart.

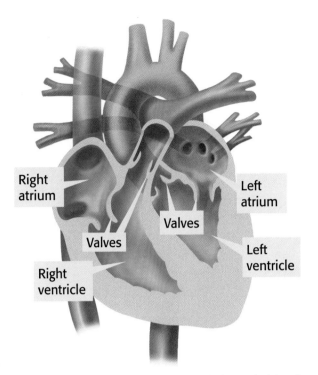

Figure 2 *The heart pumps blood through blood vessels. The vessels carrying oxygen-rich blood are shown in red. The vessels carrying oxygen-poor blood are shown in blue.*

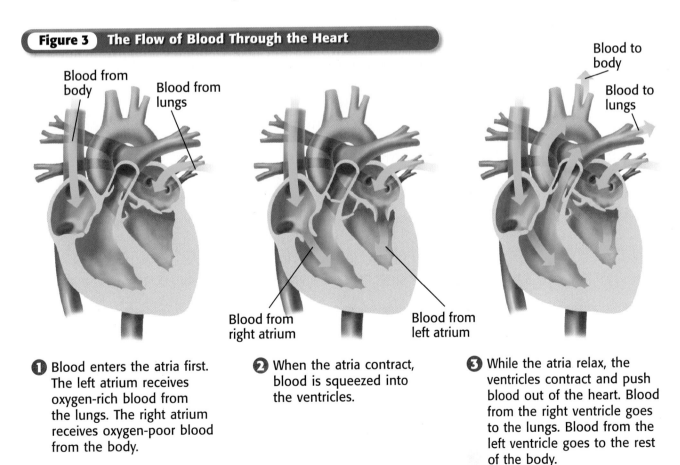

Figure 3   The Flow of Blood Through the Heart

❶ Blood enters the atria first. The left atrium receives oxygen-rich blood from the lungs. The right atrium receives oxygen-poor blood from the body.

❷ When the atria contract, blood is squeezed into the ventricles.

❸ While the atria relax, the ventricles contract and push blood out of the heart. Blood from the right ventricle goes to the lungs. Blood from the left ventricle goes to the rest of the body.

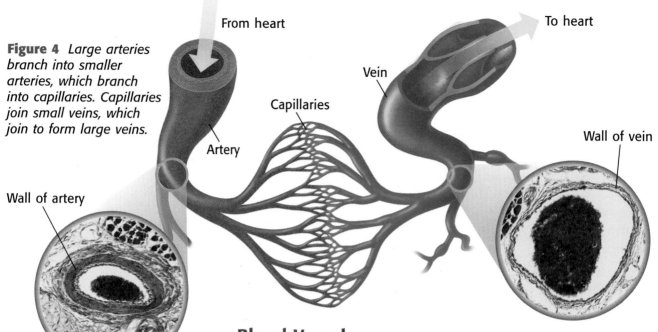

Figure 4 *Large arteries branch into smaller arteries, which branch into capillaries. Capillaries join small veins, which join to form large veins.*

From heart

To heart

Vein

Capillaries

Wall of vein

Artery

Wall of artery

Blood Vessels

Blood travels throughout your body in hollow tubes called *blood vessels*. The three types of blood vessels—arteries, capillaries, and veins—are shown in **Figure 4.**

Arteries

A blood vessel that carries blood away from the heart is an **artery.** Arteries have thick walls, which contain a layer of smooth muscle. Each heartbeat pumps blood into your arteries at high pressure. This pressure is your *blood pressure*. Artery walls stretch and are usually strong enough to stand the pressure. Your *pulse* is caused by the rhythmic change in your blood pressure.

Capillaries

Nutrients, oxygen, and other substances must leave blood and get to your body's cells. Carbon dioxide and other wastes leave body cells and are carried away by blood. A **capillary** is a tiny blood vessel that allows these exchanges between body cells and blood. These exchanges can take place because capillary walls are only one cell thick. Capillaries are so narrow that blood cells must pass through them in single file. No cell in the body is more than three or four cells away from a capillary.

Veins

After leaving capillaries, blood enters veins. A **vein** is a blood vessel that carries blood back to the heart. As blood travels through veins, valves in the veins keep the blood from flowing backward. When skeletal muscles contract, they squeeze nearby veins and help push blood toward the heart.

Reading Check Describe the three types of blood vessels.

artery a blood vessel that carries blood away from the heart to the body's organs

capillary a tiny blood vessel that allows an exchange between blood and cells in other tissue

vein in biology, a vessel that carries blood to the heart

Two Types of Circulation

Where does blood get the oxygen to deliver to your body? From your lungs! Your heart pumps blood to the lungs. In the lungs, carbon dioxide leaves the blood and oxygen enters the blood. The oxygen-rich blood then flows back to the heart. This circulation of blood between your heart and lungs is called **pulmonary circulation** (PUL muh NER ee SUHR kyoo LAY shuhn).

The oxygen-rich blood returning to the heart from the lungs is then pumped to the rest of the body. The circulation of blood between the heart and the rest of the body is called **systemic circulation** (sis TEM ik SUHR kyoo LAY shuhn). Both types of circulation are shown in **Figure 5.**

pulmonary circulation the flow of blood from the heart to the lungs and back to the heart through the pulmonary arteries, capillaries, and veins

systemic circulation the flow of blood from the heart to all parts of the body and back to the heart

Figure 5 The Flow of Blood Through the Body

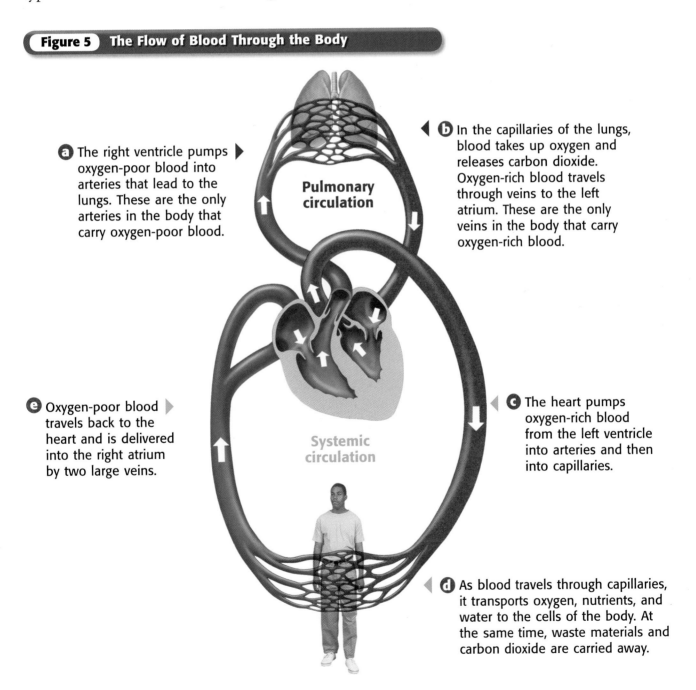

a The right ventricle pumps oxygen-poor blood into arteries that lead to the lungs. These are the only arteries in the body that carry oxygen-poor blood.

Pulmonary circulation

b In the capillaries of the lungs, blood takes up oxygen and releases carbon dioxide. Oxygen-rich blood travels through veins to the left atrium. These are the only veins in the body that carry oxygen-rich blood.

e Oxygen-poor blood travels back to the heart and is delivered into the right atrium by two large veins.

Systemic circulation

c The heart pumps oxygen-rich blood from the left ventricle into arteries and then into capillaries.

d As blood travels through capillaries, it transports oxygen, nutrients, and water to the cells of the body. At the same time, waste materials and carbon dioxide are carried away.

MATH PRACTICE

The Beat Goes On

A person's heart averages about 70 beats per minute.

1. Calculate how many times a heart beats in a day.

2. If a person lives for 75 years, how many times will his or her heart beat?

3. If an athlete's heart beats 50 times a minute, how many fewer times than an average heart will his or her heart beat in 30 days?

Cardiovascular Problems

More than just your heart and blood vessels are at risk if you have cardiovascular problems. Your whole body may be harmed. Cardiovascular problems can be caused by smoking, high levels of cholesterol in the blood, stress, physical inactivity, or heredity. Eating a healthy diet and getting plenty of exercise can reduce the risk of having cardiovascular problems.

Atherosclerosis

Heart diseases are the leading cause of death in the United States. A major cause of heart diseases is a cardiovascular disease called *atherosclerosis* (ATH uhr OH skluh ROH sis). Atherosclerosis happens when cholesterol (kuh LES tuhr AWL) builds up inside of blood vessels. This cholesterol buildup causes the blood vessels to become narrower and less elastic. **Figure 6** shows how clogged the pathway through a blood vessel can become. When an artery that supplies blood to the heart becomes blocked, the person may have a heart attack.

✓ **Reading Check** Why is atherosclerosis dangerous?

High Blood Pressure

Atherosclerosis may be caused by hypertension. *Hypertension* is abnormally high blood pressure. The higher the blood pressure, the greater the risk of a heart attack, heart failure, kidney disease, and stroke. A *stroke* is when a blood vessel in the brain becomes clogged or ruptures. As a result, that part of the brain receives no oxygen. Without oxygen, brain cells die.

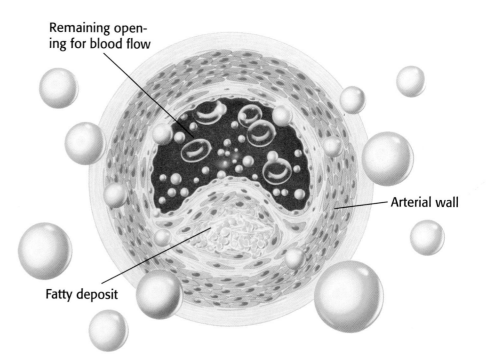

Remaining opening for blood flow

Arterial wall

Fatty deposit

Figure 6 *This illustration shows the narrowing of an artery as the result of high levels of cholesterol in the blood. Lipid deposits (yellow) build up inside the blood vessel walls and block the flow of blood. Red blood cells and lipid particles (yellow balls) are shown escaping.*

Heart Attacks and Heart Failure

Two cardiovascular problems are heart attacks and heart failure. A *heart attack* happens when heart muscle cells die and part of the heart muscle is damaged. As shown in **Figure 7,** arteries that deliver oxygen to the heart may be blocked. Without oxygen, heart muscle cells die quickly. When enough heart muscle cells die, the heart may stop.

Heart failure is different. *Heart failure* happens when the heart cannot pump enough blood to meet the body's needs. Organs, such as the brain, lungs, and kidneys, may be damaged by lack of oxygen or nutrients, or by the buildup of fluids or wastes.

Figure 7 **Heart Attack**

Artery delivering blood to heart muscle

Location of blocked artery

Area of heart damaged by lack of oxygen to heart muscle

SECTION Review

Summary

- The cardiovascular system is made up of the heart and three types of blood vessels.
- The three types of blood vessels are arteries, veins, and capillaries.
- Oxygen-poor blood flows from the heart through the lungs, where it picks up oxygen.
- Oxygen-rich blood flows from the heart to the rest of the body.
- Cardiovascular problems include atherosclerosis, hypertension, heart attacks, and strokes.

Using Key Terms

For each pair of terms, explain how the meanings of the terms differ.

1. *artery* and *vein*

2. *systemic circulation* and *pulmonary circulation*

Understanding Key Ideas

3. Which of the following is true of blood in the pulmonary veins?
   a. The blood is going to the body.
   b. The blood is oxygen poor.
   c. The blood is going to the lungs.
   d. The blood is oxygen rich.

4. What are the four parts of the cardiovascular system? Describe the functions of each part.

5. What is the difference between a heart attack and heart failure?

Math Skills

6. An adult male's heart pumps about 2.8 million liters of blood a year. If his heart beats 70 times a minute, how much blood does his heart pump with each beat?

Critical Thinking

7. **Identifying Relationships** How is the structure of capillaries related to their function?

8. **Making Inferences** One of aspirin's effects is that it prevents platelets from being too "sticky." Why might doctors prescribe aspirin for patients who have had a heart attack?

9. **Analyzing Ideas** Veins and arteries are everywhere in your body. When a pulse is taken, it is usually taken at an artery in the neck or wrist. Explain why.

10. **Making Comparisons** Why is the structure of arteries different from the structure of capillaries?

SCiLINKS®

NSTA
Developed and maintained by the National Science Teachers Association

For a variety of links related to this chapter, go to www.scilinks.org

Topic: The Cardiovascular System; Cardiovascular Problems
SciLinks code: HSM0221; HSM0220

Blood

Blood is part of the circulatory system. It travels through miles and miles of blood vessels to reach every cell in your body. So, you must have a lot of blood, right?

Well, actually, an adult human body has about 5 L of blood. Your body probably has a little less than that. All the blood in your body would not fill two 3 L soda bottles.

What Is Blood?

Your *circulatory system* is made up of your heart, your blood vessels, and blood. **Blood** is a connective tissue made up of plasma, red blood cells, platelets, and white blood cells. Blood carries oxygen and nutrients to all parts of your body.

✓ **Reading Check** **What are the four main components of blood?** (*See the Appendix for answers to Reading Checks.*)

Plasma

The fluid part of the blood is called plasma (PLAZ muh). *Plasma* is a mixture of water, minerals, nutrients, sugars, proteins, and other substances. Red blood cells, white blood cells, and platelets are found in plasma.

Red Blood Cells

Most blood cells are *red blood cells,* or RBCs. RBCs, such as the ones shown in **Figure 1,** take oxygen to every cell in your body. Cells need oxygen to carry out their functions. Each RBC has hemoglobin (HEE moh GLOH bin). *Hemoglobin* is an oxygen-carrying protein. Hemoglobin clings to the oxygen you inhale. RBCs can then transport oxygen throughout the body. Hemoglobin also gives RBCs their red color.

READING WARM-UP

Objectives

● Identify the four main components of blood.

● Describe three functions of blood.

● Explain how blood pressure is measured.

● Explain what the ABO blood types are and why they are important.

Terms to Learn

blood
blood pressure

READING STRATEGY

Reading Organizer As you read this section, create an outline of the section. Use the headings from the section in your outline.

blood the fluid that carries gases, nutrients, and wastes through the body and that is made up of plasma, red blood cells, platelets, and white blood cells

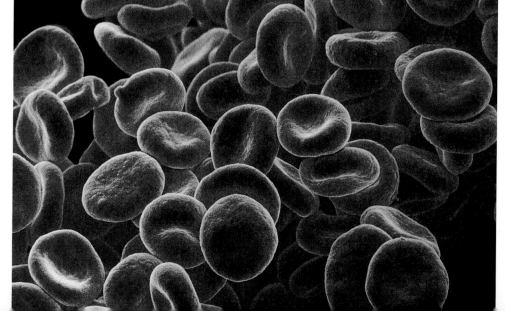

Figure 1 *Red blood cells are made in the bone marrow of certain bones. As red blood cells mature, they lose their nucleus and their DNA.*

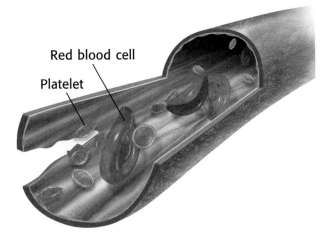

Red blood cell

Platelet

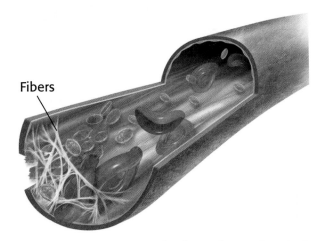

Fibers

Figure 2 *Platelets release chemicals in damaged vessels and cause fibers to form. The fibers make a "net" that traps blood cells and stops bleeding.*

Platelets

Drifting among the blood cells are tiny particles called platelets. *Platelets* are pieces of larger cells found in bone marrow. These larger cells remain in the bone marrow, but fragments are pinched off and enter the bloodstream as platelets. Platelets last for only 5 to 10 days, but they are an important part of blood. When you cut or scrape your skin, you bleed because blood vessels have been opened. As soon as bleeding starts, platelets begin to clump together in the damaged area. They form a plug that helps reduce blood loss, as shown in **Figure 2.** Platelets also release chemicals that react with proteins in plasma. The reaction causes tiny fibers to form. The fibers help create a blood clot.

White Blood Cells

Sometimes *pathogens* (PATH uh juhnz)—bacteria, viruses, and other microscopic particles that can make you sick— enter your body. When they do, they often meet *white blood cells,* or WBCs. WBCs, shown in **Figure 3,** help keep you healthy by destroying pathogens. WBCs also help clean wounds.

WBCs fight pathogens in several ways. Some WBCs squeeze out of blood vessels and move around in tissues, searching for pathogens. When they find a pathogen, they destroy it. Other WBCs release antibodies. *Antibodies* are chemicals that identify or destroy pathogens. WBCs also keep you healthy by destroying body cells that have died or been damaged. Most WBCs are made in bone marrow. Some WBCs mature in the lymphatic system.

✓ Reading Check Why are WBCs important to your health?

Figure 3 *White blood cells defend the body against pathogens. These white blood cells have been colored yellow to make their shape easier to see.*

Body Temperature Regulation

Your blood does more than supply your cells with oxygen and nutrients. It also helps regulate your body temperature. When your brain senses that your body temperature is rising, it signals blood vessels in your skin to enlarge. As the vessels enlarge, heat from your blood is transferred to your skin. This transfer helps lower your temperature. When your brain senses that your temperature is normal, it instructs your blood vessels to return to their normal size.

Blood Pressure

Every time your heart beats, it pushes blood out of the heart and into your arteries. The force exerted by blood on the inside walls of arteries is called **blood pressure.**

Blood pressure is expressed in millimeters of mercury (mm Hg). For example, a blood pressure of 110 mm Hg means the pressure on the artery walls can push a narrow column of mercury to a height of 110 mm.

Blood pressure is usually given as two numbers, such as 110/70 mm Hg. Systolic (sis TAHL ik) pressure is the first number. *Systolic pressure* is the pressure inside large arteries when the ventricles contract. The surge of blood causes the arteries to bulge and produce a pulse. The second number, *diastolic* (DIE uh STAHL ik) *pressure,* is the pressure inside arteries when the ventricles relax. For adults, a blood pressure of 120/80 mm Hg or below is considered healthy. High blood pressure can cause heart or kidney damage.

Reading Check What is the difference between systolic pressure and diastolic pressure?

Blood Types

Every person has one of four blood types: A, B, AB, or O. Your blood type refers to the type of chemicals you have on the surface of your RBCs. These surface chemicals are called *antigens* (AN tuh juhnz). Type A blood has A antigens; type B has B antigens; and type AB has both A and B antigens. Type O blood has neither the A nor the B antigen.

The different blood types have different antigens on their RBCs. They may also have different antibodies in the plasma. These antibodies react to antigens of other blood types as if the antigens were pathogens. As shown in **Figure 4,** type A blood has antibodies that react to type B blood. If a person with type A blood receives type B blood, the type B antibodies attach themselves to the type B RBCs. These RBCs begin to clump together, and the clumps may block blood vessels. A reaction to the wrong blood type may be fatal.

blood pressure the force that blood exerts on the walls of the arteries

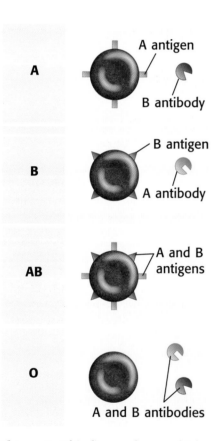

Figure 4 *This figure shows which antigens and antibodies may be present in each blood type.*

Blood Types and Transfusions

Sometimes, a person must be given a blood transfusion. A *transfusion* is the injection of blood or blood components into a person to replace blood that has been lost because of surgery or an injury. **Figure 5** shows bags of blood that may be given in a transfusion. The blood type is clearly marked. Because the ABO blood types have different antigen-antibody reactions, a person receiving blood cannot receive blood from just anyone. **Table 1** shows blood transfusion possibilities.

Table 1 Blood Transfusion Possibilities		
Type	**Can receive**	**Can donate to**
A	A, O	A, AB
B	B, O	B, AB
AB	all	AB only
O	O	all

Reading Check People with type O blood are sometimes called universal donors. Why might this be true?

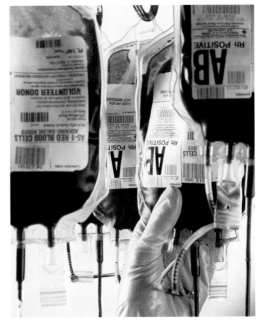

Figure 5 *The blood type must be clearly labeled on blood stored for transfusions.*

SECTION Review

Summary

- Blood's four main components are plasma, red blood cells, platelets, and white blood cells.

- Blood carries oxygen and nutrients to cells, helps protect against disease, and helps regulate body temperature.

- Blood pressure is the force blood exerts on the inside walls of arteries.

- Every person has one of four ABO blood types.

- Mixing blood types may be fatal.

Using Key Terms

1. Use each of the following terms in a separate sentence: *blood* and *blood pressure.*

Understanding Key Ideas

2. A person with type B blood can donate blood to people with which type(s) of blood?
   a. B, AB
   b. A, AB
   c. AB only
   d. All types

3. List the four main components of blood and tell what each component does.

4. Why is it important for a doctor to know a patient's blood type?

Math Skills

5. A person has a systolic pressure of 174 mm Hg. What percentage of normal (120 mm Hg) is this?

Critical Thinking

6. **Identifying Relationships** How does the body use blood and blood vessels to help maintain proper body temperature?

7. **Predicting Consequences** Some blood conditions and diseases affect the ability of red blood cells to deliver oxygen to cells of the body. Predict what might happen to a person with a disease of that type.

SCILINKS®

NSTA
Developed and maintained by the National Science Teachers Association

For a variety of links related to this chapter, go to www.scilinks.org

Topic: Blood; Blood Donations
SciLinks code: HSM0175; HSM0178

The Lymphatic System

Every time your heart pumps, a little fluid is forced out of the thin walls of the capillaries. Some of this fluid collects in the spaces around your cells. What happens to this fluid?

Most of the fluid is reabsorbed through the capillaries into your blood. But some is not. Your body has a second circulatory system called the lymphatic (lim FAT ik) system.

The **lymphatic system** is the group of organs and tissues that collect the excess fluid and return it to your blood. The lymphatic system also helps your body fight pathogens.

Vessels of the Lymphatic System

The fluid collected by the lymphatic system is carried through vessels. The smallest vessels of the lymphatic system are *lymph capillaries*. Lymph capillaries absorb some of the fluid and particles from between the cells. These particles are too large to enter blood capillaries. Some of these particles are dead cells or pathogens. The fluid and particles absorbed into lymph capillaries are called **lymph.**

As shown in **Figure 1,** lymph capillaries carry lymph into larger vessels called *lymphatic vessels.* Skeletal muscles squeeze these vessels to force lymph through the lymphatic system. Valves inside lymphatic vessels stop backflow. Lymph drains into the large neck veins of the cardiovascular system.

✓ **Reading Check** How is the lymphatic system related to the cardiovascular system? (*See the Appendix for answers to Reading Checks.*)

lymphatic system a collection of organs whose primary function is to collect extracellular fluid and return it to the blood

lymph the fluid that is collected by the lymphatic vessels and nodes

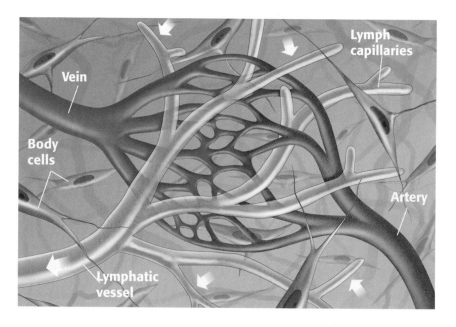

Figure 1 *The white arrows show the movement of lymph into lymph capillaries and through lymphatic vessels.*

Lymph capillaries

Vein

Body cells

Artery

Lymphatic vessel

Other Parts of the Lymphatic System

In addition to vessels and capillaries, several organs and tissues are part of the lymphatic system. These organs and tissues are shown in **Figure 2.** Bone marrow plays an important role in your lymphatic system. The other parts of the lymphatic system are the lymph nodes, the thymus gland, the spleen, and the tonsils.

Bone Marrow

Bones—part of your skeletal system—are very important to your lymphatic system. *Bone marrow* is the soft tissue inside of bones. Bone marrow is where most red and white blood cells, including lymphocytes (LIM foh SIETS), are produced. *Lymphocytes* are a type of white blood cell that helps your body fight pathogens.

Lymph Nodes

As lymph travels through lymphatic vessels, it passes through lymph nodes. **Lymph nodes** are small, bean-shaped masses of tissue that remove pathogens and dead cells from the lymph. Lymph nodes are concentrated in the armpits, neck, and groin.

Lymph nodes contain lymphocytes. Some lymphocytes—called *killer T cells*—surround and destroy pathogens. Other lymphocytes—called *B cells*—produce antibodies that attach to pathogens. These marked pathogens clump together and are then destroyed by other cells.

When bacteria or other pathogens cause an infection, WBCs may multiply greatly. The lymph nodes fill with WBCs that are fighting the infection. As a result, some lymph nodes may become swollen and painful. Your doctor may feel these swollen lymph nodes to see if you have an infection. In fact, if your lymph nodes are swollen and sore, you or your parent can feel them, too. Swollen lymph nodes are sometimes an early clue that you have an infection.

Thymus

T cells develop from immature lymphocytes produced in the bone marrow. Before these cells are ready to fight infections, they develop further in the thymus. The **thymus** is the gland that produces T cells that are ready to fight infection. The thymus is located behind the breastbone, just above the heart. Mature lymphocytes from the thymus travel through the lymphatic system to other areas of your body.

lymph node an organ that filters lymph and that is found along the lymphatic vessels

thymus the main gland of the lymphatic system; it produces mature T lymphocytes

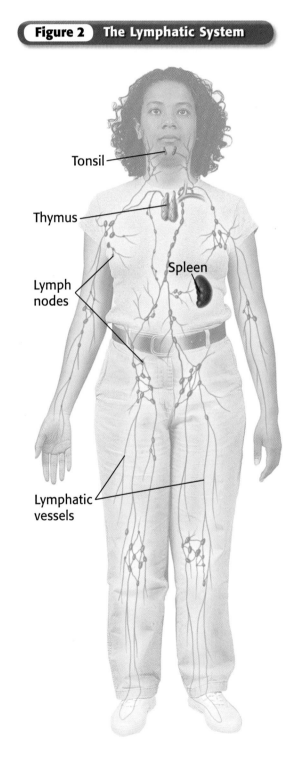

Figure 2 The Lymphatic System

Tonsil

Thymus

Spleen

Lymph nodes

Lymphatic vessels

Spleen

Your spleen is the largest lymphatic organ. The **spleen** stores and produces lymphocytes. It is a purplish organ about the size of your fist. Your spleen is soft and spongy. It is located in the upper left side of your abdomen. As blood flows through the spleen, lymphocytes attack or mark pathogens in the blood. If pathogens cause an infection, the spleen may also release lymphocytes into the bloodstream.

In addition to being part of the lymphatic system, the spleen produces, monitors, stores, and destroys blood cells. When red blood cells (RBCs) are squeezed through the spleen's capillaries, the older and more fragile cells burst. These damaged RBCs are then taken apart by some of the cells in the spleen. Some parts of these RBCs may be reused. For this reason, you can think of the spleen as the red-blood-cell recycling center.

The spleen has two important functions. The *white pulp,* shown in **Figure 3,** is part of the lymphatic system. It helps to fight infections. The *red pulp,* also shown in **Figure 3,** removes unwanted material, such as defective red blood cells, from the blood. However, it is possible to lead a healthy life without your spleen. If the spleen is damaged or removed, other organs in the body take over many of its functions.

Reading Check What are two important functions of the spleen?

spleen the largest lymphatic organ in the body

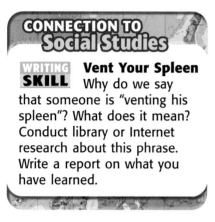

CONNECTION TO Social Studies

WRITING SKILL **Vent Your Spleen** Why do we say that someone is "venting his spleen"? What does it mean? Conduct library or Internet research about this phrase. Write a report on what you have learned.

Figure 3 **White and Red Pulp in the Spleen**

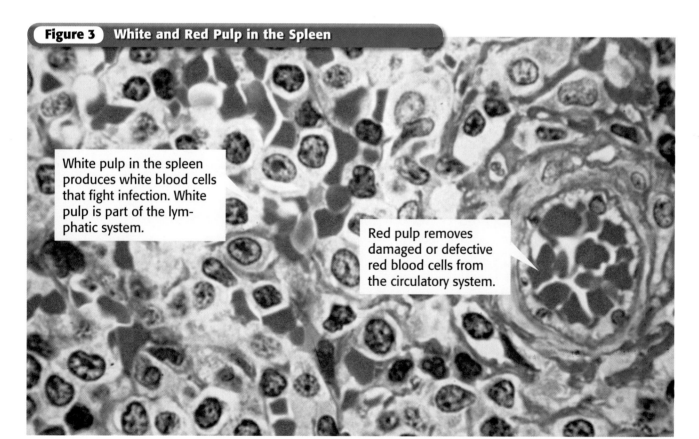

White pulp in the spleen produces white blood cells that fight infection. White pulp is part of the lymphatic system.

Red pulp removes damaged or defective red blood cells from the circulatory system.

Tonsils

The lymphatic system includes your tonsils. **Tonsils** are lymphatic tissue in the nasal cavity and at the back of the mouth on either side of the tongue. Each tonsil is about the size of a large olive.

Tonsils help defend the body against infection. Lymphocytes in the tonsils trap pathogens that enter the throat. Sometimes, tonsils become infected and are red, swollen, and very sore. Severely infected tonsils may be covered with patches of white, infected tissue. Sore, swollen tonsils, such as those in **Figure 4,** make swallowing difficult.

Sometimes, a doctor will suggest surgery to remove the tonsils. In the past, this surgery was frequently done in childhood. It is less common today. Surgery is now done only if a child has frequent, severe tonsil infections or if a child's tonsils are so enlarged that breathing is difficult.

tonsils small, rounded masses of lymphatic tissue located in the pharynx and in the passage from the mouth to the pharynx

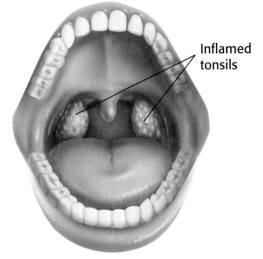

Figure 4 *Tonsils help protect your throat and lungs from infection by trapping pathogens.*

Inflamed tonsils

SECTION Review

Summary

- The lymphatic system collects fluid from between the cells and returns it to the blood.
- The lymphatic system contains cells that help the body fight disease.
- The lymphatic system consists of lymphatic vessels, lymph, and tissues and organs throughout the body.
- The thymus, spleen, and tonsils contain lymphocytes that help fight pathogens.

Using Key Terms

1. Use each of the following terms in a separate sentence: *lymph nodes, spleen,* and *tonsils.*

Understanding Key Ideas

2. Lymph
    a. is the same as blood.
    b. is fluid in the cells.
    c. drains into your muscles.
    d. is fluid collected by lymphatic vessels.

3. Name six parts of the lymphatic system. Tell what each part does.

4. How are your cardiovascular and lymphatic systems related?

Math Skills

5. One cubic millimeter of blood contains 5 million RBCs and 10,000 WBCs. How many times more RBCs are there than WBCs?

Critical Thinking

6. **Expressing Opinions** Some people have frequent, severe tonsil infections. These infections can be treated with medicine, and the infections usually go away after a few days. Do you think removing tonsils in such a case is a good idea? Explain.

7. **Analyzing Ideas** Why is it important that lymphatic tissue is spread throughout the body?

SCiLINKS.

NSTA

Developed and maintained by the National Science Teachers Association

For a variety of links related to this chapter, go to www.scilinks.org

Topic: The Lymphatic System
SciLinks code: HSM0891

The Respiratory System

Breathing—you do it all the time. You're doing it right now. You hardly ever think about it, though, unless you suddenly can't breathe.

Then, it becomes very clear that you have to breathe in order to live. But why is breathing important? Your body needs oxygen in order to get energy from the foods you eat. Breathing makes this process possible.

Respiration and the Respiratory System

The words *breathing* and *respiration* are often used to mean the same thing. However, breathing is only one part of respiration. **Respiration** is the process by which a body gets and uses oxygen and releases carbon dioxide and water. Respiration is divided into two parts. The first part is breathing, which involves inhaling and exhaling. The second part is cellular respiration, which involves chemical reactions that release energy from food.

Breathing is made possible by your respiratory system. The **respiratory system** is the group of organs that take in oxygen and get rid of carbon dioxide. The nose, throat, lungs, and passageways that lead to the lungs make up the respiratory system. **Figure 1** shows the parts of the respiratory system.

respiration the exchange of oxygen and carbon dioxide between living cells and their environment; includes breathing and cellular respiration

respiratory system a collection of organs whose primary function is to take in oxygen and expel carbon dioxide

Figure 1 *Air moves into and out of the body through the respiratory system.*

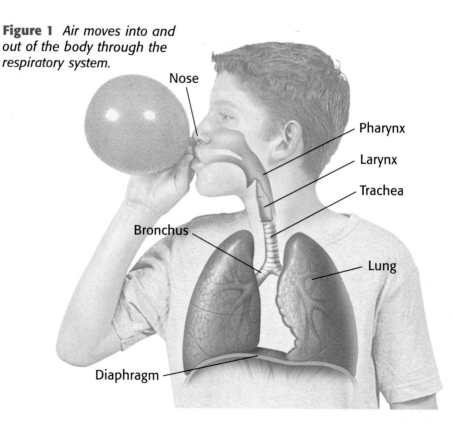

Nose

Pharynx

Larynx

Trachea

Bronchus

Lung

Diaphragm

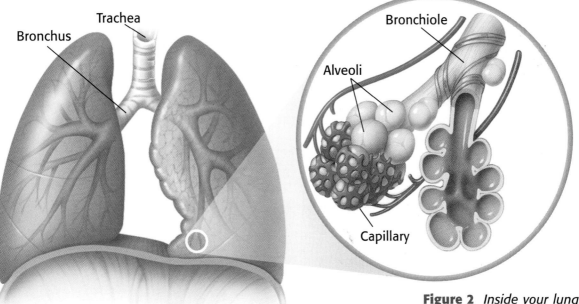

Bronchus

Trachea

Bronchiole

Alveoli

Capillary

Figure 2 *Inside your lungs, the bronchi branch into bronchioles. The bronchioles lead to tiny sacs called alveoli.*

Nose, Pharynx, and Larynx

Your *nose* is the main passageway into and out of the respiratory system. Air can be breathed in through and out of the nose. Air can also enter and leave through the mouth.

From the nose, air flows into the **pharynx** (FAR ingks), or throat. Food and drink also travel through the pharynx on the way to the stomach. The pharynx branches into two tubes. One tube, the *esophagus,* leads to the stomach. The other tube is the larynx (LAR ingks). The larynx leads to the lungs.

The **larynx** is the part of the throat that contains the vocal cords. The *vocal cords* are a pair of elastic bands that stretch across the larynx. Muscles connected to the larynx control how much the vocal cords are stretched. When air flows between the vocal cords, the cords vibrate. These vibrations make sound.

Trachea

The larynx guards the entrance to a large tube called the **trachea** (TRAY kee uh), or windpipe. Your body has two large, spongelike lungs. The trachea, shown in **Figure 2,** is the passageway for air traveling from the larynx to the lungs.

Bronchi and Alveoli

The trachea splits into two branches called **bronchi** (BRAHNG KIE) (singular, *bronchus*). One bronchus connects to each lung. Each bronchus branches into smaller tubes that are called *bronchioles* (BRAHNG kee OHLZ). In the lungs, each bronchiole branches to form tiny sacs that are called **alveoli** (al VEE uh LIE) (singular, *alveolus*).

✓ Reading Check Describe the flow of air from your nose to your alveoli. (*See the Appendix for answers to Reading Checks.*)

pharynx the passage from the mouth to the larynx and esophagus

larynx the area of the throat that contains the vocal cords and produces vocal sounds

trachea the tube that connects the larynx to the lungs

bronchus one of the two tubes that connect the lungs with the trachea

alveoli any of the tiny air sacs of the lungs where oxygen and carbon dioxide are exchanged

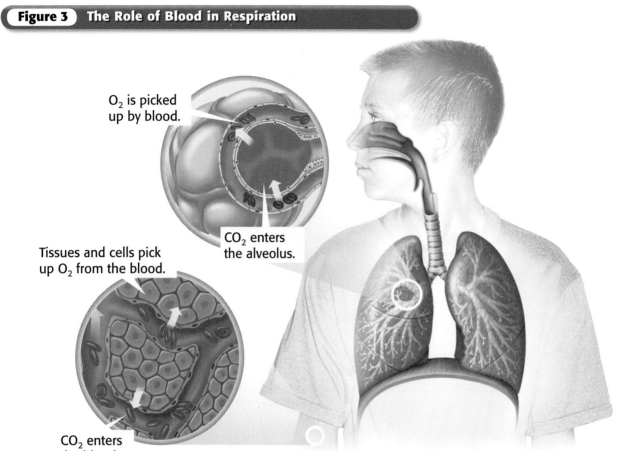

Figure 3 The Role of Blood in Respiration

O_2 is picked up by blood.

CO_2 enters the alveolus.

Tissues and cells pick up O_2 from the blood.

CO_2 enters the blood.

CONNECTION TO Chemistry

Oxygen and Blood When people who live at low elevations travel up into the mountains, they may find themselves breathing heavily even when they are not exerting themselves. Why might this happen?

Breathing

When you breathe, air is sucked into or forced out of your lungs. However, your lungs have no muscles of their own. Instead, breathing is done by the diaphragm (DIE uh FRAM) and rib muscles. The *diaphragm* is a dome-shaped muscle beneath the lungs. When you inhale, the diaphragm contracts and moves down. The chest cavity's volume increases. At the same time, some of your rib muscles contract and lift your rib cage. As a result, your chest cavity gets bigger and a vacuum is created. Air is sucked in. Exhaling is this process in reverse.

Breathing and Cellular Respiration

In *cellular respiration,* oxygen is used by cells to release energy stored in molecules of glucose. Where does the oxygen come from? When you inhale, you take in oxygen. This oxygen diffuses into red blood cells and is carried to tissue cells. The oxygen then diffuses out of the red blood cells and into each cell. Cells use the oxygen to release chemical energy. During the process, carbon dioxide (CO_2) and water are produced. Carbon dioxide is exhaled from the lungs. **Figure 3** shows how breathing and blood circulation are related.

 **Reading Check** What is cellular respiration?

Respiratory Disorders

Millions of people suffer from respiratory disorders. Respiratory disorders include asthma, emphysema, and severe acute respiratory syndrome (SARS). Asthma causes the bronchioles to narrow. A person who has asthma has difficulty breathing. An asthma attack may be triggered by irritants such as dust or pollen. SARS is caused by a virus. A person who has SARS may have a fever and difficulty breathing. Emphysema happens when the alveoli have been damaged. People who have emphysema have trouble getting the oxygen they need. **Figure 4** shows a lung damaged by emphysema.

Figure 4 *The photo on the left shows a healthy lung. The photo on the right shows the lung of a person who had emphysema.*

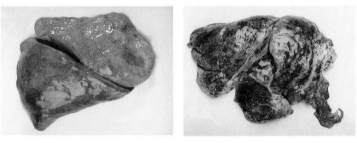

Why Do People Snore?
1. Get a **15 cm² sheet of wax paper.**
2. Hum your favorite song.
3. Then, take the wax paper and press it against your lips. Hum the song again.
4. How was your humming different when wax paper was pressed to your mouth?
5. Use your observations to guess what might cause snoring.

SECTION Review

Summary

- Air travels to the lungs through the nose or mouth, pharynx, larynx, trachea, and bronchi.
- In the lungs, the bronchi branch into bronchioles, which branch into alveoli.
- Breathing involves lungs, muscles in the rib cage, and the diaphragm.
- Oxygen enters the blood through the alveoli in the lungs. Carbon dioxide leaves the blood and is exhaled.
- Respiratory disorders include asthma, SARS, and emphysema.

Using Key Terms

For each pair of terms, explain how the meanings of the terms differ.

1. *pharynx* and *larynx*

Understanding Key Ideas

2. Which of the following are respiratory disorders?
   a. SARS, alveoli, and asthma
   b. alveoli, emphysema, and SARS
   c. larynx, asthma, and SARS
   d. SARS, emphysema, and asthma

3. Explain how breathing happens.

4. Describe how your cardiovascular and respiratory systems work together.

Math Skills

5. Total lung capacity (TLC) is about 6 L. A person can exhale about 3.6 L. What percentage of TLC cannot be exhaled?

Critical Thinking

6. **Interpreting Statistics** About 6.3 million children in the United States have asthma. About 4 million of them had an asthma attack last year. What do these statistics tell you about the relationship between asthma and asthma attacks?

7. **Identifying Relationships** If a respiratory disorder causes lungs to fill with fluid, how might this affect a person's health?

SCiLINKS.

Developed and maintained by the National Science Teachers Association

For a variety of links related to this chapter, go to www.scilinks.org
Topic: The Respiratory System; Respiratory Disorders
SciLinks code: HSM1307; HSM1306

Skills Practice Lab

Carbon Dioxide Breath

Carbon dioxide is important to both plants and animals. Plants take in carbon dioxide during photosynthesis and give off oxygen as a byproduct of the process. Animals—including you—take in oxygen during respiration and give off carbon dioxide as a byproduct of the process.

OBJECTIVES

Detect the presence of carbon dioxide in your breath.

Compare the data for carbon dioxide in your breath with the data from your classmates.

MATERIALS

- calculator (optional)
- clock with a second hand, or a stopwatch
- Erlenmeyer flask, 150 mL
- eyedropper
- gloves, protective
- graduated cylinder, 150 mL
- paper towels
- phenol red indicator solution
- plastic drinking straw
- water, 100 mL

SAFETY

Procedure

1. Put on your gloves, safety goggles, and apron.

2. Use the graduated cylinder to pour 100 mL of water into a 150 mL flask.

3. Using an eyedropper, carefully place four drops of phenol red indicator solution into the water. The water should turn orange.

4. Place a plastic drinking straw into the solution of phenol red and water. Drape a paper towel over the flask to prevent splashing.

5. Carefully blow through the straw into the solution.
   Caution: Do not inhale through the straw. Do not drink the solution, and do not share a straw with anyone.

6 Your lab partner should begin keeping time as soon as you start to blow through the straw. Have your lab partner time how long the solution takes to change color. Record the time.

Analyze the Results

1 **Describing Events** Describe what happens to the indicator solution.

2 **Examining Data** Compare your data with those of your classmates. What was the longest length of time it took to see a color change? What was the shortest? How do you account for the difference?

3 **Constructing Graphs** Make a bar graph that compares your data with the data of your classmates.

Draw Conclusions

4 **Interpreting Information** Do you think that there is a relationship between the length of time the solution takes to change color and the person's physical characteristics, such as which gender the tester is or whether the tester has an athletic build? Explain your answer.

5 **Making Predictions** Predict how exercise might affect the results of your experiment. For example, would you predict that the level of carbon dioxide in the breath of someone who was exercising would be higher or lower than the carbon dioxide level in the breath of someone who was sitting quietly? Would you predict that the level of carbon dioxide in the breath would affect the timing of any color change in the phenol solution?

Applying Your Data

Do jumping jacks or sit-ups for 3 minutes, and then repeat the experiment. Did the phenol solution still change color? Did your exercising change the timing? Describe and explain any change.

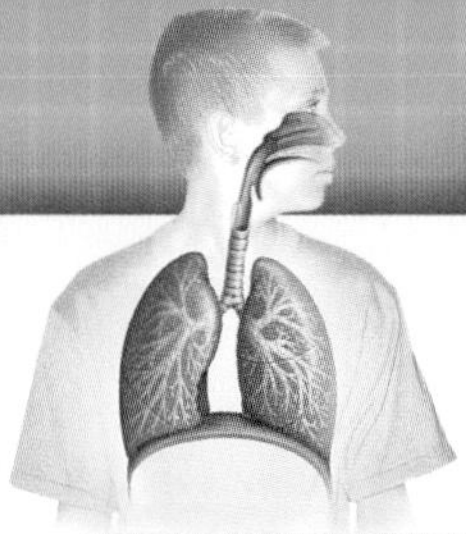

Chapter Review

USING KEY TERMS

Complete each of the following sentences by choosing the correct term from the word bank.

red blood cells	veins
white blood cells	arteries
lymphatic system	larynx
alveoli	bronchi
respiratory system	trachea

1 ___ deliver oxygen to the cells of the body.

2 ___ carry blood away from the heart.

3 The ___ helps the body fight pathogens.

4 The ___ contains the vocal cords.

5 The pathway of air through the respiratory system ends at the tiny sacs called ___.

UNDERSTANDING KEY IDEAS

Multiple Choice

6 Blood from the lungs enters the heart at the

a. left ventricle.

b. left atrium.

c. right atrium.

d. right ventricle.

7 Blood cells are made

a. in the heart.

b. from plasma.

c. from lymph.

d. in the bones.

8 Which of the following activities is a function of the lymphatic system?

a. returning excess fluid to the circulatory system

b. delivering nutrients to the cells

c. bringing oxygen to the blood

d. pumping blood to all parts of the body

9 Alveoli are surrounded by

a. veins.

b. muscles.

c. capillaries.

d. lymph nodes.

10 What prevents blood from flowing backward in veins?

a. platelets

b. valves

c. muscles

d. cartilage

11 Air moves into the lungs when the diaphragm muscle

a. contracts and moves down.

b. contracts and moves up.

c. relaxes and moves down.

d. relaxes and moves up.

Short Answer

12 What is the difference between pulmonary circulation and systemic circulation in the cardiovascular system?

13 Walton's blood pressure is 110/65. What do the two numbers mean?

14 What body process produces the carbon dioxide you exhale?

15 Describe how the circulatory system and the lymphatic system work together to keep your body healthy.

16 How is the spleen important to both the lymphatic system and the circulatory system?

17 Briefly describe the path that oxygen follows in your respiratory system and your circulatory system.

18 **Concept Mapping** Use the following terms to create a concept map: *blood, oxygen, alveoli, capillaries,* and *carbon dioxide.*

19 **Making Comparisons** Compare and contrast the functions of the circulatory system and the lymphatic system.

20 **Identifying Relationships** Why do you think there are hairs in your nose?

21 **Applying Concepts** After a person donates blood, the blood is stored in one-pint bags until it is needed for a transfusion. A healthy person has about 5 million RBCs in each cubic millimeter (1 mm^3) of blood.

  a. How many RBCs are in 1 mL of blood? (One milliliter is equal to 1 cm^3 and to 1,000 mm^3.)

  b. How many RBCs are there in 1 pt? (One pint is equal to 473 mL.)

22 **Predicting Consequences** What would happen if all of the red blood cells in your blood disappeared?

23 **Identifying Relationships** When a person is not feeling well, a doctor may examine samples of the person's blood to see how many white blood cells are present. Why would this information be useful?

The diagram below shows how the human heart would look in cross section. Use the diagram to answer the questions that follow.

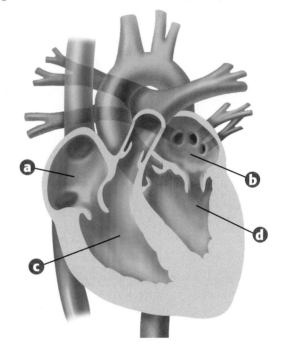

24 Which letter identifies the chamber that receives blood from systemic circulation? What is this chamber's name?

25 Which letter identifies the chamber that receives blood from the lungs? What is this chamber's name?

26 Which letter identifies the chamber that pumps blood to the lungs? What is this chamber's name?

Read each of the passages below. Then, answer the questions that follow each passage.

Passage 1 For some reason, about one in five people sneeze when they step from a dimly lit area into a brightly lit area. In fact, some may sneeze a dozen times or more! Fortunately, the sneezing usually stops relatively quickly. This sneeze reaction is called a photic sneeze reflex (FOHT ik SNEEZ REE fleks). No one knows for certain why it happens. A few years ago, some geneticists studied the photic sneeze reflex. They named it the *ACHOO syndrome*. Scientists know that the ACHOO syndrome runs in families. So, the photic sneeze may be hereditary and can be passed from parent to child. Sometimes, even the number of times in a row that each person sneezes is the same throughout a family.

1. According to the passage, the ACHOO syndrome is most likely to be which of the following?
  A contagious
  B photosynthetic
  C hereditary
  D allergic

2. In the passage, what does *photic* mean?
  F having to do with sneezing
  G having to do with plants
  H having to do with genetics
  I having to do with light

3. Which of the following statements is one clue that the photic sneeze reflex can be passed from parent to child?
  A The reflex is triggered by bright light.
  B Sneezing usually stops after a few sneezes.
  C Family members even sneeze the same number of times.
  D Scientists do not know what causes the ACHOO syndrome.

Passage 2 The two main functions of blood are transporting nutrients and oxygen from the lungs to cells and carrying carbon dioxide and other waste materials away from cells to the lungs or other organs. Blood also transfers body heat to the body surface and plays a role in defending the body against disease. The respiratory system transports gases to and from blood. The respiratory system and blood work together to carry out external respiration and internal respiration. External respiration is the exchange of gases between the atmosphere and blood. Internal respiration is the exchange of gases between blood and the cells of the body.

1. In the passage, what does *external respiration* mean?
  A the exchange of gases outdoors
  B the inhalation of gases as you breathe in
  C the exchange of gases between blood and the atmosphere
  D the exhalation of gases as you breathe out

2. Which of the following statements is a fact in the passage?
  F The respiratory system transports oxygen to all the cells of the body.
  G The respiratory system is part of the circulatory system.
  H Blood is a kind of cardiac tissue.
  I Blood transports oxygen to cells.

3. According to the passage, what are two of the roles blood plays in the human body?
  A transferring body heat and defending against disease
  B defending against disease and transporting gases to the circulatory system
  C transporting carbon dioxide to body cells and transferring body heat
  D external respiration and atmosphere

Use the graph below to answer the questions that follow.

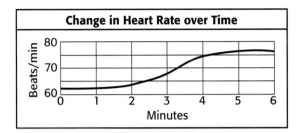

Change in Heart Rate over Time

1. What is the most likely explanation for the change seen after the two-minute mark?

   A The person started exercising.

   B The person fell asleep.

   C The person inhaled.

   D The person sat down.

2. How much faster is the heart beating during minute 5 than during minute 2?

   F 10 beats per minute more

   G 12 beats per minute more

   H 15 beats per minute more

   I 17 beats per minute more

3. About how many minutes did it take for this person's heart rate to go from 65 beats per minute to 75 beats per minute?

   A 0.7 minute

   B 1.0 minute

   C 1.7 minutes

   D 4.0 minutes

4. After how many minutes does this person's heart rate return to its resting rate?

   F 1.0 minute

   G 2.0 minutes

   H 5.0 minutes

   I There is not enough information to determine the answer.

Read each question below, and choose the best answer.

1. If Jim's heart beats 73 times every minute, Jen's heart beats 68 times every minute, and Leigh's heart beats 81 times every minute, what is the average heart rate for these 3 people?

   A 73 beats per minute

   B 74 beats per minute

   C 141 beats per minute

   D 222 beats per minute

2. The Griffith family has 4 dogs. Each of the dogs eats between 0.9 kg and 1.3 kg of food every day. Which is a reasonable estimate of the total amount of food all 4 dogs eat every day?

   F 1 kg of food

   G 3 kg of food

   H 4 kg of food

   I 8 kg of food

3. Assume that the average person's resting heart rate is 70 beats per minute. The resting heart rate of a particular person is 10 beats per minute more than the average person's. If a person with the higher heart rate lives 75 years, about how many more times will his or her heart beat than the average person's heart in that time?

   A 3,942

   B 394,200

   C 3,942,000

   D 394,200,000

4. At rest, the cells of the human body use about 250 mL of oxygen per minute. At that rate, how much oxygen would the cells of the human body use every 24 hours?

   F about 36 L

   G about 360 L

   H about 36,000 L

   I about 360,000 L

Standardized Test Preparation

Science in Action

Science, Technology, and Society

Artificial Blood

What happens when someone loses blood rapidly? Loss of blood can be fatal in a very short time, so lost blood must be replaced as quickly as possible. But what if enough blood, or blood of the right type, is not immediately available? Scientists are developing different types of artificial blood—including one based on cow hemoglobin—that may soon be used to save lives that would otherwise be lost.

Weird Science

Circular Breathing and the Didgeridoo

Do you play a musical instrument such as a clarinet, flute, or tuba? How long can you blow into it before you have to take a breath? Can you blow into it for one minute? two minutes? And what happens when you stop to breathe? The Aboriginal people of Australia have a musical instrument called the *didgeridoo* (DIJ uh ree DOO). Didgeridoo players can play for hours without stopping to take a breath. They use a technique called *circular breathing* that lets them inhale and exhale at the same time. Circular breathing lets a musician play music without having to take breaths as often. With a little practice, maybe you can do it, too.

Language Arts ACTiViTY

WRITING SKILL Imagine that you are a doctor and one of your patients needs surgery. Create a pamphlet or brochure that explains what artificial blood is and how it may be used in surgical procedures.

Social Studies ACTiViTY

WRITING SKILL Select a country from Africa or Asia. Research that country's traditional musical instruments or singing style. Write a description of how the instruments or singing style of that country differs from those of the United States. Illustrate your report.

Anthony Roberts, Jr.

Leader in Training Anthony Roberts, Jr., has asthma. When he was in the 5th grade, his school counselor told him about a summer camp—The Boggy Creek Gang Camp—that was just being built. His counselor said that the camp was designed to serve kids who have asthma or other disabilities and diseases, such as AIDS, cancer, diabetes, epilepsy, hemophilia, heart disease, kidney disease, rheumatic diseases, and sickle cell anemia. Kids, in other words, who might otherwise never go to summer camp. Anthony jumped at the chance to go. Now, Anthony is too old to be a camper, and he is too young to be a regular counselor. But he can be a *Leader in Training* (LIT). Some camps have LIT programs that help young people make the transition from camper to counselor.

For Anthony, the chance to be an LIT fit perfectly with his love of camping and with his desire to work with kids with disabilities. Anthony remembers the fun he had and wants to help other kids have the same summer fun he did.

Math ACTIVITY

Research how many children under 17 years of age in the United States have asthma. Make a bar graph that shows how the number of children who have asthma has changed since 1981. What does this graph tell you about rates of asthma among children in the United States?

To learn more about these Science in Action topics, visit go.hrw.com and type in the keyword **HL5BD2F.**

Check out Current Science® articles related to this chapter by visiting go.hrw.com. Just type in the keyword HL5CS23.

The Digestive and Urinary Systems

About the PHOTO

Is this a giant worm? No, it's an X ray of a healthy large intestine! Your large intestine helps your body preserve water. As mostly digested food passes through your large intestine, water is drawn out of the food. This water is returned to the bloodstream. The gray shadow behind the intestine is the spinal column. The areas that look empty are actually filled with organs. A special liquid helps this large intestine show up on the X ray.

PRE-READING ACTIVITY

Graphic Organizer

Chain-of-Events Chart Before you read the chapter, create the graphic organizer entitled "Chain-of-Events Chart" described in the **Study Skills** section of the Appendix. As you read the chapter, fill in the chart with details about each step of the processes that your body uses to digest food.

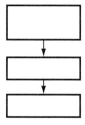

Changing Foods

The stomach breaks down food by, in part, squeezing the food. You can model the action of the stomach in the following activity.

Procedure

1. Add **200 mL of flour** and **100 mL of water** to a **resealable plastic bag.**

2. Mix **100 mL of vegetable oil** with the flour and water.

3. Seal the plastic bag.

4. Shake the bag until the flour, water, and oil are well mixed.

5. Remove as much air from the bag as you can, and reseal the bag carefully.

6. Knead the bag carefully with your hands for 5 min. Be careful to keep the bag sealed.

Analysis

1. Describe the mixture before and after you kneaded the bag.

2. How might the changes you saw in the mixture relate to how your stomach digests food?

3. Do you think this activity is a good model of how your stomach works? Explain your answer.

The Digestive System

It's your last class before lunch, and you're starving! Finally, the bell rings, and you get to eat!

You feel hungry because your brain receives signals that your cells need energy. But eating is only the beginning of the story. Your body must change a meal into substances that you can use. Your **digestive system,** shown in **Figure 1,** is a group of organs that work together to digest food so that it can be used by the body.

Digestive System at a Glance

The most obvious part of your digestive system is a series of tubelike organs called the *digestive tract.* Food passes through the digestive tract. The digestive tract includes your mouth, pharynx, esophagus, stomach, small intestine, large intestine, rectum, and anus. The human digestive tract can be more than 9 m long! The liver, gallbladder, pancreas, and salivary glands are also part of the digestive system. But food does not pass through these organs.

digestive system the organs that break down food so that it can be used by the body

Figure 1 **The Digestive System**

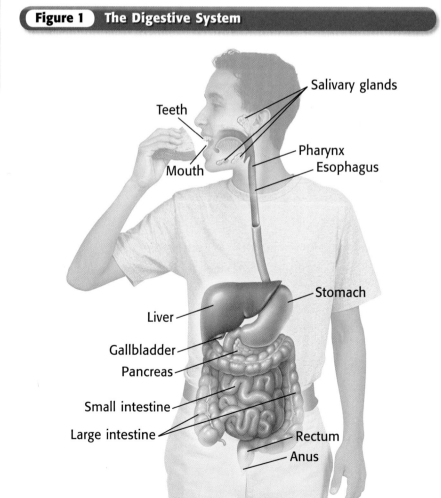

Teeth
Salivary glands
Mouth
Pharynx
Esophagus
Liver
Stomach
Gallbladder
Pancreas
Small intestine
Large intestine
Rectum
Anus

Breaking Down Food

Digestion is the process of breaking down food, such as a peanut butter and jelly sandwich, into a form that can pass from the digestive tract into the bloodstream. There are two types of digestion—mechanical and chemical. The breaking, crushing, and mashing of food is called *mechanical digestion.* In *chemical digestion,* large molecules are broken down into nutrients. Nutrients are substances in food that the body needs for normal growth, maintenance, and repair.

Three major types of nutrients—carbohydrates, proteins, and fats—make up most of the food you eat. In fact, a peanut butter and jelly sandwich contains all three of these nutrients. Substances called *enzymes* break some nutrients into smaller particles that the body can use. For example, proteins are chains of smaller molecules called *amino acids.* Proteins are too large to be absorbed into the bloodstream. So, enzymes cut up the chain of amino acids. The amino acids are small enough to pass into the bloodstream. This process is shown in **Figure 2.**

Reading Check How do enzymes help digestion? (*See the Appendix for answers to Reading Checks.*)

Break It Up!

1. Drop **one piece of hard candy** into a **clear plastic cup of water.**

2. Wrap an **identical candy** in a **towel,** and crush the candy with a **hammer.** Drop the candy into a **second clear cup of water.**

3. The next day, examine both cups. What is different about the two candies?

4. What type of digestion is represented by breaking the hard candy?

5. How does chewing your food help the process of digestion?

Figure 2 **The Role of Enzymes in Protein Digestion**

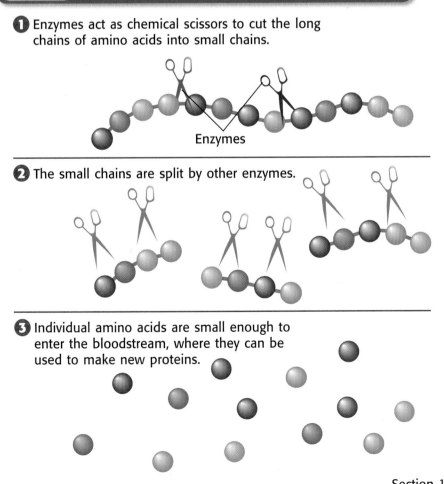

❶ Enzymes act as chemical scissors to cut the long chains of amino acids into small chains.

Enzymes

❷ The small chains are split by other enzymes.

❸ Individual amino acids are small enough to enter the bloodstream, where they can be used to make new proteins.

Digestion Begins in the Mouth

Chewing is important for two reasons. First, chewing creates small, slippery pieces of food that are easier to swallow than big, dry pieces are. Second, small pieces of food are easier to digest.

Teeth

Teeth are very important organs for mechanical digestion. With the help of strong jaw muscles, teeth break and grind food. The outermost layer of a tooth, the *enamel,* is the hardest material in the body. Enamel protects nerves and softer material inside the tooth. **Figure 3** shows a cross section of a tooth.

Have you ever noticed that your teeth have different shapes? Look at **Figure 4** to locate the different kinds of teeth. The molars are well suited for grinding food. The *premolars* are perfect for mashing food. The sharp teeth at the front of your mouth, the *incisors* and *canines,* are for shredding food.

Saliva

As you chew, the food mixes with a liquid called *saliva.* Saliva is made in salivary glands located in the mouth. Saliva contains an enzyme that begins the chemical digestion of carbohydrates. Saliva changes complex carbohydrates into simple sugars.

Leaving the Mouth

Once the food has been reduced to a soft mush, the tongue pushes it into the throat, which leads to a long, straight tube called the **esophagus** (i SAHF uh guhs). The esophagus squeezes the mass of food with rhythmic muscle contractions called *peristalsis* (PER uh STAL sis). Peristalsis forces the food into the stomach.

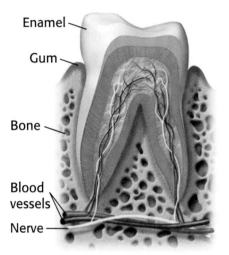

Figure 3 *A tooth, such as this molar, is made of many kinds of tissue.*

Enamel

Gum

Bone

Blood vessels

Nerve

esophagus a long, straight tube that connects the pharynx to the stomach

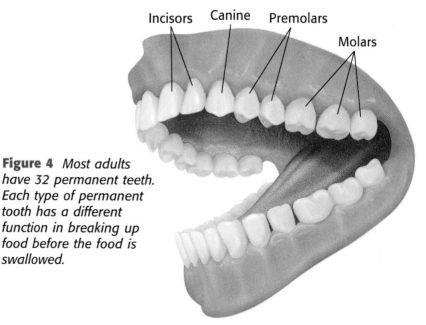

Incisors Canine Premolars Molars

Figure 4 *Most adults have 32 permanent teeth. Each type of permanent tooth has a different function in breaking up food before the food is swallowed.*

Figure 5   The Stomach

The stomach squeezes and mixes food for hours before it releases the mixture into the small intestine.

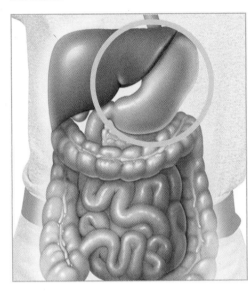

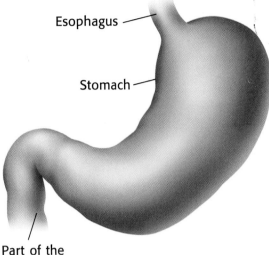

Esophagus

Stomach

Part of the small intestine

The Harsh Environment of the Stomach

The **stomach** is a muscular, saclike, digestive organ attached to the lower end of the esophagus. The stomach is shown in **Figure 5.** The stomach continues the mechanical digestion of your meal by squeezing the food with muscular contractions. While this squeezing is taking place, tiny glands in the stomach produce enzymes and acid. The enzymes and acid work together to break food into nutrients. Stomach acid also kills most bacteria that you might swallow with your food. After a few hours of combined mechanical and chemical digestion, your peanut butter and jelly sandwich has been reduced to a soupy mixture called *chyme* (KIEM).

stomach the saclike, digestive organ between the esophagus and the small intestine that breaks down food into a liquid by the action of muscles, enzymes, and acids

✓ **Reading Check** What is chyme?

Leaving the Stomach

The stomach slowly releases the chyme into the small intestine through a small ring of muscle that works like a valve. This valve keeps food in the stomach until the food has been thoroughly mixed with digestive fluids. Each time the valve opens and closes, it lets a small amount of chyme into the small intestine. Because the stomach releases chyme slowly, the intestine has more time to mix the chyme with fluids from the liver and pancreas. These fluids help digest food and stop the harsh acids in chyme from hurting the small intestine.

Tooth Truth

Young children get a first set of 20 teeth called *baby teeth*. These teeth usually fall out and are replaced by 32 permanent teeth. How many more permanent teeth than baby teeth does a person have? What is the ratio of baby teeth to permanent teeth? Be sure to express the ratio in its most reduced form.

The Pancreas and Small Intestine

Most chemical digestion takes place after food leaves the stomach. Proteins, carbohydrates, and fats in the chyme are digested by the small intestine and fluids from the pancreas.

The Pancreas

When the chyme leaves the stomach, the chyme is very acidic. The pancreas makes fluids that protect the small intestine from the acid. The **pancreas** is an oval organ located between the stomach and small intestine. The chyme never enters the pancreas. Instead, the pancreatic fluid flows into the small intestine. This fluid contains enzymes that chemically digest chyme and contains bicarbonate, which neutralizes the acid in chyme. The pancreas also functions as a part of the endocrine system by making hormones that regulate blood sugar.

The Small Intestine

The **small intestine** is a muscular tube that is about 2.5 cm in diameter. Other than having a small diameter, it is really not that small. In fact, if you stretched the small intestine out, it would be longer than you are tall—about 6 m! If you flattened out the surface of the small intestine, it would be larger than a tennis court! How is this possible? The inside wall of the small intestine is covered with fingerlike projections called *villi,* shown in **Figure 6.** The surface area of the small intestine is very large because of the villi. The villi are covered with tiny, nutrient-absorbing cells. Once the nutrients are absorbed, they enter the bloodstream.

pancreas the organ that lies behind the stomach and that makes digestive enzymes and hormones that regulate sugar levels

small intestine the organ between the stomach and the large intestine where most of the breakdown of food happens and most of the nutrients from food are absorbed

CONNECTION TO Social Studies

WRITING SKILL **Parasites** Intestinal parasites are organisms, such as roundworms and hookworms, that infect people and live in their digestive tract. Worldwide, intestinal parasites infect more than 1 billion people. Some parasites can be deadly. Research intestinal parasites in a library or on the Internet. Then, write a report on a parasite, including how it spreads, what problems it causes, how many people have it, and what can be done to stop it.

Figure 6 **The Small Intestine and Villi**

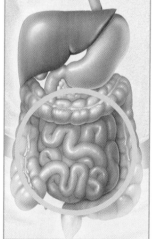

The highly folded lining of the small intestine has many fingerlike projections called *villi.*

Villi are covered with nutrient-absorbing cells that pass nutrients to the bloodstream.

Figure 7 The Liver and the Gallbladder

Food does not move through the liver, gallbladder, and pancreas even though these organs are linked to the small intestine.

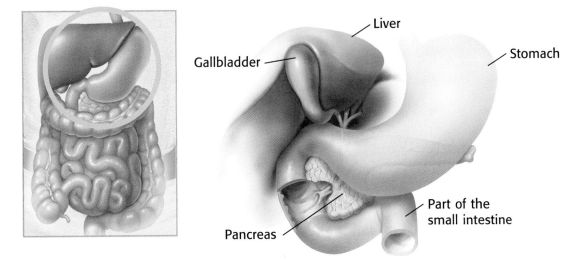

Liver

Gallbladder

Stomach

Pancreas

Part of the small intestine

The Liver and Gallbladder

The **liver** is a large, reddish brown organ that helps with digestion. A human liver can be as large as a football. Your liver is located toward your right side, slightly higher than your stomach, as shown in **Figure 7.** The liver helps with digestion in the following ways:

- It makes bile to break up fat.
- It stores nutrients.
- It breaks down toxins.

Breaking Up Fat

Although bile is made by the liver, bile is temporarily stored in a small, saclike organ called the **gallbladder,** shown in **Figure 7.** Bile is squeezed from the gallbladder into the small intestine, where the bile breaks large fat droplets into very small droplets. This mechanical process allows more fat molecules to be exposed to digestive enzymes.

✓ Reading Check How does bile help digest fat?

Storing Nutrients and Protecting the Body

After nutrients are broken down, they are absorbed into the bloodstream and carried through the body. Nutrients that are not needed right away are stored in the liver. The liver then releases the stored nutrients into the bloodstream as needed. The liver also captures and detoxifies many chemicals in the body. For instance, the liver produces enzymes that break down alcohol and many other drugs.

liver the largest organ in the body; it makes bile, stores and filters blood, and stores excess sugars as glycogen

gallbladder a sac-shaped organ that stores bile produced by the liver

Bile Model

You can model the way bile breaks down fat and oil by using dish soap. At home with a parent, put a small amount of water in a small jar. Then, add a few drops of vegetable oil to the water. Notice that the two liquids separate. Draw a picture of the jar and its contents. Next, add a few drops of dishwashing soap to the water, tighten the lid securely onto the jar, and shake the jar. What happened to the three liquids in the jar? Draw another picture of the jar and its contents.

large intestine the wider and shorter portion of the intestine that removes water from mostly digested food and that turns the waste into semisolid feces, or stool

The End of the Line

Material that can't be absorbed into the blood is pushed into the large intestine. The **large intestine** is the organ of the digestive system that stores, compacts, and then eliminates indigestible material from the body. The large intestine, shown in **Figure 8,** has a larger diameter than the small intestine. The large intestine is about 1.5 m long, and has a diameter of about 7.5 cm.

In the Large Intestine

Undigested material enters the large intestine as a soupy mixture. The large intestine absorbs most of the water in the mixture and changes the liquid into semisolid waste materials called *feces,* or *stool.*

Whole grains, fruits, and vegetables contain a carbohydrate, called *cellulose,* that humans cannot digest. We commonly refer to this material as *fiber.* Fiber keeps the stool soft and keeps material moving through the large intestine.

✓ **Reading Check** How does eating fiber help digestion?

Leaving the Body

The *rectum* is the last part of the large intestine. The rectum stores feces until they can be expelled. Feces pass to the outside of the body through an opening called the *anus.* It has taken your sandwich about 24 hours to make this journey through your digestive system.

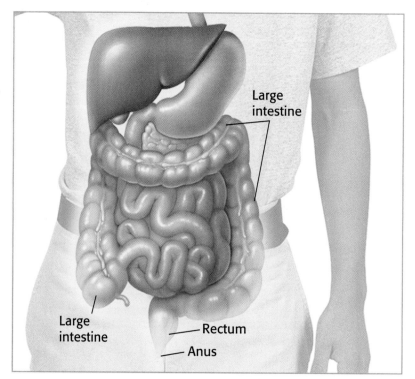

Figure 8 *The large intestine is the final organ of digestion.*

SECTION Review

Summary

- Your digestive system is a group of organs that work together to digest food so that the nutrients from food can be used by the body.

- The breaking and mashing of food is called *mechanical digestion*. Chemical digestion is the process that breaks large food molecules into simpler molecules.

- The stomach mixes food with acid and enzymes that break down nutrients. The mixture is called *chyme.*

- In the small intestine, pancreatic fluid and bile are mixed with chyme.

- From the small intestine, nutrients enter the bloodstream and are circulated to the body's cells.

- The liver makes bile, stores nutrients, and breaks down toxins.

- The large intestine absorbs water, changing liquid waste into semisolid stool, or feces.

Using Key Terms

1. Use each of the following terms in a separate sentence: *digestive system, large intestine,* and *small intestine.*

Understanding Key Ideas

2. Which of the following is NOT a function of the liver?
   a. to secrete bile
   b. to store nutrients
   c. to detoxify chemicals
   d. to compact wastes

3. What is the difference between mechanical digestion and chemical digestion?

4. What happens to the food that you eat when it gets to your stomach?

5. Describe the role of the liver, gallbladder, and pancreas in digestion.

6. Put the following steps of digestion in order.
   a. Food is chewed by the teeth in the mouth.
   b. Water is absorbed by the large intestine.
   c. Food is reduced to chyme in the stomach.
   d. Food moves down the esophagus.
   e. Nutrients are absorbed by the small intestine.
   f. The pancreas releases enzymes.

Critical Thinking

7. **Evaluating Conclusions** Explain the following statement: "Digestion begins in the mouth."

8. **Identifying Relationships** How would the inability to make saliva affect digestion?

Interpreting Graphics

9. Label and describe the function of each of the organs in the diagram below.

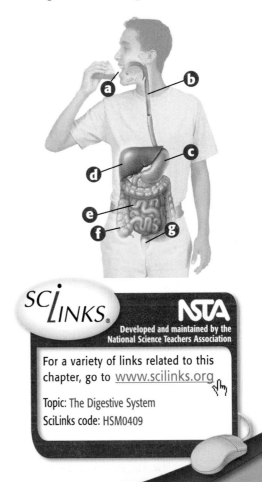

SCILINKS®

NSTA
Developed and maintained by the
National Science Teachers Association

For a variety of links related to this chapter, go to www.scilinks.org

Topic: The Digestive System
SciLinks code: HSM0409

The Urinary System

As blood travels through the tissues, it picks up waste produced by the body's cells. Your blood is like a train that comes to town to drop off supplies and take away garbage. If the waste is not removed, your body can actually be poisoned.

Excretion is the process of removing waste products from the body. Three of your body systems have a role in excretion. Your integumentary system releases waste products and water when you sweat. Your respiratory system releases carbon dioxide and water when you exhale. Finally, the **urinary system** contains the organs that remove waste products from your blood.

Cleaning the Blood

As your body performs the chemical activities that keep you alive, waste products, such as carbon dioxide and ammonia, are made. Your body has to get rid of these waste products to stay healthy. The urinary system, shown in **Figure 1,** removes these waste products from the blood.

READING WARM-UP

Objectives

● Describe the parts and functions of the urinary system.

● Explain how the kidneys filter blood.

● Describe three disorders of the urinary system.

Terms to Learn

urinary system
kidney
nephron

READING STRATEGY

Reading Organizer As you read this section, create an outline of the section. Use the headings from the section in your outline.

urinary system the organs that produce, store, and eliminate urine

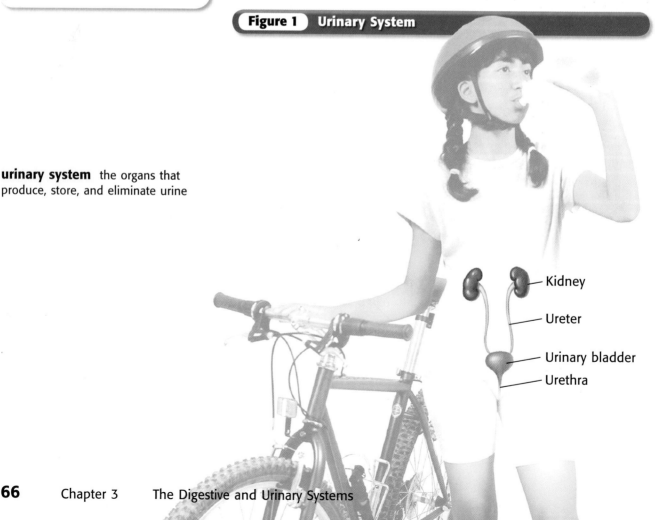

Figure 1 Urinary System

Kidney

Ureter

Urinary bladder

Urethra

The Kidneys as Filters

The **kidneys** are a pair of organs that constantly clean the blood. Your kidneys filter about 2,000 L of blood each day. Your body holds only 5.6 L of blood, so your blood cycles through your kidneys about 350 times per day!

Inside each kidney, shown in **Figure 2,** are more than 1 million nephrons. **Nephrons** are microscopic filters in the kidney that remove wastes from the blood. Nephrons remove many harmful substances. One of the most important substances removed by nephrons is urea (yoo REE uh), which contains nitrogen and is formed when cells use protein for energy.

Reading Check How are nephrons related to kidneys? (*See the Appendix for answers to Reading Checks*.)

kidney one of the pair of organs that filter water and wastes from the blood and that excrete products as urine

nephron the unit in the kidney that filters blood

Figure 2 **How the Kidneys Filter Blood**

❶ A large artery brings blood into each kidney.

❷ Tiny blood vessels branch off the main artery and pass through part of each nephron.

❸ Water and other small substances, such as glucose, salts, amino acids, and urea, are forced out of the blood vessels and into the nephrons.

❹ As these substances flow through the nephrons, most of the water and some nutrients are moved back into blood vessels that wrap around the nephrons. A concentrated mixture of waste materials is left behind in the nephrons.

❺ The cleaned blood, which has slightly less water and much less waste material, leaves each kidney in a large vein to recirculate in the body.

❻ The yellow fluid that remains in the nephrons is called *urine.* Urine leaves each kidney through a slender tube called the *ureter* and flows into the *urinary bladder,* where urine is stored.

❼ Urine leaves the body through another tube called the *urethra. Urination* is the process of expelling urine from the body.

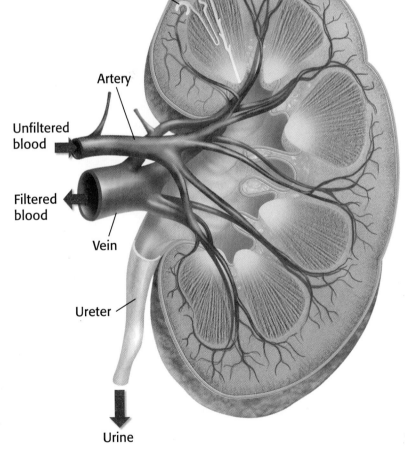

Nephron

Artery

Unfiltered blood

Filtered blood

Vein

Ureter

Urine

Figure 3 *Drinking water when you exercise helps replace the water you lose when you sweat.*

Water In, Water Out

You drink water every day. You lose water every day in sweat and urine. You need to get rid of as much water as you drink. If you don't, your body will swell up. So, how does your body keep the water levels in balance? The balance of fluids is controlled by chemical messengers in the body called *hormones*.

Sweat and Thirst

When you are too warm, as the boy in **Figure 3** is, you lose a lot of water in the form of sweat. The evaporation of water from your skin cools you down. As the water content of the blood drops, the salivary glands produce less saliva. This is one of the reasons you feel thirsty.

Antidiuretic Hormone

When you get thirsty, other parts of your body react to the water shortage, too. A hormone called *antidiuretic hormone* (AN tee DIE yoo RET ik HAWR MOHN), or ADH, is released. ADH signals the kidneys to take water from the nephrons. The nephrons return the water to the bloodstream. Thus, the kidneys make less urine. When your blood has too much water, small amounts of ADH are released. The kidneys react by allowing more water to stay in the nephrons and leave the body as urine.

Diuretics

Some beverages contain caffeine, which is a *diuretic* (DIE yoo RET ik). Diuretics cause the kidneys to make more urine, which decreases the amount of water in the blood. When you drink a beverage that contains water and caffeine, the caffeine increases fluid loss. So, your body gets to use less of the water from the caffeinated beverage than from a glass of water.

✓ **Reading Check** What are diuretics?

CONNECTION TO Language Arts

WRITING SKILL **Beverage Ban** During football season, a football coach insists that all members of the team avoid caffeinated beverages. Many of the players are upset by the news. Pretend that you are the coach. Write a letter to the members of the team explaining why it is better for them to drink water than to drink beverages that contain caffeine. Read the letter aloud to members of your family. Ask them how you could make your letter more convincing.

Urinary System Problems

The urinary system regulates body fluids and removes wastes from the blood. Any problems with water regulation can become dangerous for your body. Some common urinary system problems are described below.

- **Bacterial Infections** Bacteria can get into the bladder and ureters through the urethra and cause painful infections. Infections should be treated early, before they spread to the kidneys. Infections in the kidneys can permanently damage the nephrons.

- **Kidney Stones** Sometimes, salts and other wastes collect inside the kidneys and form kidney stones like the one in **Figure 4.** Some kidney stones interfere with urine flow and cause pain. Most kidney stones pass naturally from the body, but sometimes they must be removed by a doctor.

- **Kidney Disease** Damage to nephrons can prevent normal kidney functioning and can lead to kidney disease. If a person's kidneys do not function properly, a kidney machine can be used to filter waste from the blood.

Figure 4 *This kidney stone had to be removed from a patient's urinary system.*

SECTION Review

Summary

- The urinary system removes liquid waste as urine. The filtering structures in the kidney are called *nephrons.*

- Most of the water in the blood is returned to the bloodstream. Urine passes through the ureter, into the bladder, and out of the body through the urethra.

- Disorders of the urinary system include infections, kidney stones, and kidney disease.

Using Key Terms

1. In your own words, write a definition for the term *urinary system.*

Understanding Key Ideas

2. Which event happens first?
   a. Water is absorbed into blood.
   b. A large artery brings blood into the kidney.
   c. Water enters the nephrons.
   d. The nephron separates water from wastes.

3. How do kidneys filter blood?

4. Describe three disorders of the urinary system.

Math Skills

5. A study has shown that 75% of teenage boys drink 34 oz of soda per day. How many 12 oz cans of soda would a boy drink in a week if he drank 34 oz per day?

Critical Thinking

6. **Applying Concepts** Which of the following contains more water: the blood going into the kidney or the blood leaving it?

7. **Predicting Consequences** When people have one kidney removed, their other kidney can often keep their blood clean. But the remaining kidney often changes. Predict how the remaining kidney may change to do the work of two kidneys.

SCILINKS®

NSTA
Developed and maintained by the National Science Teachers Association

For a variety of links related to this chapter, go to www.scilinks.org
Topic: The Urinary System; Urinary System Ailments
SciLinks code: HSM1583; HSM1584

Skills Practice Lab

As the Stomach Churns

The stomach, as you know, performs not only mechanical digestion but also chemical digestion. As the stomach churns, which moves the food particles around, the digestive fluids—acid and enzymes—are added to begin protein digestion.

Commercially prepared meat tenderizers contain enzymes from plants that break down, or digest, proteins. Two types of meat tenderizer are commonly available at grocery stores. One type of tenderizer contains an enzyme called *papain,* from papaya. Another type of tenderizer contains an enzyme called *bromelain,* from pineapple. In this lab, you will test the effects of these two types of meat tenderizers on beef stew meat.

Ask a Question

1 Determine which question you will answer through your experiment. That question may be one of the following: Which meat tenderizer will work faster? Which one will make the meat more tender? Will the meat tenderizers change the color of the meat or water? What might these color changes, if any, indicate?

Form a Hypothesis

2 Form a hypothesis from the question you formed in step 1. **Caution:** Do not taste any of the materials in this activity.

Test the Hypothesis

3 Identify all variables and controls present in your experiment. In your notebook, make a data table that includes these variables and controls. Use this data table to record your observations and results.

4 Label one test tube with the name of one tenderizer, and label the other test tube with the name of the other tenderizer. Label the third test tube "Control." What will the test tube labeled "Control" contain?

OBJECTIVES

Demonstrate chemical digestion in the stomach.

Investigate three forms of chemical digestion.

MATERIALS

- beef stew meat, 1 cm cubes (3)
- eyedropper
- gloves, protective
- graduated cylinder, 25 mL
- hydrochloric acid, very dilute, 0.1 M
- measuring spoon, 1/4 tsp
- meat tenderizer, commercially prepared, containing bromelain
- meat tenderizer, commercially prepared, containing papain
- tape, masking
- test tubes (4)
- test-tube marker
- test-tube rack
- water

SAFETY

5 Pour 20 mL of water into each test tube.

6 Use the eyedropper to add four drops of very dilute hydrochloric acid to each test tube. **Caution:** Hydrochloric acid can burn your skin. If any acid touches your skin, rinse the area with running water and tell your teacher immediately.

7 Use the measuring spoon to add 1/4 tsp of each meat tenderizer to its corresponding test tube.

8 Add one cube of beef to each test tube.

9 Record your observations for each test tube immediately, after 5 min, after 15 min, after 30 min, and after 24 h.

Analyze the Results

1 **Describing Events** Did you immediately notice any differences in the beef in the three test tubes? At what time interval did you notice a significant difference in the appearance of the beef in the test tubes? Explain the differences.

2 **Examining Data** Did one meat tenderizer perform better than the other? Explain how you determined which performed better.

Draw Conclusions

3 **Evaluating Results** Was your hypothesis supported? Explain your answer.

4 **Applying Conclusions** Many animals that sting have venom composed of proteins. Explain how applying meat tenderizer to the wound helps relieve the pain of such a sting.

Chapter Review

USING KEY TERMS

Complete each of the following sentences by choosing the correct term from the word bank.

pancreas	digestive system
large intestine	stomach
kidney	small intestine
nephron	urinary system

1 The ____ secretes juices into the small intestine.

2 The saclike organ at the end of the esophagus is called the ____.

3 The ___ is an organ that contains millions of nephrons.

4 A group of organs that removes waste from the blood and excretes it from the body is called the ____.

5 The ____ is a group of organs that work together to break down food.

6 Indigestible material is formed into feces in the ____.

UNDERSTANDING KEY IDEAS

Multiple Choice

7 The hormone that signals the kidneys to make less urine is

a. urea.　　c. ADH.
b. caffeine.　　d. ATP.

8 Which of the following organs aids digestion by producing bile?

a. stomach　　c. small intestine
b. pancreas　　d. liver

9 The part of the kidney that filters the blood is the

a. artery.　　c. nephron.
b. ureter.　　d. urethra.

10 The fingerlike projections that line the small intestine are called

a. emulsifiers.

b. fats.

c. amino acids.

d. villi.

11 Which of the following is NOT part of the digestive tract?

a. mouth　　c. stomach
b. kidney　　d. rectum

12 The soupy mixture of food, enzymes, and acids in the stomach is called

a. chyme.　　c. urea.
b. villi.　　d. vitamins.

13 The stomach helps with

a. storing food.

b. chemical digestion.

c. physical digestion.

d. All of the above

14 The gall bladder stores

a. food.　　c. bile.
b. urine.　　d. villi.

15 The esophagus connects the

a. pharynx to the stomach.

b. stomach to the small intestine.

c. kidneys to the nephrons.

d. stomach to the large intestine.

Short Answer

16 Why is it important for the pancreas to release bicarbonate into the small intestine?

17 How does the structure of the small intestine help the small intestine absorb nutrients?

18 What is a kidney stone?

CRITICAL THINKING

19 **Concept Mapping** Use the following terms to create a concept map: *teeth, stomach, digestion, bile, saliva, mechanical digestion, gallbladder,* and *chemical digestion.*

20 **Predicting Consequences** How would digestion be affected if the liver were damaged?

21 **Analyzing Processes** When you put a piece of carbohydrate-rich food, such as bread, a potato, or a cracker, into your mouth, the food tastes bland. But if this food sits on your tongue for a while, the food will begin to taste sweet. What digestive process causes this change in taste?

22 **Making Comparisons** The recycling process for one kind of plastic begins with breaking the plastic into small pieces. Next, chemicals are used to break the small pieces of plastic down to its building blocks. Then, those building blocks are used to make new plastic. How is this process both like and unlike human digestion?

INTERPRETING GRAPHICS

The bar graph below shows how long the average meal spends in each portion of your digestive tract. Use the graph below to answer the questions that follow.

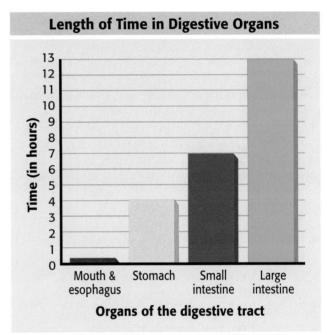

Length of Time in Digestive Organs

Time (in hours) / Organs of the digestive tract

23 In which part of your digestive tract does the food spend the longest amount of time?

24 On average, how much longer does food stay in the small intestine than in the stomach?

25 Which organ mixes food with special substances to make chyme? Approximately how long does food remain in this organ?

26 Bile breaks large fat droplets into very small droplets. How long is the food in your body before it comes into contact with bile?

Standardized Test Preparation

Read the passage below. Then, read each question that follows the passage. Decide which is the best answer to each question.

Passage 1 When you lose water, your blood becomes <u>more concentrated</u>. Think about how you make a powdered drink, such as lemonade. If you use the same amount of powder in 1 L of water as you do in 2 L of water, the drinks will taste different. The lemonade made with 1 L of water will be stronger because it is more concentrated. Losing water through sweating increases the concentration of sodium and potassium in your blood. The kidneys force the extra potassium out of the blood stream and into nephrons. From the nephrons, the potassium is eliminated from the body in urine.

1. The words *more concentrated* in this passage refer to
   A the same amount of water with different amounts of material dissolved in it.
   B small amounts of material dissolved in small amounts of water.
   C large amounts of material dissolved in large amounts of water.
   D a given amount of material dissolved in a smaller amount of water.

2. Which of the following statements is a fact from the passage?
   F Blood contains both potassium and sodium.
   G Losing too much sodium is dangerous.
   H Potassium and sodium can be replaced by drinking an exercise drink.
   I Tears contain sodium.

Passage 2 Three major types of nutrients—carbohydrates, proteins, and fats—make up most of the food you eat. Chemical substances called *enzymes* break these nutrients into smaller particles for the body to use. For example, proteins, which are chains of smaller molecules called *amino acids,* are too large to be absorbed into the bloodstream. So, enzymes cut the chain of amino acids. These amino acids are small enough to pass into the bloodstream to be used by the body.

1. According to the passage, what is a carbohydrate?
   A an enzyme
   B a substance made of amino acids
   C a nutrient
   D the only substance in a healthy diet

2. Which of the following statements is a fact from the passage?
   F Carbohydrates, fats, and proteins are three major types of nutrients.
   G Proteins are made of fats and carbohydrates.
   H Some enzymes create chains of proteins.
   I Fats are difficult to digest.

3. Which of the following can be inferred from the passage?
   A To be useful to the body, nutrients must be small enough to enter the bloodstream.
   B Carbohydrates are made of amino acids.
   C Amino acids are made of proteins.
   D Without enough protein, the body cannot grow.

Use the figure below to answer the questions that follow.

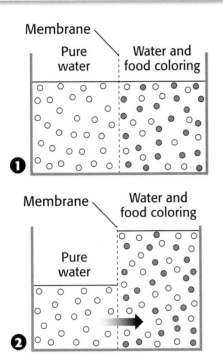

Membrane

Pure water — Water and food coloring

❶

Membrane — Water and food coloring

Pure water

❷

1. The container is divided by a membrane. What can you conclude from the diagram?

A Water molecules can pass through the membrane.

B Food-coloring molecules can pass through the membrane.

C Both water molecules and food-coloring molecules can pass through the membrane.

D Neither water molecules nor food-coloring molecules can pass through the membrane.

2. If the membrane has holes that separate molecules by size,

F food-coloring molecules are larger than water molecules.

G water molecules are larger than food-coloring molecules.

H water molecules and food-coloring molecules are the same size.

I the holes are smaller than both water molecules and food-coloring molecules.

3. The concentration of food-coloring molecules in the columns labeled "Water and food coloring"

A is greater in 2 than in 1.

B is greater in 1 than in 2.

C is the same in 1 and 2.

D cannot change.

MATH

Read each question below, and choose the best answer.

1. Cora is 1.5 m tall. Cora's small intestine is 6 m long. How many times longer is Cora's small intestine than her height?

A 3 times longer

B 4 times longer

C 5 times longer

D 6 times longer

2. During a water-balance study that was performed for one day, a woman drank 1,500 mL of water. The food she ate contained 750 mL of water, and her body produced 250 mL of water internally during normal body processes. She lost 900 mL of water in sweat, 1,500 mL in urine, and 100 mL in feces. Overall, how much water did she gain or lose during the day?

F She gained 1,500 mL of water.

G She lost 900 mL of water.

H She gained as much water as she lost.

I She lost twice as much water as she gained.

3. There are 6 blue marbles, 2 red marbles, and 4 green marbles in a bag. If someone selects 1 marble at random from the bag, what is the probability that the marble will be blue?

A 1/5

B 1/4

C 1/3

D 1/2

Science in Action

Weird Science

Tapeworms

What if you found out that you had a constant mealtime companion who didn't want just a bite but wanted it all? And what if that companion never asked for your permission? This mealtime companion might be a tapeworm. Tapeworms are invertebrate flatworms. These flatworms are parasites. A parasite is an organism that obtains its food by living in or on another organism. A tapeworm doesn't have a digestive tract of its own. Instead, a tapeworm absorbs the nutrients digested by the host. Some tape worms can grow to be over 10 m long. Cooking beef, pork, and fish properly can help prevent people from getting tapeworms. People or animals who get tapeworms can be treated with medicines.

Science, Technology, and Society

Pill Cameras

Open wide and say "Ahhhh." When you have a problem with your mouth or teeth, doctors can examine you pretty easily. But when people have problems that are further down their digestive tract, examination becomes more difficult. So, some doctors have recently created a tiny, disposable camera that patients can swallow. As the camera travels down the digestive tract, the camera takes pictures and sends them to a tiny recorder that patients wear on their belt. The camera takes about 57,000 images during its trip. Later, doctors can review the pictures and see the pictures of the patient's entire digestive tract.

Social Studies ACTIVITY

WRITING SKILL The World Health Organization and the Pan American Health Organization have made fighting intestinal parasites in children a high priority. Conduct library or Internet research on Worm Busters, which is a program for fighting parasites. Write a brief report of your findings.

Math ACTIVITY

If a pill camera takes 57,000 images while it travels through the digestive system and takes about two pictures per second, how many hours is the camera in the body?

Christy Krames

Medical Illustrator Christy Krames is a medical illustrator. For 19 years, she has created detailed illustrations of the inner workings of the human body. Medical illustrations allow doctors and surgeons to share concepts, theories, and techniques with colleagues and allow students to learn about the human body.

Medical illustrators often draw tiny structures or body processes that would be difficult or impossible to photograph. For example, a photograph of a small intestine can show the entire organ. But a medical illustrator can add to the photograph an enlarged drawing of the tiny villi inside the intestine. Adding details helps to better explain how small parts of organs work together so that the organs can function.

Medical illustration requires knowledge of both art and science. So, Christy Krames studied both art and medicine in college. Often, Krames must do research before she draws a subject. Her research may include reading books, observing surgical procedures, or even dissecting a pig's heart. This research results in accurate and educational drawings of the inner body.

Language Arts ACTIVITY

WRITING SKILL Pretend you are going to publish an atlas of the human body. Write a classified advertisement to hire medical illustrators. Describe the job, and describe the qualities that the best candidates will have. As you write the ad, remember you are trying to persuade the best illustrators to contact you.

To learn more about these Science in Action topics, visit **go.hrw.com** and type in the keyword **HL5BD3F**.

Current Science

Check out Current Science® articles related to this chapter by visiting go.hrw.com. Just type in the keyword **HL5CS24**.

Communication and Control

About the PHOTO

This picture may look like it shows a flower garden or a coral reef. But it really shows something much closer to home. It shows the human tongue (magnified thousands of times, of course). Those round bumps are taste buds. You use taste and other senses to gather information about your surroundings.

PRE-READING ACTIVITY

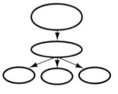

Graphic Organizer

Concept Map Before you read the chapter, create the graphic organizer entitled "Concept Map" described in the **Study Skills** section of the Appendix. As you read the chapter, fill in the concept map with details about each part or division of the nervous system. Include details about what each part or division does.

Act Fast!

If you want to catch an object, your brain sends a message to the muscles in your arm. In this exercise, you will see how long sending that message takes.

Procedure

1. Sit in a **chair** with one arm in a "handshake" position. Your partner should stand facing you, holding a **meterstick** vertically. The stick should be positioned so that it will fall between your thumb and fingers.

2. Tell your partner to let go of the meterstick without warning you. Catch the stick between your thumb and fingers. Your partner should catch the meterstick if it tips over.

3. Record the number of centimeters that the stick dropped before you caught it. That distance represents your reaction time.

4. Repeat steps 1–3 three times. Calculate the average distance.

5. Repeat steps 1–4 with your other hand.

6. Trade places with your partner, and repeat steps 1–5.

Analysis

1. Compare the reaction times of your own hands. Why might one hand react more quickly than the other?

2. Compare your results with your partner's. Why might one person react more quickly than another?

The Nervous System

Which of the following activities do NOT involve your nervous system: eating, playing a musical instrument, reading a book, running, or sleeping?

This is a trick question. All of these activities involve your nervous system. In fact, your nervous system controls almost everything you do.

Two Systems Within a System

The nervous system acts as the body's central command post. It has two basic functions. First, it gathers and interprets information. This information comes from inside your body and from the world outside your body. Then, the nervous system responds to that information as needed.

The nervous system has two parts: the central nervous system and the peripheral (puh RIF uhr uhl) nervous system. The **central nervous system** (CNS) is your brain and spinal cord. The CNS processes and responds to all messages coming from the peripheral nervous system. The **peripheral nervous system** (PNS) is all of the parts of the nervous system except for the brain and the spinal cord. The PNS connects all parts of the body to the CNS. The PNS uses specialized structures, called *nerves*, to carry information between your body and your CNS. **Figure 1** shows the major divisions of the nervous system.

✓ Reading Check **Explain the difference between the CNS and the PNS.** (*See the Appendix for answers to Reading Checks.*)

central nervous system (CNS) the brain and the spinal cord

peripheral nervous system (PNS) all of the parts of the nervous system except for the brain and the spinal cord

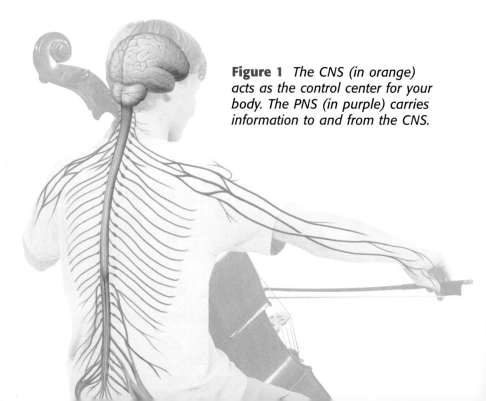

Figure 1 *The CNS (in orange) acts as the control center for your body. The PNS (in purple) carries information to and from the CNS.*

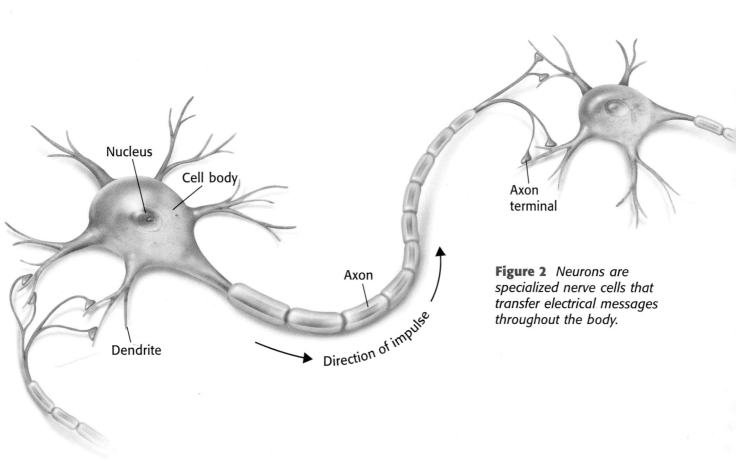

Nucleus

Cell body

Axon terminal

Axon

Dendrite

Direction of impulse

Figure 2 *Neurons are specialized nerve cells that transfer electrical messages throughout the body.*

The Peripheral Nervous System

Messages about your environment travel through the nervous system along neurons. A **neuron** (NOO RAHN) is a nerve cell that is specialized to transfer messages in the form of fast-moving electrical energy. These electrical messages are called *impulses*. Impulses may travel as fast as 150 m/s or as slow as 0.2 m/s. **Figure 2** shows a typical neuron transferring an impulse.

Neuron Structure

In many ways, a neuron is similar to other cells. A neuron has a large region in its center called the *cell body*. The cell body has a nucleus and cell organelles. But neurons also have special structures called dendrites and axons. *Dendrites* are usually short, branched extensions of the cell. Neurons receive information from other cells through their dendrites. A neuron may have many dendrites, which allows it to receive impulses from thousands of other cells.

Impulses are carried away from the cell body by axons. *Axons* are elongated extensions of a neuron. They can be very short or quite long. Some long axons extend almost 1 m from your lower back to your toes. The end of an axon often has branches that allow information to pass to other cells. The tip of each branch is called an *axon terminal*.

Reading Check In your own words, describe a neuron.

neuron a nerve cell that is specialized to receive and conduct electrical impulses

Time to Travel

To calculate how long an impulse takes to travel a certain distance, you can use the following equation:

$$time = \frac{distance}{speed}$$

If an impulse travels 100 m/s, about how long would it take an impulse to travel 10 m?

Information Collection

Remember that neurons are a type of nerve cell that carries impulses. Some neurons are *sensory neurons*. These neurons gather information about what is happening in and around your body. They have specialized nerve endings called *receptors*. Receptors detect changes inside and outside the body. For example, receptors in your eyes detect light. Sensory neurons then send this information to the CNS for processing.

Delivering Orders

Neurons that send impulses from the brain and spinal cord to other systems are called *motor neurons*. When muscles get impulses from motor neurons, they respond by contracting. For example, motor neurons cause muscles around your eyes to contract when you are in bright light. These muscles make you squint. Squinting lets less light enter the eyes. Motor neurons also send messages to your glands, such as sweat glands. These messages tell sweat glands to start or stop making sweat.

Nerves

The central nervous system is connected to the rest of your body by nerves. A **nerve** is a collection of axons bundled together with blood vessels and connective tissue. Nerves are everywhere in your body. Most nerves have axons of both sensory neurons and motor neurons. Axons are parts of nerves, but nerves are more than just axons. **Figure 3** shows the structure of a nerve. The axon in this nerve transmits information from the spinal cord to muscle fibers.

Reading Check What is a nerve?

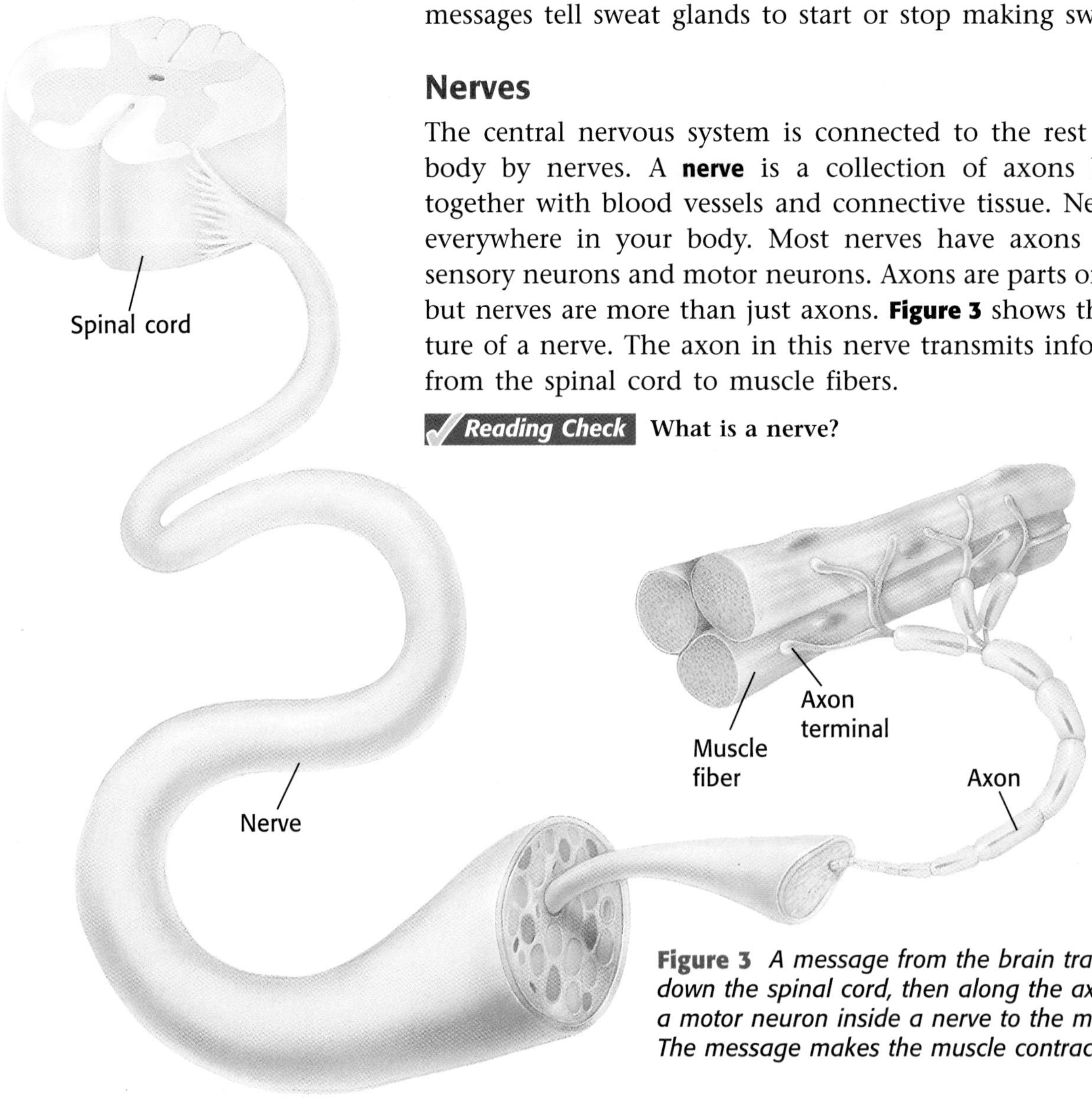

nerve a collection of nerve fibers (axons) through which impulses travel between the central nervous system and other parts of the body

Spinal cord

Nerve

Muscle fiber

Axon terminal

Axon

Figure 3 *A message from the brain travels down the spinal cord, then along the axon of a motor neuron inside a nerve to the muscle. The message makes the muscle contract.*

Somatic and Autonomic Nervous Systems

Remember, the PNS connects your CNS to the rest of your body. And the PNS has two main parts—the sensory part (sensory neurons) and the motor part (motor neurons). You know that sensory nerves collect information from your senses and send that information to the CNS. You also know that motor nerves carry out the CNS's responses to that sensory information. To carry those responses, the motor part of the PNS has two kinds of nerves: somatic nerves and autonomic nerves.

Somatic Nervous System

Most of the neurons that are part of the *somatic nervous system* are under your conscious control. These are the neurons that stimulate skeletal muscles. They control voluntary movements, such as writing, talking, smiling, or jumping.

Autonomic Nervous System

Autonomic nerves do not need your conscious control. These neurons are part of the autonomic nervous system. The *autonomic nervous system* controls body functions that you don't think about, such as digestion and heart rate (the number of times your heart beats per minute).

The main job of the autonomic nervous system is to keep all the body's functions in balance. Depending on the situation, the autonomic nervous system can speed up or slow down these functions. The autonomic nervous system has two divisions: the *sympathetic nervous system* and the *parasympathetic nervous system*. These two divisions work together to keep your internal environment stable. This is called *homeostasis*. Some of these functions are shown in **Table 1.**

✓ Reading Check Describe three functions of the PNS.

CONNECTION TO Chemistry

Keeping Your Balance The autonomic nervous system has two parts—the sympathetic division and the parasympathetic division. These parts of your nervous system help keep all of your body systems in balance. Research these two parts of the nervous system, and make a poster showing how they keep your body healthy.

ACTIVITY

Table 1	Effects of the Autonomic Nervous System on the Body	
Organ	Effect of sympathetic division	Effect of parasympathetic division
Eyes	pupils dilate (grow larger; makes it easier to see objects)	pupils constrict (vision normal)
Heart	heart rate increases (increases blood flow)	heart rate slows (blood flow slows)
Lungs	bronchioles dilate (grow larger; increases oxygen in blood)	bronchioles constrict
Blood vessels	blood vessels dilate (increases blood flow except to digestion)	little or no effect
Intestines	digestion slows (reduces blood flow to stomach and intestines)	digestion returns to normal

The Central Nervous System

The central nervous system receives information from the sensory neurons. Then it responds by sending messages to the body through motor neurons in the PNS.

The Control Center

brain the mass of nerve tissue that is the main control center of the nervous system

The largest organ in the nervous system is the brain. The **brain** is the main control center of the nervous system. Many processes that the brain controls happen automatically. These processes are called *involuntary*. For example, you couldn't stop digesting food even if you tried. On the other hand, some actions controlled by your brain are *voluntary*. When you want to move your arm, your brain sends signals along motor neurons to muscles in your arm. Then, the muscles contract, and your arm moves. The brain has three main parts—the cerebrum (suh REE bruhm), the cerebellum (SER uh BEL uhm), and the medulla (mi DUHL uh). Each part has its own job.

Reading Check What is the difference between a voluntary action and an involuntary action?

The Cerebrum

The largest part of your brain is called the *cerebrum*. It looks like a mushroom cap. This dome-shaped area is where you think and where most memories are stored. It controls voluntary movements and allows you to sense touch, light, sound, odors, taste, pain, heat, and cold.

The cerebrum has two halves, called *hemispheres*. The left hemisphere directs the right side of the body, and the right hemisphere directs the left side of the body. **Figure 4** shows some of the activities that each hemisphere controls. However, most brain activities use both hemispheres.

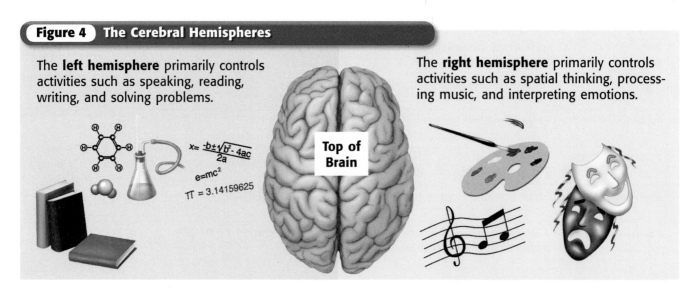

Figure 4 **The Cerebral Hemispheres**

The **left hemisphere** primarily controls activities such as speaking, reading, writing, and solving problems.

$x \approx \frac{-b \pm \sqrt{b^2 - 4ac}}{2a}$

$e = mc^2$

$\pi = 3.14159625$

Top of Brain

The **right hemisphere** primarily controls activities such as spatial thinking, processing music, and interpreting emotions.

The Cerebellum

The second-largest part of your brain is the *cerebellum*. It lies beneath the back of the cerebrum. The cerebellum processes sensory information from your body, such as from skeletal muscles and joints. This allows the brain to keep track of your body's position. If you begin to lose your balance, the cerebellum sends impulses telling different skeletal muscles to contract. Those muscles shift a person's weight and keep a person, such as the girl in **Figure 5,** from losing her balance.

The Medulla

The *medulla* is the part of your brain that connects to your spinal cord. The medulla is about 3 cm long, and you can't live without it. The medulla controls involuntary processes, such as blood pressure, body temperature, heart rate, and involuntary breathing.

Your medulla constantly receives sensory impulses from receptors in your blood vessels. It uses this information to regulate your blood pressure. If your blood pressure gets too low, the medulla sends out impulses that tell blood vessels to tighten up. As a result, blood pressure rises. The medulla also sends impulses to the heart to make the heart beat faster or slower. **Figure 6** shows the location of the parts of the brain and some of the functions of each part.

Reading Check Explain why the medulla is important.

Figure 5 *Your cerebellum causes skeletal muscles to make adjustments so that you will stay upright.*

Figure 6 Areas of the Brain at Work

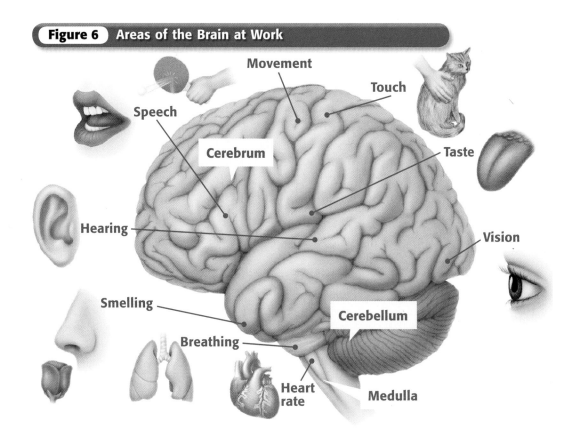

Movement

Touch

Speech

Taste

Cerebrum

Hearing

Vision

Smelling

Cerebellum

Breathing

Heart rate

Medulla

The Spinal Cord

Your spinal cord, which is part of your central nervous system, is about as big around as your thumb. The spinal cord is made of neurons and bundles of axons that pass impulses to and from the brain. As shown in **Figure 7,** the spinal cord is surrounded by protective bones called *vertebrae* (VUHR tuh BRAY).

The nerve fibers in your spinal cord allow your brain to communicate with your peripheral nervous system. Sensory neurons in your skin and muscles send impulses along their axons to your spinal cord. The spinal cord carries impulses to your brain. The brain interprets these impulses as pain, temperature, or other sensations. The brain then responds to the situation. Impulses moving from the brain down the spinal cord are relayed to motor neurons. Motor neurons carry the impulses along their axons to muscles and glands all over your body.

Reading Check Describe the path of an impulse from the skin to the brain and the path of the response.

Spinal Cord Injury

A spinal cord injury may block all information to and from the brain. Sensory information coming from below the injury may not get to the brain. For example, a spinal cord injury may block all sensory impulses from the feet and legs. People with such an injury would not be able to sense pain, touch, or temperature with their feet. And motor commands from the brain to the injured area may not reach the peripheral nerves. So, the person would not be able to move his or her legs.

Each year, thousands of people are paralyzed by spinal cord injuries. Many of these injuries happen in car accidents and could be avoided by wearing a seat belt. Among young people, spinal cord injuries are sometimes related to sports or other activities. These injuries might be prevented by wearing proper safety equipment.

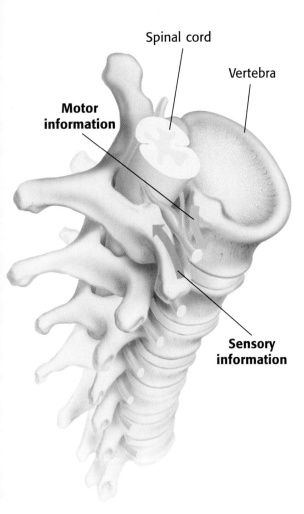

Motor information

Spinal cord

Vertebra

Sensory information

Figure 7 *The spinal cord carries information to and from the brain. Vertebrae protect the spinal cord.*

Building a Neuron

1. Your teacher will provide at least four different colors of **modeling clay.** Build a model of a neuron by using different-colored clay for the various parts of the neuron.

2. Use **tape** to attach your model neuron to a **piece of plain white paper.**

3. On the paper, label each part of the neuron. Draw an arrow from the label to the part.

4. Using a **colored pencil, marker,** or **crayon,** draw arrows showing the path of an impulse traveling in your neuron. Tell whether the impulse is a sensory impulse or a motor impulse. Then, describe what will happen when the impulse reaches its destination.

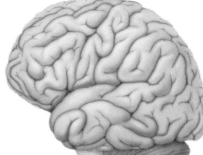

Summary

- The central nervous system (CNS) includes the brain and the spinal cord.
- The peripheral nervous system (PNS) is all the parts of the nervous system except the brain and spinal cord.
- The peripheral nervous system has nerves made up of axons of neurons.
- Sensory neurons have receptors that detect information about the body and its environment. Motor neurons carry messages from the brain and spinal cord to other parts of the body.

- The PNS has two types of motor nerves—somatic nerves and autonomic nerves.
- The cerebrum is the largest part of the brain and controls thinking, sensing, and voluntary movement.
- The cerebellum is the part of the brain that keeps track of the body's position and helps maintain balance.
- The medulla controls involuntary processes, such as heart rate, blood pressure, body temperature, and breathing.

Using Key Terms

1. In your own words, write a definition for each of the following terms: *neuron* and *nerve*.

2. Use the following terms in the same sentence: *brain* and *peripheral nervous system*.

Understanding Key Ideas

3. Someone touches your shoulder and you turn around. Which sequence do your impulses follow?
   a. motor neuron, sensory neuron, CNS response
   b. motor neuron, CNS response, sensory neuron
   c. sensory neuron, motor neuron, CNS response
   d. sensory neuron, CNS response, motor neuron

4. Describe one function of each part of the brain.

5. Compare the somatic nervous system with the autonomic nervous system.

6. Explain how a severe injury to the spinal cord can affect other parts of the body.

Critical Thinking

7. **Applying Concepts** Some medications slow a person's nervous system. These drugs are often labeled "May cause drowsiness." Explain why a person needs to know about this side effect.

8. **Predicting Consequences** Explain how your life would change if your autonomic nervous system suddenly stopped working.

Interpreting Graphics

Use the figure below to answer the questions that follow.

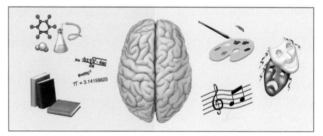

9. Which hemisphere of the brain recognizes and processes words, numbers, and letters? faces, places, and objects?

10. For a person whose left hemisphere is primarily in control, would it be easier to learn to play a new computer game by reading the rules and following instructions or by watching a friend play and imitating his actions?

SCILINKS®

Developed and maintained by the National Science Teachers Association

For a variety of links related to this chapter, go to www.scilinks.org

Topic: Nervous System
SciLinks code: HSM1023

Responding to the Environment

You feel a tap on your shoulder. Who tapped you? You turn to look, hoping to see a friend. Your senses are on the job!

The tap produces impulses in sensory receptors on your shoulder. These impulses travel to your brain. Once the impulses reach your brain, they create an awareness called a *sensation*. In this case, the sensation is of your shoulder being touched. But you still do not know who tapped you. So, you turn around. The sensory receptors in your eyes send impulses to your brain. Now, your brain recognizes your best friend.

Sense of Touch

Touch is what you feel when sensory receptors in the skin are stimulated. It is the sensation you feel when you shake hands or feel a breeze. As shown in **Figure 1,** skin has different kinds of receptors. Each kind of receptor responds mainly to one kind of stimulus. For example, *thermoreceptors* respond to temperature change. Each kind of receptor produces a specific sensation of touch, such as pressure, temperature, pain, or vibration. Skin is part of the integumentary (in TEG yoo MEN tuhr ee) system. The **integumentary system** protects the body from damage. It includes hair, skin, and nails.

✓ **Reading Check** List four sensations that your skin can detect. (*See the Appendix for answers to Reading Checks.*)

integumentary system the organ system that forms a protective covering on the outside of the body

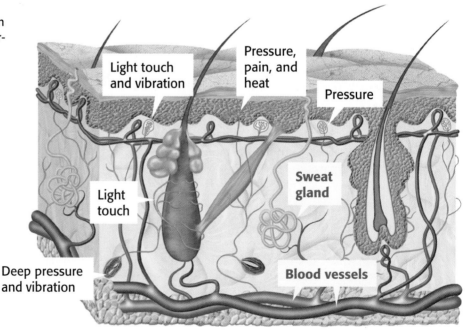

Figure 1 *Each type of receptor in your skin has its own structure and function.*

Light touch and vibration

Pressure, pain, and heat

Pressure

Light touch

Sweat gland

Deep pressure and vibration

Blood vessels

Responding to Sensory Messages

When you step on something sharp, as the man in **Figure 2** did, pain receptors in your foot or toe send impulses to your spinal cord. Almost immediately, a message to move your foot travels back to the muscles in your leg and foot. Without thinking, you quickly lift your foot. This immediate, involuntary action is called a **reflex.** Your brain isn't telling your leg to move. In fact, by the time the message reaches your brain, your leg and foot have already moved. If you had to wait for your brain to act, you toes might be seriously hurt!

✓ **Reading Check** Why are reflexes important?

Feedback Mechanisms

Most of the time, the brain processes information from skin receptors. For example, on a hot day, heat receptors in your skin detect an increase in your temperature. The receptors send impulses to the brain. Your brain responds by sending messages to your sweat glands to make sweat. As sweat evaporates, it cools your body. Your brain also tells the blood vessels in your skin to dilate (open wider). Blood flow increases. Thermal energy from the blood in your skin moves to your surroundings. This also cools your body. As your body cools, it sends messages to your brain. The brain responds by sending messages to sweat glands and blood vessels to reduce their activity.

This cooling process is one of your body's feedback mechanisms. A **feedback mechanism** is a cycle of events in which information from one step controls or affects a previous step. The temperature-regulating feedback mechanism helps keep your body temperature within safe limits. This cooling mechanism works like a thermostat on an air conditioner. Once a room reaches the right temperature, the thermostat sends a message to the air conditioner to stop blowing cold air.

reflex an involuntary and almost immediate movement in response to a stimulus

feedback mechanism a cycle of events in which information from one step controls or affects a previous step

Figure 2 *A reflex, such as lifting your foot when you step on something sharp, is one way your nervous system responds to your environment.*

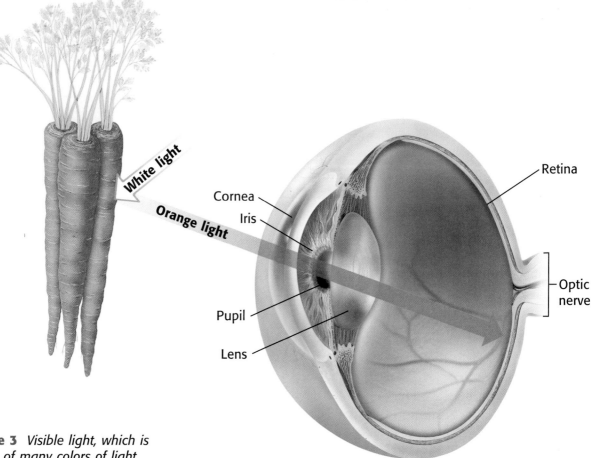

Figure 3 *Visible light, which is made of many colors of light, hits the carrots. Carrots look orange because they reflect orange light to your eyes.*

retina the light-sensitive inner layer of the eye; it receives images formed by the lens and transmits them through the optic nerve to the brain

For another activity related to this chapter, go to **go.hrw.com** and type in the keyword **HL5BD4W.**

Sense of Sight

Sight is the sense that allows you to see the size, shape, motion, and color of objects around you. You see an object when it sends or reflects visible light toward your eyes. Your eyes detect this light, which enables your brain to form visual images.

Your eyes are complex sensory organs, as you can see in **Figure 3.** The front of the eye is covered by a clear membrane called the *cornea.* The cornea protects the eye but allows light to enter. Light from an object enters the front of your eye through an opening called the *pupil.* The light then travels through the lens to the back of the eye. There, the light strikes the **retina,** a layer of light-sensitive cells.

The retina is packed with photoreceptors. A *photoreceptor* is a special neuron that changes light into electrical impulses. The retina has two kinds of photoreceptors: rods and cones. Rods are very sensitive to dim light. They are important for night vision. Impulses from rods are interpreted as black-and-white images. Cones are very sensitive to bright light. Impulses from cones allow you to see fine details and colors.

Impulses from the rods and cones travel along axons. The impulses leave the back of each eye through an optic nerve. The optic nerve carries the impulses to your brain, where the impulses are interpreted as the images that you see.

✓ Reading Check Describe how light and sight are related.

Reacting to Light

Your pupil looks like a black dot in the center of your eye. In fact, it is an opening that lets light enter the eye. The pupil is surrounded by the *iris,* a ring of muscle. The iris controls the amount of light that enters the eye and gives the eye its color. In bright light, the iris contracts, which makes the pupil smaller. A smaller pupil reduces the amount of light entering the eye and passing onto the retina. In dim light, the iris opens the pupil and lets in more light.

✓ Reading Check How does your iris react to bright light?

Focusing the Light

Light travels in straight lines until it passes through the cornea and the lens. The *lens* is an oval-shaped piece of clear, curved material behind the iris. Muscles in the eye change the shape of the lens in order to focus light onto the retina. When you look at objects close to the eye, the lens becomes more curved. When you look at objects far away, the lens gets flatter.

Figure 4 shows some common vision problems. In some eyes, the lens focuses the light in front of the retina, which results in nearsightedness. If the lens focuses the light just behind the retina, the result is farsightedness. Glasses, contact lenses, or surgery can usually correct these vision problems.

Where's the Dot?

1. Hold your **book** at arm's length, and close your right eye. Focus your left eye on the black dot below.

   ◯   ●

2. Slowly move the book toward your face until the white dot disappears. You may need to try a few times to get this result. The white dot doesn't always disappear for every person.

3. Describe your observations.

4. Use the library or the Internet to research the optic nerve and to find out why the white dot disappears.

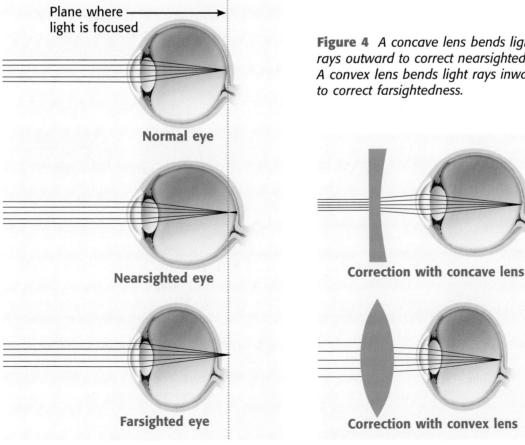

Plane where light is focused

Normal eye

Nearsighted eye

Farsighted eye

Figure 4 *A concave lens bends light rays outward to correct nearsightedness. A convex lens bends light rays inward to correct farsightedness.*

Correction with concave lens

Correction with convex lens

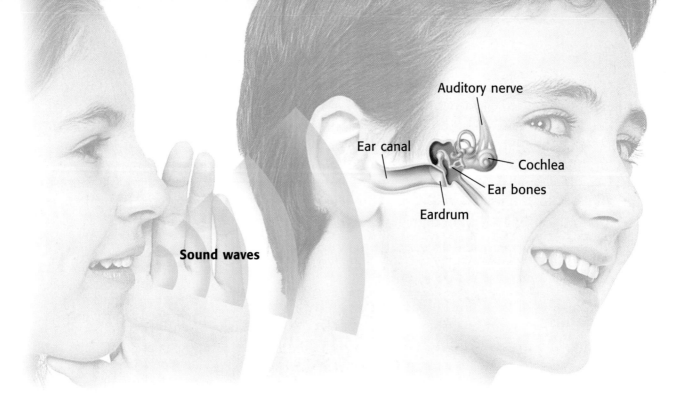

Sound waves

Auditory nerve

Ear canal

Cochlea

Ear bones

Eardrum

Figure 5 *A sound wave travels into the outer ear. It is converted into bone vibrations in the middle ear, then into liquid vibrations in the inner ear, and finally, into nerve impulses that travel to the brain.*

cochlea a coiled tube that is found in the inner ear and that is essential to hearing

CONNECTION TO Physics

WRITING SKILL **Elephant Talk** Sound is produced by vibrating objects. Some sounds, called *infrasonic sounds*, are too low for human ears to detect. Research how elephants use infrasonic sounds to communicate with each other, and write a report about what you learn.

Sense of Hearing

Sound is produced when something, such as a drum, vibrates. Vibrations push on nearby air particles, which push on other air particles. The vibrations create waves of sound energy. Hearing is the sense that allows you to experience sound energy.

Ears are organs specialized for hearing. Each ear has an outer, middle, and inner portion, as shown in **Figure 5.** Sound waves reaching the outer ear are funneled into the middle ear. There, the waves make the eardrum vibrate. The eardrum is a thin membrane separating the outer ear from the middle ear. The vibrating eardrum makes tiny bones in the middle ear vibrate. One of these bones vibrates against the **cochlea** (KAHK lee uh), a fluid-filled organ of the inner ear. Inside the cochlea, vibrations make waves just like the waves you make by tapping on a glass of water. Neurons in the cochlea change the waves into electrical impulses. These impulses travel along the auditory nerve to the area of the brain that interprets sound.

✓ *Reading Check* **Why is the cochlea important to hearing?**

Sense of Taste

Taste is the sense that allows you to detect chemicals and distinguish flavors. Your tongue is covered with tiny bumps called *papillae* (puh PIL ee). Most papillae contain taste buds. Taste buds contain clusters of *taste cells,* the receptors for taste. Taste cells respond to dissolved food molecules. Taste cells react to four basic tastes: sweetness, sourness, saltiness, and bitterness. When the brain combines information from all of the taste buds, you taste a "combination" flavor.

Sense of Smell

As you can see in **Figure 6,** receptors for smell are located on *olfactory cells* in the upper part of your nasal cavity. An olfactory cell is a nerve cell that responds to chemical molecules in the air. You smell something when the receptors react to molecules that have been inhaled. The molecules dissolve in the moist lining of the nasal cavity and trigger an impulse. Olfactory cells send those impulses to the brain, which interprets the impulses as odors.

Taste buds and olfactory cells both detect dissolved molecules. Your brain combines information from both senses to give you sensations of flavor.

Figure 6 *Olfactory cells line the nasal cavity. These cells are sensory receptors that react to chemicals in the air.*

Brain

Olfactory cell

Nasal passage

SECTION Review

Summary

- Touch allows you to respond to temperature, pressure, pain, and vibration on the skin.
- Reflexes and feedback mechanisms help you respond to your environment.
- Sight allows you to respond to light energy.
- Hearing allows you to respond to sound energy.
- Taste allows you to distinguish flavors.
- Smell allows you to perceive different odors.

Using Key Terms

1. In your own words, write a definition for each of the following terms: *reflex* and *feedback mechanism.*

2. Use each of the following terms in a separate sentence: *retina* and *cochlea.*

Understanding Key Ideas

3. Three sensations that receptors in the skin detect are
   a. light, smell, and sound.
   b. touch, pain, and odors.
   c. temperature, pressure, and pain.
   d. pressure, sound, and touch.

4. Explain how light and sight are related.

5. Describe how your senses of hearing, taste, and smell work.

6. Explain why you might have trouble seeing bright colors at a candlelit dinner.

7. How is your sense of taste similar to your sense of smell, and how do these senses work together?

8. Describe how the feedback mechanism that regulates body temperature works.

Math Skills

9. Suppose a nerve impulse must travel 0.90 m from your toe to your central nervous system. If the impulse travels at 150 m/s, calculate how long it will take the impulse to arrive. If the impulse travels at 0.2 m/s, how long will it take the impulse to arrive?

Critical Thinking

10. **Making Inferences** Why is it important for the human body to have reflexes?

11. **Applying Concepts** Rods help you detect objects and shapes in dim light. Explain why it is important for human eyes to have both rods and cones.

SCiLINKS.

NSTA
Developed and maintained by the National Science Teachers Association

For a variety of links related to this chapter, go to www.scilinks.org

Topic: The Senses; The Eye
SciLinks code: HSM1378; HSM0560

The Endocrine System

Have you ever heard of an epinephrine (EP uh NEPH rin) rush? You might have had one without realizing it. Exciting situations, such as riding a roller coaster or watching a scary movie, can cause your body to release epinephrine.

Epinephrine is one of the body's chemical messengers made by the endocrine system. Your endocrine system regulates body processes, such as fluid balance, growth, and development.

Hormones as Chemical Messengers

The **endocrine system** controls body functions by using chemicals that are made by the endocrine glands. A **gland** is a group of cells that make special chemicals for your body. Chemical messengers made by the endocrine glands are called hormones. A **hormone** is a chemical messenger made in one cell or tissue that causes a change in another cell or tissue in another part of the body. Hormones flow through the bloodstream to all parts of the body. Thus, an endocrine gland near your brain can control an organ that is somewhere else in your body.

Endocrine glands may affect many organs at one time. For example, in the situation shown in **Figure 1,** the adrenal glands release the hormone *epinephrine*, which is sometimes called *adrenaline.* Epinephrine increases your heartbeat and breathing rate. This response is called the "fight-or-flight" response. When you are frightened, angry, or excited, the "fight-or-flight" response prepares you to fight the danger or to run from it.

READING WARM-UP

Objectives

● Explain why the endocrine system is important to the body.

● Identify five glands of the endocrine system, and describe what their hormones do.

● Describe how feedback mechanisms stop and start hormone release.

● Name two hormone imbalances.

Terms to Learn

endocrine system
gland
hormone

READING STRATEGY

Discussion Read this section silently. Write down questions that you have about this section. Discuss your questions in a small group.

endocrine system a collection of glands and groups of cells that secrete hormones that regulate growth, development, and homeostasis

gland a group of cells that make special chemicals for the body

Figure 1 *When you have to move quickly to avoid danger, your adrenal glands make more blood glucose available for energy.*

More Endocrine Glands

Your body has several other endocrine glands. Some of these glands have many functions. For example, your pituitary gland stimulates skeletal growth and helps the thyroid gland work properly. It also regulates the amount of water in the blood. And the pituitary gland stimulates the birth process in women.

Your thyroid gland is very important during infancy and childhood. Thyroid hormones control the secretion of growth hormones for normal body growth. Thyroid hormones also control the development of the central nervous system. And they control your metabolism. *Metabolism* is the sum of all the chemical processes that take place in an organism.

Your thymus gland is important to your immune system. Cells called *killer T cells* grow and mature in the thymus gland. These T cells help destroy or neutralize cells or substances that invade your body. The names and some of the functions of endocrine glands are shown in **Figure 2**.

✓ Reading Check Name two endocrine glands, and explain why they are important to your body. *(See the Appendix for answers to Reading Checks.)*

hormone a substance that is made in one cell or tissue and that causes a change in another cell or tissue in a different part of the body

CONNECTION TO Language Arts

WRITING SKILL **Fight or Flight?** Write a paragraph describing a time when you had a fight-or-flight experience. Include in your description the following terms: *hormones, fight-or-flight,* and *epinephrine.* If you cannot think of a personal experience, write a short story describing someone else's fight-or-flight experience.

Figure 2 Endocrine Glands and Their Functions

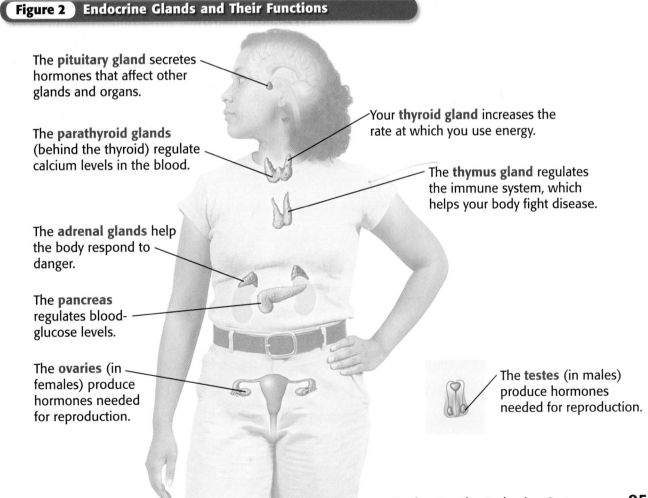

The **pituitary gland** secretes hormones that affect other glands and organs.

The **parathyroid glands** (behind the thyroid) regulate calcium levels in the blood.

The **adrenal glands** help the body respond to danger.

The **pancreas** regulates blood-glucose levels.

The **ovaries** (in females) produce hormones needed for reproduction.

Your **thyroid gland** increases the rate at which you use energy.

The **thymus gland** regulates the immune system, which helps your body fight disease.

The **testes** (in males) produce hormones needed for reproduction.

Controlling the Endocrine Glands

Do you remember the feedback mechanisms at work in the nervous system? Endocrine glands control similar feedback mechanisms. For example, the pancreas has specialized cells that make two different hormones, *insulin* and *glucagon*. As shown in **Figure 3,** these two hormones control the level of glucose in the blood. Insulin lowers blood-glucose levels by telling the liver to convert glucose into glycogen and to store glycogen for future use. Glucagon has the opposite effect. It tells the liver to convert glycogen into glucose and to release the glucose into the blood.

✓ **Reading Check** What does insulin do?

Figure 3 Blood-Glucose Feedback Control

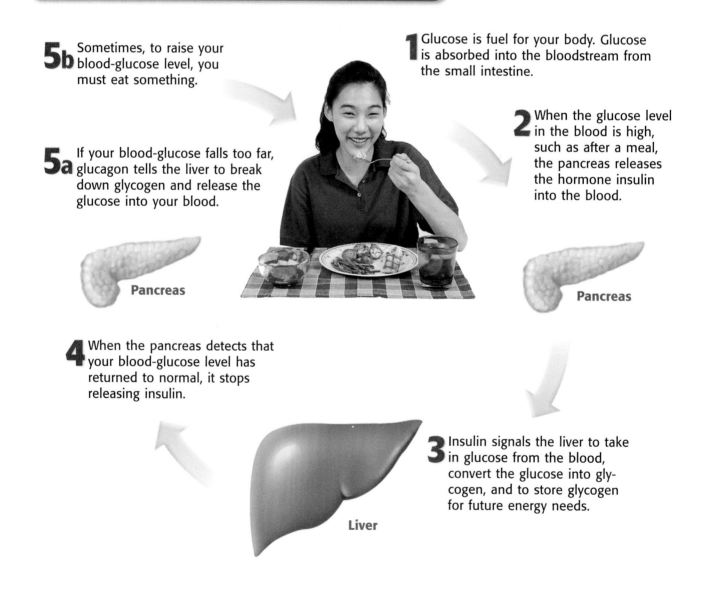

5b Sometimes, to raise your blood-glucose level, you must eat something.

1 Glucose is fuel for your body. Glucose is absorbed into the bloodstream from the small intestine.

5a If your blood-glucose falls too far, glucagon tells the liver to break down glycogen and release the glucose into your blood.

2 When the glucose level in the blood is high, such as after a meal, the pancreas releases the hormone insulin into the blood.

Pancreas

Pancreas

4 When the pancreas detects that your blood-glucose level has returned to normal, it stops releasing insulin.

3 Insulin signals the liver to take in glucose from the blood, convert the glucose into glycogen, and to store glycogen for future energy needs.

Liver

Hormone Imbalances

Occasionally, an endocrine gland makes too much or not enough of a hormone. For example, when a person's blood-glucose level rises, the pancreas secretes insulin. Insulin sends a message to the liver to convert glucose into glycogen. The liver stores glycogen for future use. But a person whose body does not use insulin properly or whose pancreas does not make enough insulin has a condition called *diabetes mellitus* (DIE uh BEET EEZ muh LIET uhs). A person who has diabetes may need daily injections of insulin to keep his or her blood-glucose levels within safe limits. Some patients, such as the woman in **Figure 4,** receive their insulin automatically from a small machine worn next to the body.

Another hormone imbalance is when a child's pituitary gland doesn't make enough growth hormone. As a result, the child's growth is stunted. Fortunately, if the problem is detected early, a doctor can prescribe growth hormone and monitor the child's growth. If the pituitary makes too much growth hormone, a child may grow taller than expected.

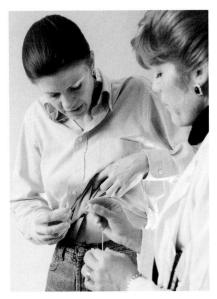

Figure 4 *This woman has diabetes and receives insulin from a device that monitors her blood-glucose level.*

SECTION Review

Summary

- Glands in the endocrine system use chemical messengers called *hormones.*

- Hormones regulate body functions by causing changes in cells or tissues.

- Feedback mechanisms tell endocrine glands when to turn hormones on and off.

- A hormone imbalance is when a gland releases too much or too little of a hormone.

Using Key Terms

1. Use the following terms in the same sentence: *endocrine system, glands,* and *hormone.*

Understanding Key Ideas

2. Identify five endocrine glands, and explain why their hormones are important to your body.

3. Hormone imbalances may cause
   a. feedback and insulin.
   b. diabetes and stunted growth.
   c. thyroid and pituitary.
   d. glucose and glycogen.

4. How do feedback mechanisms control hormone production?

Math Skills

5. One's bedtime blood-glucose level is normally 140 mg/dL. Ty's blood-glucose level is 189 mg/dL at bedtime. What percentage above 140 mg/dL is Ty's level?

Critical Thinking

6. **Making Inferences** Glucose is a source of energy. Epinephrine quickly increases the blood-glucose level. Why is epinephrine important in times of stress?

7. **Applying Concepts** The hormone glucagon is released when glucose levels fall below normal. Explain how the hormones glucagon and insulin work together to control blood-glucose levels.

SCLINKS®

NSTA
Developed and maintained by the National Science Teachers Association

For a variety of links related to this chapter, go to www.scilinks.org

Topic: Hormones
SciLinks code: HSM0758

Skills Practice Lab

You've Gotta Lotta Nerve

OBJECTIVES

Locate areas on the skin that respond to certain stimuli.

Determine which areas on the skin are more sensitive to certain kinds of stimuli.

MATERIALS

- dissecting pin with a small piece of cork or a small rubber stopper covering the sharp end
- eyedropper, plastic
- paper, graphing
- pens or markers, washable, fine point
- ruler, metric
- tap water, hot
- water, very cold

SAFETY

Your skin has thousands of nerve receptors that detect sensations, such as temperature, pain, and pressure. Your brain is designed to filter out or ignore most of the input it receives from these skin receptors. If the brain did not filter input, simply wearing clothes would trigger so many responses that you couldn't function.

Some areas of the skin, such as the back of your hand, are more sensitive than others. In this activity, you will map the skin receptors for heat, cold, and pressure on the back of your hand.

Procedure

1 Form a group of three. One of you will volunteer the back of your hand for testing, one will do the testing, and the third will record the results.

2 Use a fine-point, washable marker or pen and a metric ruler to mark a 3 cm × 3 cm square on the back of one person's hand. Draw a grid within the area. Space the lines approximately 0.5 cm apart. You will have 36 squares in the grid when you are finished, as shown in the photograph below.

3 Mark off three 3 cm × 3 cm areas on a piece of graph paper. Make a grid in each area exactly as you did on the back of your partner's hand. Label one grid "Cold," another grid "Hot," and the third grid "Pressure."

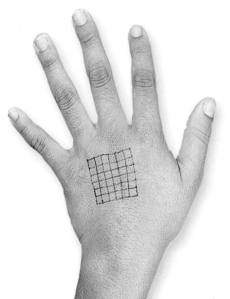

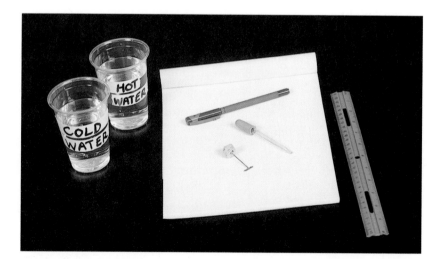

4. Use the eyedropper to apply one small droplet of cold water on each square in the grid on your partner's hand. Your partner should turn away while being tested. On your graph paper, mark an X on the "Cold" grid to show where your partner felt the cold droplet. Carefully blot the water off your partner's hand after several drops.

5. Repeat the test using hot-water droplets. The hot water should not be hot enough to hurt your partner. Mark an X on the "Hot" grid to indicate where your partner felt the hot droplet.

6. Repeat the test by using the head (not the point!) of the pin. Touch the skin to detect pressure receptors. Use a very light touch. On the graph paper, mark an X on the "Pressure" grid to indicate where your partner felt the pressure.

Analyze the Results

1. **Organizing Data** Count the number of Xs in each grid. How many heat receptor responses are there per 3 cm^2? How many cold receptor responses are there? How many pressure receptor responses are there?

2. **Explaining Events** Do you have areas on the back of your hand where the receptors overlap? Explain your answer.

3. **Recognizing Patterns** How do you think the results of this experiment would be similar or different if you mapped an area of your forearm? of the back of your neck? of the palm of your hand?

Draw Conclusions

4. **Interpreting Information** Prepare a written report that includes a description of your investigation and a discussion of your answers to items 1–3. What conclusions can you draw from your results?

Applying Your Data

Use the library or the Internet to research what happens if a receptor is continuously stimulated. Does the kind of receptor make a difference? Does the intensity or strength of the stimulus make a difference? Explain your answers.

Complete each of the following sentences by choosing the correct term from the word bank.

insulin	axon
hormone	nerve
retina	central nervous
neuron	system
reflex	

1 The two parts of your _____ are your brain and spinal cord.

2 Sensory receptors in the _____ detect light.

3 Epinephrine is a(n) _____ that triggers the fight-or-flight response.

4 A(n) _____ is an involuntary and almost immediate movement in response to a stimulus.

5 One hormone that helps to regulate blood-glucose levels is _____ .

6 A(n) _____ is a specialized cell that receives and conducts electrical impulses.

Multiple Choice

7 Which of the following has receptors for smelling?

a. cochlea cells
b. thermoreceptors
c. olfactory cells
d. optic nerve

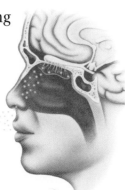

8 Which of the following allow you to see the world in color?

a. cones
b. rods
c. lenses
d. retinas

9 Which of the following glands makes insulin?

a. adrenal gland
b. pituitary gland
c. thyroid gland
d. pancreas

10 The peripheral nervous system does NOT include

a. the spinal cord.
b. axons.
c. sensory receptors.
d. motor neurons.

11 Which part of the brain regulates blood pressure?

a. right cerebral hemisphere
b. left cerebral hemisphere
c. cerebellum
d. medulla

12 The process in which the endocrine system, the digestive system, and the circulatory system control the level of blood glucose is an example of

a. a reflex.
b. an endocrine gland.
c. the fight-or-flight response.
d. a feedback mechanism.

Short Answer

13 What is the difference between the somatic nervous system and the autonomic nervous system? Why are both systems important to the body?

14 Why is the endocrine system important to your body?

15 What is the relationship between the CNS and the PNS?

16 What is the function of the bones in the middle ear?

17 Describe two interactions between the endocrine system and the body that happen when a person is frightened.

CRITICAL THINKING

18 **Concept Mapping** Use the following terms to create a concept map: *nervous system, spinal cord, medulla, peripheral nervous system, brain, cerebrum, central nervous system,* and *cerebellum.*

19 **Making Comparisons** Compare a feedback mechanism with a reflex.

20 **Analyzing Ideas** Why is it important to have a lens that can change shape inside the eye?

21 **Applying Concepts** Why it is important that reflexes happen without thinking about them?

22 **Predicting Consequences** What would happen if your autonomic nervous system stopped working?

23 **Making Comparisons** How are the nervous system and the endocrine system similar? How are they different?

INTERPRETING GRAPHICS

Use the diagram below to answer the questions that follow.

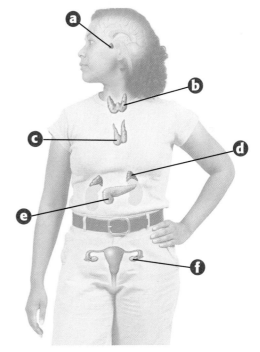

24 Which letter identifies the gland that regulates blood-glucose level?

25 Which letter identifies the gland that releases a hormone that stimulates the birth process?

26 Which letter identifies the gland that helps the body fight disease?

READING

Read each of the passages below. Then, answer the questions that follow each passage.

Passage 1 The axon terminals of neurons usually do not touch the other cells. There is a small gap between an axon terminal and another cell. This space where a neuron meets another cell is called a *synapse*. When a nerve impulse arrives at an axon terminal, the impulse cannot cross the gap. Instead, the impulse triggers the release of chemicals called *neurotransmitters*. These neurotransmitters cross the synapse between the axon terminal and the cell. When neurotransmitters reach the next cell, they signal the cell to react in a certain way. There are many kinds of neurotransmitters. Some neurotransmitters tell cells to start an action. Other neurotransmitters tell cells to stop an action.

1. What is the space between a neuron terminal and a receiving cell called?

  A a neurotransmitter

  B a synapse

  C an axon

  D a nerve

2. Why are neurotransmitters necessary?

  F They tell muscle cells to contract or relax.

  G They create a gap that axons must cross.

  H They carry messages across the synapse.

  I They release chemical signals called *impulses*.

3. Which of the following statements is a fact in the passage?

  A A synapse is an extension of a nerve cell.

  B The space between an axon terminal and another cell is filled with neurons.

  C Nerve impulses jump from an axon to another cell.

  D There are many kinds of neurotransmitters.

Passage 2 Hormones are chemical messengers released by cells that <u>regulate</u> other cells in the body. Hormones regulate many body processes. Hormones control growth, direct the production and use of energy, keep body temperature within normal limits, and direct responses to stimuli outside the body. Hormones carry chemical messages that tell cells to change their activities. For example, one hormone tells the heart to beat faster. Another hormone tells certain cells to make proteins and stimulates bone and muscle growth. Each hormone communicates with specific cells. Each hormone is like a key that opens only one kind of lock. A hormone's message can be received only by cells that have the right kind of lock. Hormones control many important body functions, so their messages must be delivered properly.

1. According to the passage, which of the following statements about hormones is true?

  A Hormones tell cells to change their activities.

  B Hormones are electrical messengers.

  C Hormones are like locks.

  D Hormones are not important to your body.

2. What does the word *regulate* mean?

  F to control or direct

  G to beat faster

  H to raise your temperature

  I to reverse

3. According to the passage, what are two ways that one particular hormone affects the body?

  A controls your temperature and heart rate

  B responds to stimuli and makes proteins

  C stimulates bone growth and makes proteins

  D coordinates energy production and use and decreases temperature

The diagram below shows a typical neuron. Use the diagram below to answer the questions that follow.

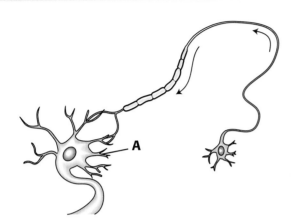

1. What does A represent?

A a cell body   **C** a dendrite

B an axon   **D** an axon terminal

2. Which of the following represents the path that an impulse in a neuron travels?

F dendrite, cell body, axon, axon terminal

G axon, axon terminal, cell body, dendrite

H dendrite, nucleus, cell body, axon

I nucleus, cell body, nucleus, axon

3. To where is an impulse that reaches an axon terminal transmitted?

A another axon terminal

B the brain

C a reflex

D dendrites of another neuron

4. What does having many dendrites allow a neuron to do?

F to be locked into place in the body

G to receive impulses from many other cells

H to send impulses to surrounding cells

I to get necessary nutrition

5. Which of the following statements about an axon is true?

A An axon is part of a gland.

B An axon connects the cell body to the axon terminal.

C An axon detects sights and sounds.

D An axon carries chemical messages.

Read each question below, and choose the best answer.

1. Sound travels about 335 m/s. How many kilometers would a sound travel in 1 min? (One kilometer is equal to 1,000 meters.)

A 335,000 km

B 20,100 km

C 20.1 km

D 0.335 km

2. Some axons send one impulse every 2.5 milliseconds. How many impulses could one of these axons send every second? (One second is equal to 1,000 milliseconds.)

F 4 impulses

G 40 impulses

H 400 impulses

I 4,000 impulses

3. The table below shows the results of Miguel's blood-glucose tests. Miguel ate lunch at 12:00 noon. His blood glucose was measured every hour after that time. What was the average hourly decrease in blood-glucose level?

Blood Glucose	
Time tested	Blood-glucose level (mg/1,000 mL)
1:00 P.M.	178
2:00 P.M.	112
3:00 P.M.	100
4:00 P.M.	89

A approximately 160 mg/1,000 mL

B approximately 120 mg/1,000 mL

C approximately 30 mg/1,000 mL

D approximately 22 mg/1,000 mL

4. Your brain has about 1 billion neurons. How is 1 billion expressed in scientific notation?

F 1×10^3

G 1×10^6

H 1×10^9

I 1×10^{12}

Science in Action

Scientific Discoveries

The Placebo Effect

A placebo (pluh SEE boh) is an inactive substance, such as a sugar pill, used in experimental drug trials. Some of the people who are test subjects are given a placebo as if it were the drug being tested. Usually, neither the doctor conducting the trial nor the test subjects know whether a person is taking a placebo or the test drug. In theory, any change in a subject's condition should be the result of the test drug. But for many years, scientists have known about the *placebo effect,* the effect of feeling better after taking the placebo pill. What makes someone who takes the placebo feel better? By studying brain activity, scientists are beginning to understand the placebo effect.

Science, Technology, and Society

Robotic Limbs

Cyborgs, or people that are part human and part robot, have been part of science fiction for many years and usually have super-human strength and X-ray vision. Meanwhile there are ordinary people on Earth who have lost the use of their arms and legs and could use some robot power. However, until recently, they have had to settle for clumsy mechanical limbs that were not a very good substitute for a real arm or hand. Today, thanks to advances in technology, scientists are developing artificial limbs—and eyes and ears—that can be wired directly into the nervous system and can be controlled by the brain. In the near future, artificial limbs and some artificial organs will be much more like the real thing.

Social Studies ACTIVITY

Research the differences and similarities between ancient Chinese medical practices and traditional Western medical treatment. Both types of treatment rely in part on a patient's mental and emotional response to treatment. How might the placebo effect be part of both medical traditions? Create a poster showing the results of your research.

Language Arts ACTIVITY

WRITING SKILL At the library or on the Internet, find examples of optical or visual illusions. Research how the brain processes visual information and how the brain "sees" and interprets these illusions. Write a report about why the brain seems to be fooled by visual tricks. How can understanding the brain's response to illusions help scientists create artificial vision?

Bertha Madras

Studying Brain Activity The brain is an amazing organ. Sometimes, though, drugs or disease keep the brain from working properly. Bertha Madras is a biochemist who studies drug addiction. Dr. Madras studies brain activity to see how substances, such as cocaine, target cells or areas in the brain. Using a variety of brain scanning techniques, Dr. Madras can observe a brain on drugs. She can see how a drug affects the normal activity of the brain. During her research, Dr. Madras realized that some of her results could be applied to Parkinson's disease and to attention deficit hyperactivity disorder (ADHD) in adults. Her research has led to new treatments for both problems.

Math ACTIVITY

Using a search engine on a computer connected to the Internet, search the Internet for "reaction time experiment." Go to one of the Web sites and take the response-time experiment. Record the time that it took you to respond. Repeat the test nine more times, and record your response time for each trial. Then, make a line graph or a bar graph of your response times. Did your response times change? In what way did they change?

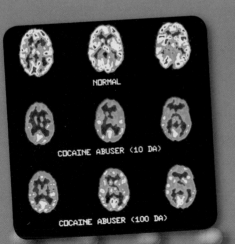

NORMAL

COCAINE ABUSER (10 DA)

COCAINE ABUSER (100 DA)

To learn more about these Science in Action topics, visit **go.hrw.com** and type in the keyword **HL5BD4F.**

Check out Current Science® articles related to this chapter by visiting go.hrw.com. Just type in the keyword **HL5CS25.**

5
Reproduction and Development

About the

If someone had taken your picture when your mother was about 13 weeks pregnant with you, that picture would have looked much like this photograph. You have changed a lot since then, haven't you? You started out as a single cell, and you became a complete person. And you haven't stopped growing and changing yet. In fact, you will continue to change for the rest of your life.

PRE-READING ACTIVITY

Graphic Organizer **Spider Map** Before you read the chapter, create the graphic organizer entitled "Spider Map" described in the **Study Skills** section of the Appendix. Label the circle "Reproduction and Development." Create a leg for each section title. As you read the chapter, fill in the map with details about reproduction and development from each section.

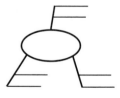

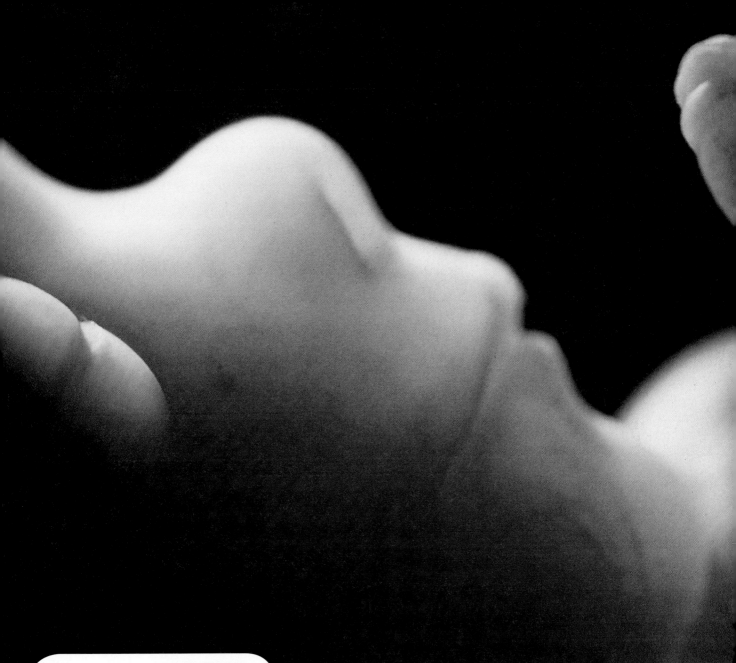

START-UP ACTIVITY

How Grows It?

As you read this paragraph, you are slowly aging. Your body is growing into the body of an adult. But does your body have the same proportions that an adult's body has? Complete this activity to find out.

Procedure

1. Have a classmate use a **tape measure** and **meterstick** to measure your total height, head height, and leg length. Your teacher will tell you how to take these measurements.

2. Use the following equations to calculate your head height–to–total body height proportion and your leg length–to–total body height proportion.

$$\text{head proportion} = \frac{\text{head height}}{\text{body height}} \times 100$$

$$\text{leg proportion} = \frac{\text{leg length}}{\text{body height}} \times 100$$

3. Your teacher will give you the head, body, and leg measurements of three adults. Calculate the head-body and leg-body proportions of each of the three adults. Record all of the measurements and calculations.

Analysis

1. Compare your proportions with the proportions of the three adults.

Animal Reproduction

The life span of some living things is short compared with ours. For example, a fruit fly lives only about 40 days. Other organisms live much longer than we do. Some bristlecone pine trees, for example, are nearly 5,000 years old.

But all living things eventually die. If a species is to survive, its members must reproduce.

Asexual Reproduction

Some animals, particularly simpler ones, reproduce asexually. In **asexual reproduction,** a single parent has offspring that are genetically identical to the parent.

One kind of asexual reproduction is called budding. *Budding* happens when a part of the parent organism pinches off and forms a new organism. The new organism separates from the parent and lives independently. The hydra, shown in **Figure 1,** reproduces by budding. The new hydra is genetically identical to its parent.

Fragmentation is a second kind of asexual reproduction. In *fragmentation,* parts of an organism break off and then develop into a new individual that is identical to the original one. Certain organisms, such as flatworms called *planaria,* reproduce by fragmentation. A third type of asexual reproduction, similar to fragmentation, is *regeneration.* When an organism capable of regeneration, such as the sea star in **Figure 2,** loses a body part, that part may develop into an entirely new organism.

asexual reproduction reproduction that does not involve the union of sex cells and in which a single parent produces offspring that are genetically identical to the parent

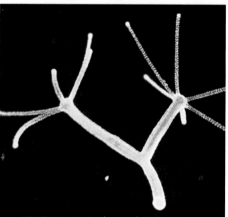

Figure 1 *The hydra bud will separate from its parent. Buds from other organisms, such as certain corals, remain attached to the parent.*

Figure 2 *The largest arm on this sea star was a fragment, from which a new sea star will regenerate. In time, all of the sea star's arms will grow to the same size.*

Sexual Reproduction

Most animals reproduce sexually. In **sexual reproduction,** off-spring are formed when genetic information from more than one parent combines. Sexual reproduction in animals usually requires two parents—a male and a female. The female parent produces sex cells called **eggs.** The male parent produces sex cells called **sperm.** When an egg's nucleus and a sperm's nucleus join, a fertilized egg, called a *zygote* (ZIE GOHT), is created. This joining of an egg and sperm is known as *fertilization.*

Human cells—except eggs and sperm and mature red blood cells—contain 46 chromosomes. Eggs and sperm are formed by a process called *meiosis.* In humans, meiosis is the division of one cell that has 46 chromosomes into four cells that have 23 chromosomes each. When an egg and a sperm join to form a zygote, the original number of 46 chromosomes is restored.

Genetic information is found in *genes*. Genes are located on *chromosomes* (KROH muh SOHMZ) made of the cell's DNA. During fertilization, the egg and sperm each contribute chromosomes to the zygote. The combination of genes from the two parents results in a zygote that grows into a unique individual. **Figure 3** shows how genes mix through three generations.

Reading Check What is sexual reproduction? (*See the Appendix for answers to Reading Checks.*)

sexual reproduction reproduction in which sex cells from two parents unite to produce offspring that share traits from both parents

egg a sex cell produced by a female

sperm the male sex cell

Figure 3 | **Inheriting Genes**

Eggs and sperm contain chromosomes. You inherit chromosomes—and the genes on them—from both of your parents. Your parents each inherited chromosomes from their parents.

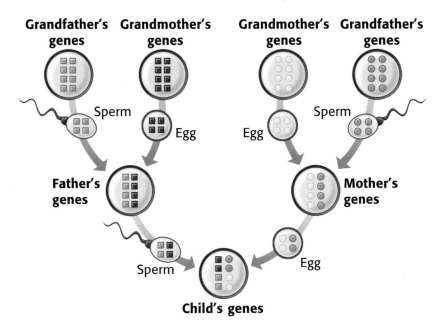

Grandfather's genes   Grandmother's genes   Grandmother's genes   Grandfather's genes

Sperm   Egg   Egg   Sperm

Father's genes   Mother's genes

Sperm   Egg

Child's genes

CONNECTION TO Language Arts

WRITING SKILL **Nature or Nurture?** Scientists debate whether genetics or upbringing is more important in shaping people. Use the Internet or library to research the issue of "nature versus nurture." Find information about identical twins who were raised apart. When you finish your research, write a persuasive essay supporting one side of the debate. Include evidence to support your argument.

Figure 4 *Some fish, such as these clownfish, fertilize their eggs externally. The eggs are the orange mass on the rock.*

external fertilization the union of sex cells outside the bodies of the parents

internal fertilization fertilization of an egg by sperm that occurs inside the body of a female

Figure 5 *This zebra has just been born, but he is already able to stand. Within an hour, he will be able to run.*

Internal and External Fertilization

Fertilization can happen either outside or inside the female's body. When the sperm fertilizes the eggs outside the female's body, the process is called **external fertilization.** External fertilization must take place in a moist environment so that the delicate zygotes won't dry out. Some fishes, such as those in **Figure 4,** reproduce by external fertilization.

Many amphibians, such as frogs, use external fertilization. For example, the female frog releases her eggs. At the same time, the male frog releases his sperm over the eggs to fertilize them. Frogs usually leave the zygotes to develop on their own. In about two weeks, the fertilized eggs hatch into tadpoles.

Internal Fertilization

When the egg and sperm join inside the female's body, the process is called **internal fertilization**. Internal fertilization allows the female animal to protect the developing egg inside her body. Reptiles, birds, mammals, and some fishes reproduce by internal fertilization. Many animals that use internal fertilization can lay fertilized eggs. Female chickens, for example, usually lay one or two eggs after internal fertilization has taken place.

In most mammals, one or more fertilized eggs develop inside the mother's body. Many mammals give birth to young that are well developed. Young zebras, such as the one in **Figure 5,** can stand up and nurse almost immediately after birth.

Reading Check What is the difference between external and internal fertilization?

Mammals

All mammals reproduce sexually. All mammals nurture their young with milk. And all mammals reproduce in one of the following three ways:

- **Monotreme** *Monotremes* (MAHN oh TREEMZ) are mammals that lay eggs. After the eggs are incubated and hatch, the young are nourished by milk that oozes from pores on the mother's belly. Echidnas and platypuses are monotremes.

- **Marsupial** Mammals that give birth to partially developed live young, such as the kangaroo in **Figure 6,** are *marsupials* (mahr SOO pee uhlz). Most marsupials have pouches where their young continue to develop after birth. Opossums, koalas, wombats, and Tasmanian devils are marsupials.

- **Placental Mammal** There are more than 4,000 species of placental mammals, including armadillos, humans, and bats. Placental mammals are nourished inside their mother's body before birth. Newborn placental mammals are more developed than newborn monotremes or marsupials are.

✓ Reading Check Name two ways that all mammals are alike.

Figure 6 *The red kangaroo is a marsupial. A young kangaroo, such as this one in its mother's pouch, is called a* joey.

SECTION Review

Summary

- In asexual reproduction, a single parent produces offspring that are genetically identical to the parent.
- In sexual reproduction, an egg from one parent combines with a sperm from the other parent.
- Fertilization can be external or internal.
- All mammals reproduce sexually and nurture their young with milk.

Using Key Terms

For each pair of terms, explain how the meanings of the terms differ.

1. *internal fertilization* and *external fertilization*

2. *asexual reproduction* and *sexual reproduction*

Understanding Key Ideas

3. In humans, each egg and each sperm contain
   - **a.** 23 chromosomes.
   - **b.** 46 chromosomes.
   - **c.** 69 chromosomes.
   - **d.** 529 chromosomes.

4. List three types of asexual reproduction.

5. How do monotremes differ from marsupials?

6. Describe the process of meiosis.

7. Are humans placental mammals, monotremes, or marsupials? Explain.

Math Skills

8. Some bristlecone pine needles last 40 years. If a tree lives for 3,920 years, how many sets of needles might it grow?

Critical Thinking

9. **Making Inferences** Why is reproduction as important to a bristlecone pine as it is to a fruit fly?

10. **Applying Concepts** Describe one advantage of internal fertilization over external fertilization.

SCLINKS **NSTA**
Developed and maintained by the National Science Teachers Association

For a variety of links related to this chapter, go to www.scilinks.org
Topic: Reproduction
SciLinks code: HSM1293

Human Reproduction

About nine months after a human sperm and egg combine, a mother gives birth to her baby. But how do humans make eggs and sperm?

The Male Reproductive System

The male reproductive system, shown in **Figure 1,** produces sperm and delivers it to the female reproductive system. The **testes** (singular, *testis*) are a pair of organs that make sperm and testosterone (tes TAHS tuhr OHN). Testosterone is the main male sex hormone. It helps regulate the production of sperm and the development of male characteristics.

As sperm leave a testis, they are stored in a tube called an *epididymis* (EP uh DID i mis). Sperm mature in the epididymis. Another tube, called a *vas deferens* (vas DEF uh RENZ), passes from the epididymis into the body and through the *prostate gland*. The prostate gland surrounds the neck of the bladder. As sperm move through the vas deferens, they mix with fluids from several glands, including the prostate gland. This mixture of sperm and fluids is called *semen.*

To leave the body, semen passes through the vas deferens into the *urethra* (yoo REE thruh). The urethra is the tube that runs through the penis. The **penis** is the external organ that transfers semen into the female's body.

✓ **Reading Check** Describe the path that sperm take from the testes to the penis. (*See the Appendix for answers to Reading Checks.*)

testes the primary male reproductive organs, which produce sperm and testosterone (singular, *testis*)

penis the male organ that transfers sperm to a female and that carries urine out of the body

Figure 1 **The Male Reproductive System**

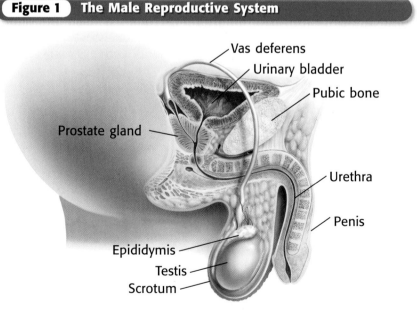

Vas deferens
Urinary bladder
Pubic bone
Prostate gland
Urethra
Penis
Epididymis
Testis
Scrotum

Figure 2 The Female Reproductive System

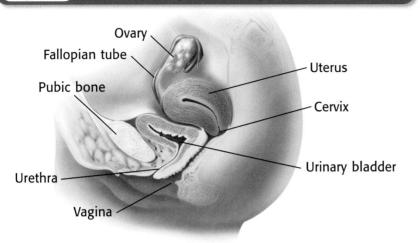

Ovary
Fallopian tube
Pubic bone
Uterus
Cervix
Urinary bladder
Urethra
Vagina

The Female Reproductive System

The female reproductive system, shown in **Figure 2,** produces eggs, nurtures fertilized eggs (zygotes), and gives birth. The two **ovaries** are the organs that make eggs. Ovaries also release estrogen (ES truh juhn) and progesterone (proh JES tuhr OHN), the main female sex hormones. These hormones regulate the release of eggs and development of female characteristics.

The Egg's Journey

During *ovulation* (AHV yoo LAY shuhn), an egg is released from an ovary and passes into a *fallopian* (fuh LOH pee uhn) *tube.* A fallopian tube leads from each ovary to the uterus. The egg passes through the fallopian tube into the uterus. Fertilization usually happens in the fallopian tube. If the egg is fertilized, the resulting zygote enters the uterus. The zygote may become embedded in the thickened lining of the uterus. The **uterus** is the organ in which a zygote develops into a baby.

When a baby is born, he or she passes from the uterus through the vagina and emerges outside the body. The **vagina** is the canal between the outside of the body and the uterus.

Menstrual Cycle

From puberty through her late 40s or early 50s, a woman's reproductive system goes through monthly changes. These changes prepare the body for pregnancy and are called the *menstrual cycle* (MEN struhl SIE kuhl). The first day of *menstruation* (MEN STRAY shuhn), the monthly discharge of blood and tissue from the uterus, is counted as the first day of the cycle. Menstruation lasts about 5 days. When menstruation ends, the lining of the uterus thickens. Ovulation occurs on about the 14th day of the cycle. If the egg is not fertilized within a few days, menstruation begins and flushes the egg away. The cycle—which usually takes about 28 days—starts again.

ovary in the female reproductive system of animals, an organ that produces eggs

uterus in female mammals, the hollow, muscular organ in which a fertilized egg is embedded and in which the embryo and fetus develop

vagina the female reproductive organ that connects the outside of the body to the uterus

Counting Eggs

1. The average woman ovulates each month from about age 12 to about age 50. How many mature eggs could she produce from age 18 to age 50?

2. A female's ovaries typically contain 2 million immature eggs. If she ovulates regularly from age 12 to age 50, what percentage of her eggs will mature?

Multiple Births

Have you ever seen identical twins? Sometimes, they are so similar that even their parents have trouble telling them apart. The boys in **Figure 3** are identical twins. Fraternal twins, the other type of twins, are more common than identical twins are. Fraternal twins can look very different from each other. In every 1,000 births, there are about 30 sets of twins. About one-third of all twin births are identical twins.

Twins are the most common multiple births. But humans sometimes have triplets (3 babies). In the United States, there are about two sets of triplets in every 1,000 births. Humans also have quadruplets (4 babies), quintuplets (5 babies), and more. These types of multiple births are rare. Births of quintuplets or more happen only once in about 53,000 births.

Reading Check What is the frequency of twin births?

Figure 3 *Identical twins have genes that are exactly the same. Many identical twins who are raised apart have similar personalities and interests.*

Reproductive System Problems

In most cases, the reproductive system functions flawlessly. But like any body system, the reproductive system sometimes has problems. These problems include disease and infertility.

STDs

Chlamydia, herpes, and hepatitis B are common sexually transmitted diseases. A *sexually transmitted disease,* or STD, is a disease that can pass from a person who is infected with the STD to an uninfected person during sexual contact. STDs are also called *sexually transmitted infections,* or STIs. These diseases affect many people each year, as shown in **Table 1.**

An STD you may have heard of is *acquired immune deficiency syndrome* (AIDS). AIDS is caused by *human immunodeficiency virus* (HIV). But you may not have heard of the STD *hepatitis B,* a liver disease also caused by a virus. This virus is spread in several ways, including sexual contact. In the United States, about 140,000 new cases of hepatitis B happen each year.

Table 1 The Spread of STDs in the United States	
STD	**Approximate number of new cases each year**
Chlamydia	3 to 10 million
Genital HPV (human papillomavirus)	5.5 million
Genital herpes	1 million
Gonorrhea	650,000
Syphilis	70,000
HIV/AIDS	40,000 to 50,000

SCHOOL to HOME

Twins and More

With a parent, discuss some challenges that are created by the birth of twins, triplets, quadruplets, or other multiples. Include financial, mental, emotional, and physical challenges.

Create a poster that shows these challenges and ways to meet them.

If twins or other multiples are in your family, discuss how the individuals differ and how they are alike.

ACTIVITY

Cancer

Sometimes, cancer happens in reproductive organs. *Cancer* is a disease in which cells grow at an uncontrolled rate. Cancer cells start out as normal cells. Then, something triggers uncontrolled cell growth. Different kinds of cancer have different triggers.

In men, the two most common reproductive system cancers are cancer of the testes and cancer of the prostate gland. In women, the two most common reproductive system cancers are breast cancer and cancer of the cervix. The *cervix* is the lower part, or neck, of the uterus. The cervix opens to the vagina.

Infertility

In the United States, about 15% of married couples have difficulty producing offspring. Many of these couples are *infertile*, or unable to have children. Men may be infertile if they do not produce enough healthy sperm. Women may be infertile if they do not ovulate normally.

Sexually transmitted diseases, such as gonorrhea and chlamydia, can lead to infertility in women. STD-related infertility occurs in men, but not as commonly as it does in women.

CONNECTION TO Social Studies

Understanding STDs Select one of the STDs in **Table 1.** Make a poster or brochure that identifies the cause of the disease, describes its symptoms, explains how it affects the body, and tells how it can be treated. Include a bar graph that shows the number of cases in different age groups.

ACTIVITY

SECTION Review

Summary

- The male reproductive system produces sperm and delivers it to the female reproductive system.
- The female reproductive system produces eggs, nurtures zygotes, and gives birth.
- Humans usually have one child per birth, but multiple births, such as those of twins or triplets, are possible.
- Human reproduction can be affected by cancer, infertility, and disease.

Using Key Terms

1. Use the following terms in the same sentence: *uterus* and *vagina*.

Understanding Key Ideas

2. Describe two problems of the reproductive system.

3. Identify the structures and functions of the male and female reproductive systems.

4. Identical twins happen once in 250 births. How many pairs of these twins might be at a school with 2,750 students?
   a. 1
   b. 11
   c. 22
   d. 250

Math Skills

5. In one country, 7 out of 1,000 infants die before their first birthday. Convert this figure to a percentage. Is your answer greater than or less than 1%?

Critical Thinking

6. **Making Inferences** What is the purpose of the menstrual cycle?

7. **Applying Concepts** Twins can happen when a zygote splits in two or when two eggs are fertilized. How can these two ways of twin formation explain how identical twins differ from fraternal twins?

8. **Predicting Consequences** How might cancer of the testes affect a man's ability to make sperm?

SCILINKS

NSTA
Developed and maintained by the National Science Teachers Association

For a variety of links related to this chapter, go to www.scilinks.org
Topic: Reproduction System Irregularities or Disorders
SciLinks code: HSM1298

Growth and Development

Every one of us started out as a single cell. How did that cell become a person made of trillions of cells?

A single cell divides many times and develops into a baby. But the development of a baby from a single cell is only the first stage of human development. Think about how you will change between now and when you become a grandparent!

From Fertilization to Embryo

Ordinarily, the process of human development starts when a man deposits millions of sperm into a woman's vagina. A few hundred sperm make it through the uterus into a fallopian tube. There, a few sperm cover the egg. Usually, only one sperm gets through the outer coating of the egg. When this happens, it triggers a response—a membrane forms around the egg to keep other sperm from entering. When the sperm's nucleus joins with the nucleus of the egg, the egg becomes fertilized.

The fertilized egg (zygote) travels down the fallopian tube toward the uterus. This journey takes 5 to 6 days. During the trip, the zygote undergoes cell division many times. Eleven to 12 days after fertilization, the zygote has become a tiny ball of cells called an **embryo.** The embryo implants itself in the uterus. *Implantation* happens when the zygote embeds itself in the thick, nutrient-rich lining of the uterus. Fertilization and implantation are outlined in **Figure 1.**

✔️ **Reading Check** Describe the process of fertilization and implantation. (*See the Appendix for answers to Reading Checks.*)

embryo a developing human, from fertilization through the first 8 weeks of development (the 10th week of pregnancy)

placenta the partly fetal and partly maternal organ by which materials are exchanged between fetus and mother

Figure 1 Fertilization and Implantation

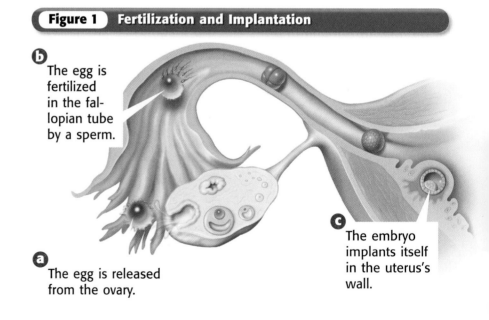

b The egg is fertilized in the fallopian tube by a sperm.

c The embryo implants itself in the uterus's wall.

a The egg is released from the ovary.

From Embryo to Fetus

After implantation, the placenta (pluh SEN tuh) begins to grow. The **placenta** is a special two-way exchange organ. It has a network of blood vessels that provides the embryo with oxygen and nutrients from the mother's blood. Wastes produced by the embryo are removed in the placenta. They are carried by the mother's blood so that her body can excrete them. The embryo's blood and the mother's blood flow very near each other in the placenta, but they normally do not mix.

✓ Reading Check Why is the placenta important?

Weeks 1 and 2

Doctors commonly count the time of a woman's pregnancy as starting from the first day of her last menstrual period. Even though fertilization has not yet taken place, that day is a convenient date from which to start counting. A normal pregnancy lasts about 280 days, or 40 weeks, from that day.

Weeks 3 and 4

Fertilization takes place at about the end of week 2. In week 3, after fertilization, the zygote moves to the uterus. As the zygote travels, it divides many times. It becomes a ball of cells that implants itself in the wall of the uterus. The zygote is now called an *embryo*. At the end of week 4, implantation is complete and the woman is pregnant. The embryo's blood cells begin to form. At this point, the embryo is about 0.2 mm long.

Weeks 5 to 8

Weeks 5 to 8 of pregnancy are weeks 3 to 6 of embryonic development. In this stage, the embryo becomes surrounded by a thin membrane called the *amnion* (AM nee AHN). The amnion is filled with amniotic fluid and protects the growing embryo from bumps and injury. During week 5, the umbilical cord forms. The **umbilical cord** (uhm BIL i kuhl KAWRD) is a cord that connects the embryo to the placenta. **Figure 2** shows the umbilical cord, amnion, and placenta.

In this stage, the heart, brain, other organs, and blood vessels start to form. They grow quickly. In weeks 5 and 6, eyes and ears take shape. The spinal cord begins to develop. In week 6, tiny limb buds appear. These buds will become arms and legs. In week 8, muscles start developing. Nerves grow into the shoulders and upper arms. Fingers and toes start to form. The embryo, now about 16 mm long, can swallow and blink.

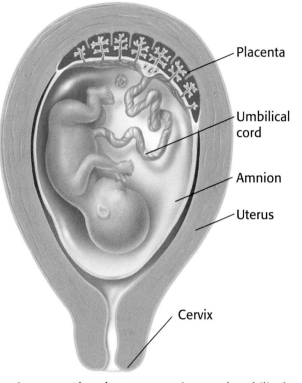

Placenta

Umbilical cord

Amnion

Uterus

Cervix

Figure 2 *The placenta, amnion, and umbilical cord are the life support system for the fetus. This fetus is about 20 to 22 weeks old.*

umbilical cord the structure that connects the fetus to the placenta

SCHOOL to HOME

Growing Up

With a parent, discuss the physical and mental changes that you went through between your birth and your first day of school. Make a poster illustrating those changes.

ACTIVITY

fetus a developing human from seven or eight weeks after fertilization until birth

Weeks 9 to 16

At week 9, the fetus may begin to make tiny movements. After week 10, the embryo is called a **fetus** (FEET uhs). In about week 13, the fetus's face begins to look more human. During this stage, fetal muscles grow stronger. As a result, the fetus can make a fist and begins to move. The fetus grows rapidly during this stage. It doubles, and then triples, its size within a month. For example, in week 10, the fetus is about 36 mm long. A little later, at week 16, the fetus is about 108 mm to 116 mm long. Use **Figure 3** to follow some of the changes that take place in the fetus as it develops.

 **Reading Check** Describe three changes the fetus undergoes during weeks 9 to 16.

Weeks 17 to 24

By week 17, the fetus can make faces. Usually, in week 18, the fetus starts to make movements that the mother can feel. By week 18, the fetus can hear sounds through the mother's uterus. It may even jump at loud noises. By week 23, the fetus's movements may be quite vigorous! If the fetus were born after week 24, it might survive. But babies born at 24 weeks require a lot of help. In weeks 17 to 24, the fetus grows to between 25 cm and 30 cm in length.

Weeks 25 to 36

At about 25 or 26 weeks, the fetus's lungs are well developed but not fully mature. The fetus still gets oxygen from its mother through the placenta. The fetus will not take its first breath of air until it is born. By the 32nd week, the fetus's eyes can open and close. Studies of fetal heart rate and brain activity show that fetuses respond to light. Some scientists have observed brain activity and eye movements in sleeping fetuses that resemble those activities in sleeping children or adults. These scientists think that a sleeping fetus may dream. After 36 weeks, the fetus is almost ready to be born.

Birth

At 37 to 38 weeks, the fetus is fully developed. A full-term pregnancy usually lasts about 40 weeks. Typically, as birth begins, the mother's uterus begins a series of muscular contractions called *labor*. Usually, these contractions push the fetus through the mother's vagina, and the baby is born. The newborn is still connected to the placenta by its umbilical cord, which is tied and cut. All that will remain of the point where the umbilical cord was attached is the baby's navel. Soon, the mother expels the placenta, and labor is complete.

CONNECTION TO Physics

Using Ultrasound Doctors often use ultrasound to view a fetus in the uterus. Research how an ultrasound machine works, and make a poster explaining how sound waves can show what is happening inside a human body.

 ACTIVITY

Figure 3 **Pregnancy Timeline**

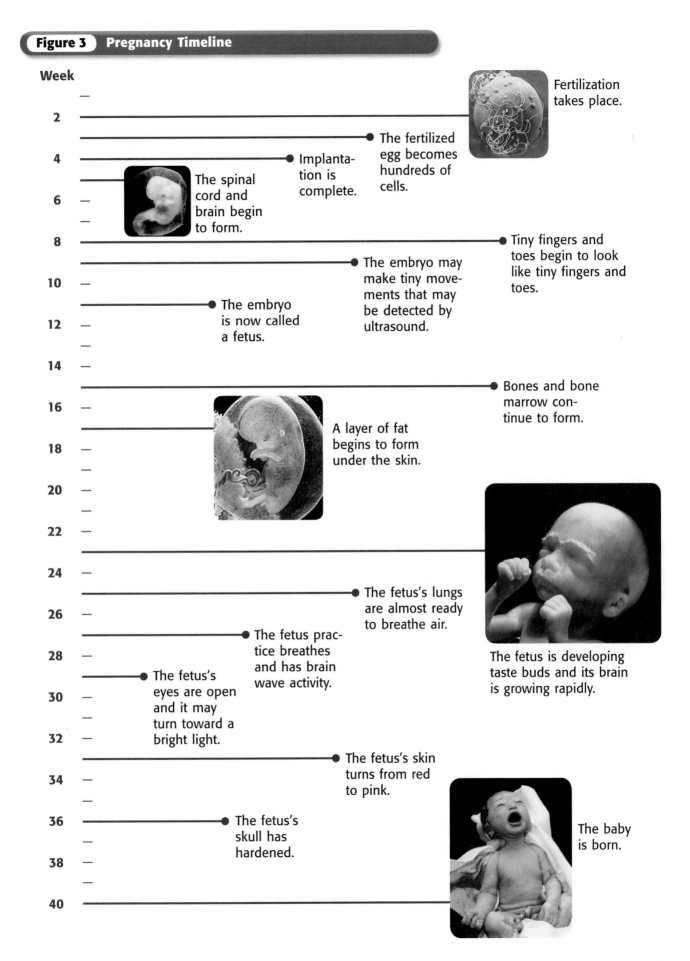

Week

2

4
Fertilization takes place.

The fertilized egg becomes hundreds of cells.

Implantation is complete.

The spinal cord and brain begin to form.

6

8
Tiny fingers and toes begin to look like tiny fingers and toes.

The embryo may make tiny movements that may be detected by ultrasound.

10

The embryo is now called a fetus.

12

14

16
Bones and bone marrow continue to form.

A layer of fat begins to form under the skin.

18

20

22

24

26
The fetus's lungs are almost ready to breathe air.

The fetus practice breathes and has brain wave activity.

28

The fetus's eyes are open and it may turn toward a bright light.

The fetus is developing taste buds and its brain is growing rapidly.

30

32

34
The fetus's skin turns from red to pink.

36
The fetus's skull has hardened.

The baby is born.

38

40

Figure 4 Stages of Human Development

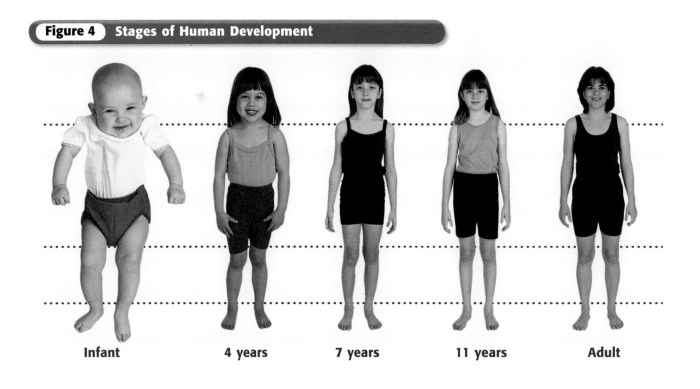

| Infant | 4 years | 7 years | 11 years | Adult |

From Birth to Death

After birth, the human body goes through several stages of development. Some of those stages are shown in **Figure 4.**

Infancy and Childhood

Generally, infancy is the stage from birth to age 2. During infancy, you grew quickly and your baby teeth appeared. As your nervous system developed, you became more coordinated and started to walk.

Childhood—another period of fast growth—lasts from age 2 to puberty. Your baby teeth were replaced by permanent teeth. And your muscles became more coordinated, which allowed you to ride a bicycle, jump rope, and do other activities.

Adolescence

The stage from puberty to adulthood is adolescence. During puberty, a person's reproductive system becomes mature. In most boys, puberty takes place between the ages of 11 and 16. During this time, the young male's body becomes more muscular, his voice becomes deeper, and body and facial hair appear. In most girls, puberty takes place between the ages of 9 and 14. During puberty in females, the amount of fat in the hips and thighs increases, the breasts enlarge, body hair appears, and menstruation begins.

✓ **Reading Check** Name an important change that takes place during adolescence.

Life Grows On

Use **Figure 4** to complete this activity.

1. Use a **ruler** to measure the infant's head height. Then, measure the infant's entire height, including the head.

2. Calculate the ratio of the infant's head height to the infant's total height.

3. Repeat these measurements and calculations for the other stages.

4. Does a baby's head grow faster or slower than the rest of the body? Why do you think this is so?

Adulthood

From about age 20 to age 40, you will be a young adult. You will be at the peak of your physical development. Beginning around age 30, changes associated with aging begin. These changes are gradual and different for everyone. Some early signs of aging include loss of flexibility in muscles, deterioration of eyesight, increase in body fat, and some loss of hair.

The aging process continues in middle age (between 40 and 65 years old). During this time, hair may turn gray, athletic abilities will decline, and skin may wrinkle. A person who is more than 65 years old is considered an older adult. Although the aging process continues, many older adults lead very active lives, as is shown in **Figure 5.**

Figure 5 *Older adults can still enjoy activities that they enjoyed when they were younger.*

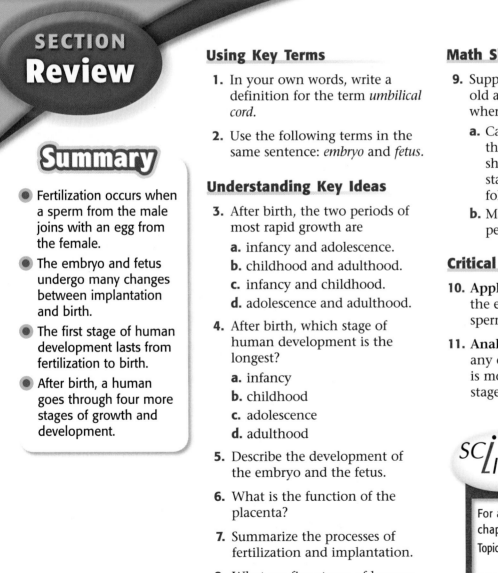

SECTION Review

Summary

- Fertilization occurs when a sperm from the male joins with an egg from the female.

- The embryo and fetus undergo many changes between implantation and birth.

- The first stage of human development lasts from fertilization to birth.

- After birth, a human goes through four more stages of growth and development.

Using Key Terms

1. In your own words, write a definition for the term *umbilical cord*.

2. Use the following terms in the same sentence: *embryo* and *fetus*.

Understanding Key Ideas

3. After birth, the two periods of most rapid growth are
   a. infancy and adolescence.
   b. childhood and adulthood.
   c. infancy and childhood.
   d. adolescence and adulthood.

4. After birth, which stage of human development is the longest?
   a. infancy
   b. childhood
   c. adolescence
   d. adulthood

5. Describe the development of the embryo and the fetus.

6. What is the function of the placenta?

7. Summarize the processes of fertilization and implantation.

8. What are five stages of human development?

Math Skills

9. Suppose a person is 80 years old and that puberty took place when he or she was 12 years old.
   a. Calculate the percentage of the person's life that he or she spent in each of the four stages of development that follow birth.
   b. Make a bar graph showing the percentage for each stage.

Critical Thinking

10. **Applying Concepts** Why does the egg's covering change after a sperm has entered the egg?

11. **Analyzing Ideas** Do you think any one stage of development is more important than other stages? Explain your answer.

Skills Practice Lab

OBJECTIVES

Construct a model of a human uterus protecting a fetus.

Compare the protection that a bird's egg gives a developing baby bird with the protection that a human uterus gives a fetus.

MATERIALS

- computer (optional)
- cotton, soft fabric, or other soft materials
- eggs, soft-boiled and in the shell (2 to 4)
- eggs, soft-boiled and peeled (3 or 4)
- gloves, protective
- mineral oil, cooking oil, syrup, or other thick liquid
- plastic bags, sealable
- water

SAFETY

It's a Comfy, Safe World!

Before birth, baby birds live inside a hard, protective shell until the baby has used up all the food supply. Most mammal babies develop within their mother's uterus, in which they are surrounded by fluid and connected to a placenta, before they are born. Before human babies are born, they lead a comfy life. By the seventh month, they lie around sucking their thumb, blinking their eyes, and perhaps even dreaming.

Ask a Question

1 Inside which structure is a developing organism better protected from bumps and blows: the uterus of a placental mammal or the egg of a bird?

Form a Hypothesis

2 A placental mammal's uterus protects a developing organism from bumps and blows better than a bird's egg does.

Test the Hypothesis

3 Brainstorm several ideas about how you will construct and test your model of a mammalian uterus. Then, use the materials provided by your teacher to build your model. A peeled, soft-boiled egg will represent the fetus inside your model uterus.

4 Make a data table similar to **Table 1** below. Test your model, examine the egg for damage, and record your results.

Table 1 First Model Test	
Original model	**Modified model**
DO NOT WRITE	
IN BOOK	

5 Modify your model as necessary; test this modified model using another peeled, soft-boiled egg; and record your results.

6 When you are satisfied with the design of your model, obtain another peeled, soft-boiled egg and an egg in the shell. The egg in the shell represents the baby bird inside the egg.

7 Make a data table similar to **Table 2** below. Test your new eggs, examine them for damage, and record your results in your data table.

Table 2 **Final Model Test**	
	Test Results
Model	DO NOT WRITE IN BOOK
Egg in shell	

Analyze the Results

1 **Explaining Events** Explain any differences in the test results for the model and the egg in a shell.

2 **Analyzing Results** What modification to your model was the most effective in protecting the fetus?

Draw Conclusions

3 **Evaluating Data** Review your hypothesis. Did your data support your hypothesis? Why or why not?

4 **Evaluating Models** What modifications to your model might make it more like a uterus?

Applying Your Data

Use the Internet or the library to find information about the development of monotremes, such as the echidna or the platypus, and marsupials, such as the koala or the kangaroo. Then, using what you have learned in this lab, compare the development of placental mammals with that of marsupials and monotremes.

Chapter Review

USING KEY TERMS

For each pair of terms, explain how the meanings of the terms differ.

1 *internal fertilization* and *external fertilization*

2 *testes* and *ovaries*

3 *asexual reproduction* and *sexual reproduction*

4 *fertilization* and *implantation*

5 *umbilical cord* and *placenta*

UNDERSTANDING KEY IDEAS

Multiple Choice

6 The sea star reproduces asexually by

  a. fragmentation.

  b. budding.

  c. external fertilization.

  d. internal fertilization.

7 Which list shows in order sperm's path through the male reproductive system?

  a. testes, epididymis, urethra, vas deferens

  b. epididymis, urethra, testes, vas deferens

  c. testes, vas deferens, epididymis, urethra

  d. testes, epididymis, vas deferens, urethra

8 Identical twins are the result of

  a. a fertilized egg splitting in two.

  b. two separate eggs being fertilized.

  c. budding in the uterus.

  d. external fertilization.

9 If the onset of menstruation is counted as the first day of the menstrual cycle, on what day of the cycle does ovulation typically occur?

  a. 2nd day

  b. 5th day

  c. 14th day

  d. 28th day

10 How do monotremes differ from placental mammals?

  a. Monotremes are not mammals.

  b. Monotremes have hair.

  c. Monotremes nurture their young with milk.

  d. Monotremes lay eggs.

11 All of the following are sexually transmitted diseases EXCEPT

  a. chlamydia.

  b. AIDS.

  c. infertility.

  d. genital herpes.

12 Where do fertilization and implantation, respectively, take place?

  a. uterus, fallopian tube

  b. fallopian tube, vagina

  c. uterus, vagina

  d. fallopian tube, uterus

Short Answer

13 Which human reproductive organs produce sperm? produce eggs?

14 Explain how the fetus gets oxygen and nutrients and how it gets rid of waste.

15 What are four stages of human life following birth?

16 Name three problems that can affect the human reproductive system, and explain why each is a problem.

17 Draw a diagram showing the structures of the male and female reproductive systems. Label each structure, and explain how each structure contributes to fertilization and implantation.

CRITICAL THINKING

18 Concept Mapping Use the following terms to create a concept map: *asexual reproduction, budding, external fertilization, fragmentation, reproduction, internal fertilization,* and *sexual reproduction.*

19 Identifying Relationships The environment in which organisms live may change over time. For example, a wet, swampy area may gradually become a grassy area with a small pond. Explain how sexual reproduction may give species that live in a changing environment a survival advantage.

20 Applying Concepts What is the function of the uterus? How is this function related to the menstrual cycle?

21 Making Inferences In most human body cells, the 46 chromosomes are duplicated during cell division so that each new cell receives 46 chromosomes. Cells that make eggs and sperm also split and duplicate their 46 chromosomes. But then, in the process of meiosis, the two cells split again to form four cells (egg or sperm) that each have 23 chromosomes. Why is meiosis important to human reproduction and to the human species?

INTERPRETING GRAPHICS

The following graph illustrates the cycles of the female hormone estrogen and the male hormone testosterone. The blue line shows the estrogen level in a female over 28 days. The red line shows the testosterone level in a male over the same amount of time. Use the graph below to answer the questions that follow.

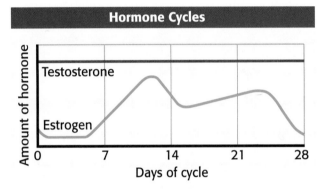

22 What is the major difference between the levels of the two hormones over the 28 days?

23 What cycle do you think estrogen affects?

24 Why might the level of testosterone stay the same?

25 Do you think that the above estrogen cycle would change in a pregnant woman? Explain your answer.

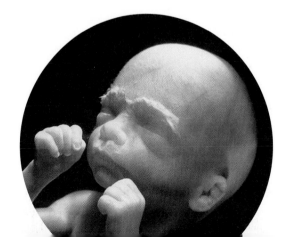

Standardized Test Preparation

Read each of the passages below. Then, answer the questions that follow each passage.

Passage 1 The male reproductive system is made up of internal and external organs. The <u>external</u> organs of this system are the penis and the scrotum. The scrotum is a skin-covered sac that hangs outside the body. Normal human body temperature is about 37°C. Normal sperm production and development cannot take place at that temperature. Normal sperm production and development takes place at lower temperatures. That is why the testes rest in the scrotum, outside the body. The scrotum is about 2°C cooler than the body. Inside each testis are masses of tightly coiled tubes, called *seminiferous tubules,* in which sperm are produced when conditions are right.

1. In this passage, what does the word *external* mean?
   A not part of the body
   B outside the body
   C inside the body
   D lasting a long time

2. Which of the following statements is a fact according to the passage?
   F The temperature in the scrotum is higher than body temperature.
   G Testes are internal organs of the male reproductive system.
   H Normal sperm production cannot take place at normal body temperature.
   I Normal human body temperature is about 37°F.

3. What are the tubes in which sperm are made called?
   A testes
   B scrotum
   C seminiferous tubules
   D external organs

Passage 2 In a normal pregnancy, the fertilized egg travels to the uterus and implants itself in the uterus's wall. But, in about 7 out of 1,000 pregnancies in the United States, a woman has an <u>ectopic pregnancy</u>. The term *ectopic* is from two Greek words meaning "out of place." In an ectopic pregnancy, the fertilized egg implants itself in an ovary, a fallopian tube, or another area of the female reproductive system that is not the lining of the uterus. Because the zygote cannot develop properly outside of the uterus, an ectopic pregnancy can be very dangerous for both the mother and zygote. As the zygote grows, it causes the mother pain and bleeding. For example, an ectopic pregnancy in a fallopian tube can rupture the tube and cause abdominal bleeding. If an ectopic pregnancy is not treated quickly enough, the mother may die.

1. In the passage, what does the term *ectopic pregnancy* probably mean?
   A a pregnancy that takes place at the wrong time
   B a type of pregnancy that happens about 7 out of 100 times in the United States
   C a type of pregnancy caused by a problem with a fallopian tube
   D a pregnancy in which the zygote implants itself in the wrong place

2. Which of the following statements is a fact according to the passage?
   F Ectopic pregnancies take place in about 7% of all pregnancies.
   G The ectopic pregnancy rate in the United States is less than 1%.
   H Ectopic pregnancies take place in the uterus.
   I An ectopic pregnancy is harmless.

Use the diagrams below to answer the questions that follow.

A.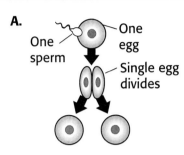

One sperm · One egg · Single egg divides

B. Two sperm

Two eggs

1. Which diagram of cell division would produce identical twins: A or B?

   A diagram B, because each egg is fertilized by a separate sperm cell

   B both diagram A and diagram B, because twins result in both cases

   C diagram A, because a single fertilized egg separates into two halves

   D diagram B, because two eggs are released by an ovary

2. Which of the following could describe fraternal twins?

   F both boys

   G both girls

   H one girl and one boy

   I any of these combinations

3. Which diagram of cell division could explain triplets, two of whom are identical and one of whom is fraternal?

   A diagram A

   B diagram B

   C either diagram A or diagram B

   D neither diagram A or diagram B

Read each question below, and choose the best answer.

1. Identify the group that contains equivalent fractions, decimals, and percents.

   A 7/10, 0.7, 7%

   B 1/2, 0.5, 50%

   C 3/8, 0.38, 38%

   D 3/100, 0.3, 33%

2. A geologist was exploring a cave. She spent 2.7 h exploring on Saturday and twice as many hours exploring on Sunday. Which equation could be used to find n, the total number of hours the geologist spent exploring the cave on those 2 days?

   F $n = 2 \div 2.7$

   G $n = 2.7 + (2 \times 2.7)$

   H $n = 2.7 + 2.7 + 2$

   I $n = 2 \times 2.7$

3. Which of the following story problems can be solved by the equation below?

$$(60 + 70 + 68 + 80 + x) \div 5 = 70$$

   A The heights of four buildings in South Braintree are 60 ft, 70 ft, 68 ft, and 80 ft. Find x, the average height of the buildings.

   B The weights of four dogs Jason is raising are 60 lb, 70 lb, 68 lb, and 80 lb. Find x, the sum of the weights of the four dogs.

   C Kayla's first four handmade bracelets sold for $60, $70, $68, and $80. Find x, the amount for which Kayla needs to sell her fifth bracelet to have an average selling price of $70.

   D The times it took Taylor to complete each of four 100 m practice swims were 60 s, 70 s, 68 s, and 80 s. Find x, the average time it took Taylor to complete his practice swims.

Standardized Test Preparation

Science in Action

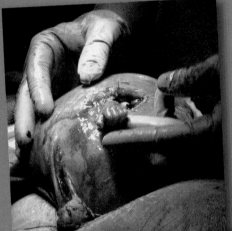

Doctors operated on a fetus, whose hand is visible in this photo, to correct spina bifida.

Science, Technology, and Society

Fetal Surgery

Sometimes, a developing fetus has a serious medical problem. In many cases, surgery after birth can correct the problem. But some problems can be treated while the fetus is still in the uterus. For example, fetal surgery may be used to correct spina bifida (part of the spinal cord is exposed because the backbone doesn't form properly). Doctors now can fix several types of problems before a baby is born.

Social Studies ACTiViTy

WRITING SKILL Research the causes of spina bifida. Write a brochure telling expectant mothers what precautions they can take to prevent spina bifida.

Scientific Discoveries

Lasers and Acne

Many people think that acne affects only teenagers, but acne can strike at any age. Some acne is mild, but some is severe. Now, for some severe cases of acne, lasers may provide relief. That's right—lasers can be used to treat acne! Surgeons who specialize in the health and diseases of the skin use laser light to treat the skin disease known as *acne*.

In addition, laser treatments may stimulate the skin cells that produce collagen. Collagen is a protein found in connective tissue. Increased production of collagen in the skin improves the skin's texture and helps smooth out acne scars.

Language Arts ACTiViTy

WRITING SKILL Write a story about how severe acne affects a teen's life. Tell what happens when a doctor refers the teen to a specialist for laser treatment and how the successful treatment changes the teen's life.

Reva Curry

Diagnostic Medical Sonographer Sounds are everywhere in our world. But only some of those sounds—such as your favorite music playing on the stereo or the dog barking next door—are sounds that we can hear. There are sound waves whose frequency is too high for us to hear. These high-pitched sounds are called *ultrasound*. Some animals, such as bats, use ultrasound to hunt and to avoid midair collisions.

Humans use ultrasound, too. Ultrasound machines can peer inside the human body to look at hearts, blood vessels, and fetuses. Diagnostic medical sonographers are people who use sonography equipment to diagnose medical problems and to follow the growth and development of a fetus before it is born. One of the leading professionals in the field of diagnostic medical sonography is Dr. Reva Curry. Dr. Curry spent many years as a sonographer. Her primary job was to use high-tech instruments to create ultrasound images of parts of the body and interpret the results for other medical professionals. Today, Dr. Curry works with students as the dean of a community college.

Math ACTiViTY

At 20°C, the speed of sound in water is 1,482 m/s and in steel is 5,200 m/s. How long would it take a sound to travel 815.1 m in water? In that same length of time, how far would a sound travel in a steel beam?

To learn more about these Science in Action topics, visit go.hrw.com and type in the keyword **HL5BD5F**.

Check out Current Science® articles related to this chapter by visiting go.hrw.com. Just type in the keyword HL5CS26.

6

Body Defenses and Disease

About the

No, this photo is not from a sci-fi movie. It is not an alien insect soldier. This is, in fact, a greatly enlarged image of a house dust mite that is tinier than the dot of an *i*. Huge numbers of these creatures live in carpets, beds, and sofas in every home. Dust mites often cause problems for people who have asthma or allergies. The body's immune system fights diseases and alien factors, such as dust mites, that cause allergies.

PRE-READING ACTIVITY

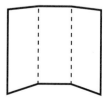

FOLDNOTES **Tri-Fold** Before you read the chapter, create the FoldNote entitled "Tri-Fold" described in the **Study Skills** section of the Appendix. Write what you know about the body's defenses in the column labeled "Know." Then, write what you want to know in the column labeled "Want." As you read the chapter, write what you learn about the body's defenses in the column labeled "Learn."

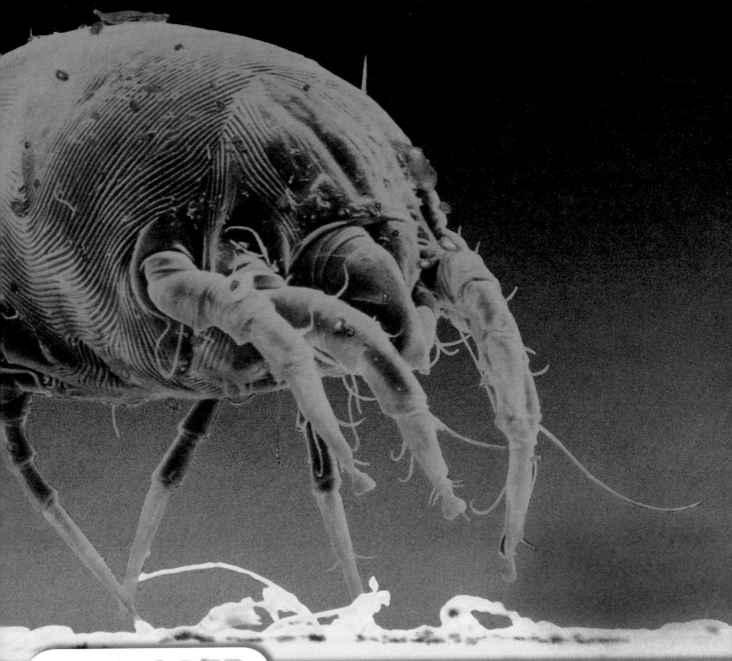

START-UP ACTIVITY

Invisible Invaders

In this activity, you will see tiny organisms grow.

Procedure

1. Obtain **two Petri dishes containing nutrient agar.** Label them "Washed" and "Unwashed."

2. Rub **two marbles** between the palms of your hands. Observe the appearance of the marbles.

3. Roll one marble in the Petri dish labeled "Unwashed."

4. Put on a pair of **disposable gloves.** Wash the other marble with **soap** and **warm water** for 4 min.

5. Roll the washed marble in the Petri dish labeled "Washed."

6. Secure the lids of the Petri dishes with **transparent tape.** Place the dishes in a warm, dark place. Do not open the Petri dishes after they are sealed.

7. Record changes in the Petri dishes for 1 week.

Analysis

1. How did the washed and unwashed marbles compare? How did the Petri dishes differ after several days?

2. Why is it important to wash your hands before eating?

Disease

You've probably heard it before: "Cover your mouth when you sneeze!" "Wash your hands!" "Don't put that in your mouth!"

What is all the fuss about? When people say these things to you, they are concerned about the spread of disease.

Causes of Disease

When you have a *disease,* your normal body functions are disrupted. Some diseases, such as most cancers and heart disease, are not spread from one person to another. They are called **noninfectious diseases.**

Noninfectious diseases can be caused by a variety of factors. For example, a genetic disorder causes the disease hemophilia (HEE moh FIL ee uh), in which a person's blood does not clot properly. Smoking, lack of physical activity, and a high-fat diet can greatly increase a person's chances of getting certain noninfectious diseases. Avoiding harmful habits may help you avoid noninfectious diseases.

A disease that can be passed from one living thing to another is an **infectious disease.** Infectious diseases are caused by agents called **pathogens.** Viruses and some bacteria, fungi, protists, and worms may all cause diseases. **Figure 1** shows some enlarged images of common pathogens.

noninfectious disease a disease that cannot spread from one individual to another

infectious disease a disease that is caused by a pathogen and that can be spread from one individual to another

pathogen a virus, microorganism, or other organism that causes disease

Figure 1 **Pathogens**

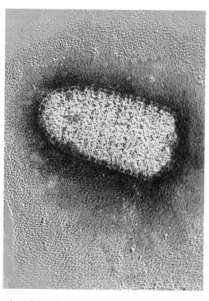

▲ This virus causes rabies.

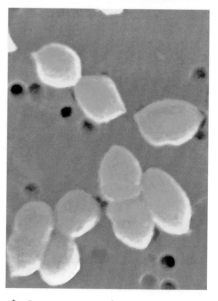

▲ *Streptococcus* bacteria can cause strep throat.

Pathways to Pathogens

There are many ways pathogens can be passed from one person to another. Being aware of them can help you stay healthy.

Air

Some pathogens travel through the air. For example, a single sneeze, such as the one shown in **Figure 2,** releases thousands of tiny droplets of moisture that can carry pathogens.

Contaminated Objects

You may already know that if you drink from a glass that an infected person has just used, you could become infected with a pathogen. A person who is sick may leave bacteria or viruses on many other objects, too. For example, contaminated doorknobs, keyboards, combs, and towels can pass pathogens.

Person to Person

Some pathogens are spread by direct person-to-person contact. You can become infected with some illnesses by kissing, shaking hands, or touching the sores of an infected person.

Animals

Some pathogens are carried by animals. For example, humans can get a fungus called *ringworm* from handling an infected dog or cat. Also, ticks may carry bacteria that cause Lyme disease or Rocky Mountain spotted fever.

Food and Water

Drinking water in the United States is generally safe. But water lines can break, or treatment plants can become flooded. These problems may allow microorganisms to enter the public water supply. Bacteria growing in foods and beverages can cause illness, too. For example, meat, fish, and eggs that are not cooked enough can still contain dangerous bacteria or parasites. Even leaving food out at room temperature can give bacteria such as salmonella the chance to grow and produce toxins in the food. Refrigerating foods can slow the growth of many of these pathogens. Because bacteria grow in food, washing all used cooking surfaces and tools is also important.

✓ Reading Check Why must you cook meat and eggs thoroughly? (*See the Appendix for answers to Reading Checks.*)

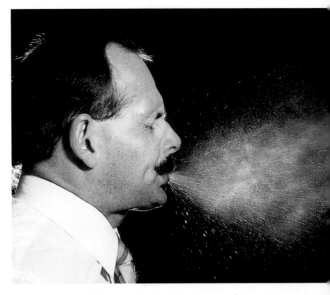

Figure 2 *A sneeze can force thousands of pathogen-carrying droplets out of your body at up to 160 km/h.*

CONNECTION TO Social Studies

Disease and History Many diseases have shaped history. For example, yellow fever, which is caused by a virus that is spread by mosquitoes, was one of the obstacles in building the Panama Canal. Only after people learned how to prevent the spread of the yellow fever virus could the canal be completed.

Use information from Internet and library research to create a poster describing how one infectious disease affected history.

ACTIVITY

Putting Pathogens in Their Place

Until the twentieth century, surgery patients often died of bacterial infections. But doctors learned that simple cleanliness could help prevent the spread of some diseases. Today, hospitals and clinics use a variety of technologies to prevent the spread of pathogens. For example, ultraviolet radiation, boiling water, and chemicals are used to kill pathogens in health facilities.

Label Check

At home or in a local store, find a product that has been pasteurized. In your **science journal,** write down other safety information you find on the label, including the product's refrigeration needs. Why do you think most products that require pasteurization also require refrigeration?

Pasteurization

During the mid-1800s, Louis Pasteur, a French scientist, discovered that microorganisms caused wine to spoil. The uninvited microorganisms were bacteria. Pasteur devised a method of using heat to kill most of the bacteria in the wine. This method is called *pasteurization* (PAS tuhr i ZAY shuhn), and it is still used today. The milk that the girl in **Figure 3** is drinking has been pasteurized.

immunity the ability to resist or to recover from an infectious disease

Vaccines and Immunity

In the late 1700s, no one knew what a pathogen was. During this time, Edward Jenner studied a disease called *smallpox*. He observed that people who had been infected with cowpox seemed to have protection against smallpox. These people had a resistance to the disease. The ability to resist or recover from an infectious disease is called **immunity.** Jenner's work led to the first modern vaccine. A *vaccine* is a substance that helps your body develop immunity to a disease.

Today, vaccines are used all over the world to prevent many serious diseases. Modern vaccines contain pathogens that are killed or specially treated so that they can't make you very sick. The vaccine is enough like the pathogen to allow your body to develop a defense against the disease.

Figure 3 *Today, pasteurization is used to kill pathogens in many different types of food, including dairy products, shellfish, and juices.*

Antibiotics

Have you ever had strep throat? If so, you have had a bacterial infection. Bacterial infections can be a serious threat to your health. Fortunately, doctors can usually treat these kinds of infections with antibiotics. An *antibiotic* is a substance that can kill bacteria or slow the growth of bacteria. Antibiotics may also be used to treat infections caused by other microorganisms, such as fungi. You may take an antibiotic when you are sick. Always take antibiotics according to your doctor's instructions to ensure that all the pathogens are killed.

Viruses, such as those that cause colds, are not affected by antibiotics. Antibiotics can kill only living things, and viruses are not alive. The only way to destroy viruses in your body is to locate and kill the cells they have invaded.

✓ Reading Check Frank caught a bad cold just before the opening night of a school play. He visited his doctor and asked her to prescribe antibiotics for his cold. The doctor politely refused and advised Frank to stay home and get plenty of rest. Why do you think the doctor refused to give Frank antibiotics?

Epidemic!

You catch a cold and return to your school while sick. Your friends don't have immunity to your cold. On the first day, you expose five friends to your cold. The next day, each of those friends passes the virus to five more people. If this pattern continues for 5 more days, how many people will be exposed to the virus?

SECTION Review

Summary

● Noninfectious diseases cannot be spread from one person to another.

● Infectious diseases are caused by pathogens that are passed from one living thing to another.

● Pathogens can travel through the air or can be spread by contact with other people, contaminated objects, animals, food, or water.

● Cleanliness, pasteurization, vaccines, and antibiotics help control the spread of pathogens.

Using Key Terms

1. In your own words, write a definition for each of the following terms: *infectious disease, noninfectious disease,* and *immunity.*

Understanding Key Ideas

2. Vaccines contain
   a. treated pathogens.
   b. heat.
   c. antibiotics.
   d. pasteurization.

3. List five ways that you might come into contact with a pathogen.

4. Name four ways to help keep safe from pathogens.

Math Skills

5. If 10 people with the virus each expose 25 more people to the virus, how many people will be exposed to the virus?

Critical Thinking

6. **Identifying Relationships** Why might the risk of infectious disease be high in a community that has no water treatment facility?

7. **Analyzing Methods** Explain what might happen if a doctor did not wear gloves when treating patients.

8. **Applying Concepts** Why do vaccines for diseases in animals help prevent some illnesses in people?

Developed and maintained by the National Science Teachers Association

For a variety of links related to this chapter, go to www.scilinks.org

Topic: Pathogens; What Causes Diseases?
SciLinks code: HSM1118; HSM1653

SECTION 2

Your Body's Defenses

Bacteria and viruses can be in the air, in the water, and on all the surfaces around you.

Your body must constantly protect itself against pathogens that are trying to invade it. But how does your body do that? Luckily, your body has its own built-in defense system.

READING WARM-UP

Objectives

- Describe how your body keeps out pathogens.
- Explain how the immune system fights infections.
- Describe four challenges to the immune system.

Terms to Learn

immune system
macrophage
T cell
B cell
antibody
memory B cell
allergy
autoimmune disease
cancer

READING STRATEGY

Reading Organizer As you read this section, make a flowchart of the steps of how your body responds to a virus.

First Lines of Defense

For a pathogen to harm you, it must attack a part of your body. Usually, though, very few of the pathogens around you make it past your first lines of defense.

Many organisms that try to enter your eyes or mouth are destroyed by special enzymes. Pathogens that enter your nose are washed down the back of your throat by mucus. The mucus carries the pathogens to your stomach, where most are quickly digested.

Your skin is made of many layers of flat cells. The outermost layers are dead. As a result, many pathogens that land on your skin have difficulty finding a live cell to infect. As **Figure 1** shows, the dead skin cells are constantly dropping off your body as new skin cells grow from beneath. As the dead skin cells flake off, they carry away viruses, bacteria, and other microorganisms. In addition, glands secrete oil onto your skin's surface. The oil contains chemicals that kill many pathogens.

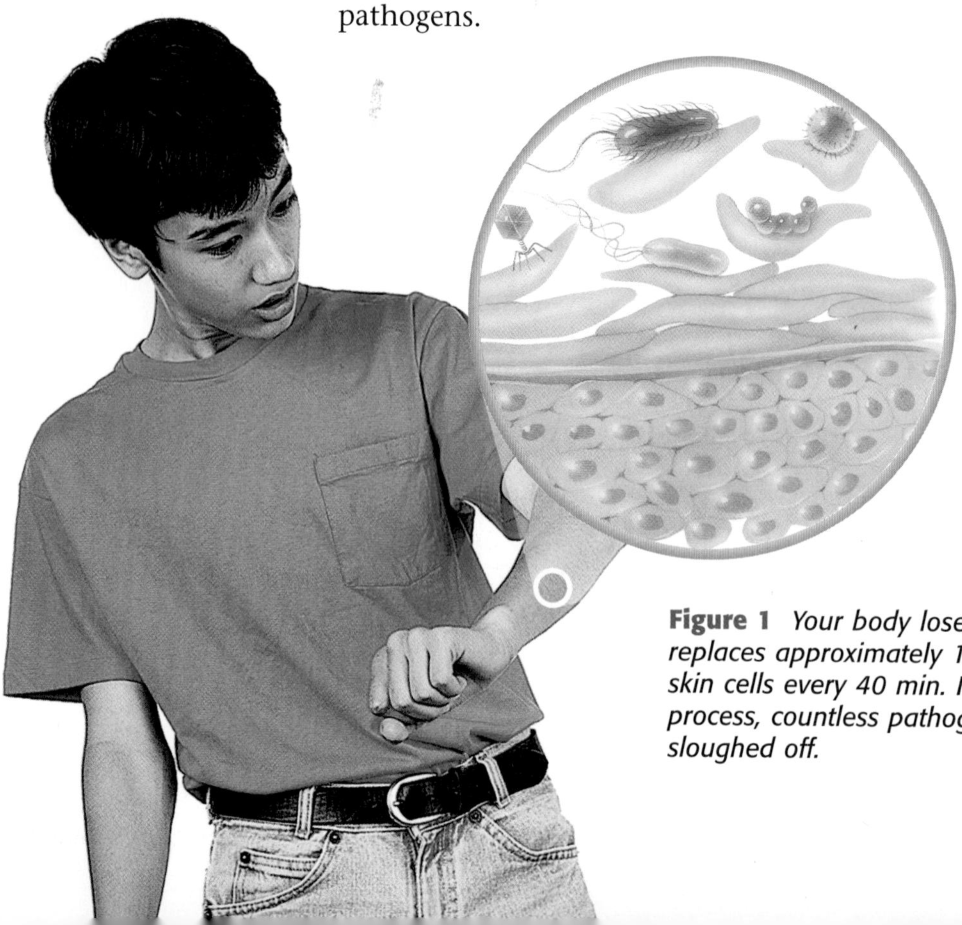

Figure 1 *Your body loses and replaces approximately 1 million skin cells every 40 min. In the process, countless pathogens are sloughed off.*

Failure of First Lines

Sometimes, skin is cut or punctured and pathogens can enter the body. The body acts quickly to keep out as many pathogens as possible. Blood flow to the injured area increases. Cell parts in the blood called *platelets* help seal the open wound so that no more pathogens can enter.

The increased blood flow also brings cells that belong to the **immune system,** the body system that fights pathogens. The immune system is not localized in any one place in your body. It is not controlled by any one organ, such as the brain. Instead, it is a team of individual cells, tissues, and organs that work together to keep you safe from invading pathogens.

Cells of the Immune System

The immune system consists mainly of three kinds of cells. One kind is the macrophage (MAK roh FAYJ). **Macrophages** engulf and digest many microorganisms or viruses that enter your body. If only a few microorganisms or viruses have entered a wound, the macrophages can easily stop them.

The other two main kinds of immune-system cells are T cells and B cells. **T cells** coordinate the immune system and attack many infected cells. **B cells** are immune-system cells that make antibodies. **Antibodies** are proteins that attach to specific antigens. *Antigens* are substances that stimulate an immune response. Your body is capable of making billions of different antibodies. Each antibody usually attaches to only one kind of antigen, as illustrated in **Figure 2.**

✔ **Reading Check** How do macrophages help fight disease? (*See the Appendix for answers to Reading Checks.*)

immune system the cells and tissues that recognize and attack foreign substances in the body

macrophage an immune system cell that engulfs pathogens and other materials

T cell an immune system cell that coordinates the immune system and attacks many infected cells

B cell a white blood cell that makes antibodies

antibody a protein made by B cells that binds to a specific antigen

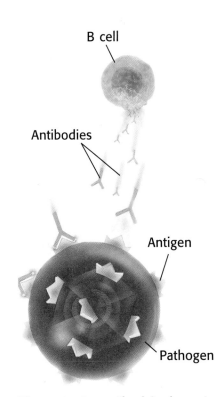

Figure 2 *An antibody's shape is very specialized. It matches an antigen like a key fits a lock.*

Only Skin Deep

1. Cut an **apple** in half.
2. Place **plastic wrap** over each half. The plastic wrap will act as skin.
3. Use **scissors** to cut the plastic wrap on one of the apple halves, and then use an **eyedropper** to drip **food coloring** on each apple half. The food coloring represents pathogens coming into contact with your body.
4. What happened to each apple half?
5. How is the plastic wrap similar to skin?
6. How is the plastic wrap different from skin?

Responding to a Virus

If virus particles enter your body, some of the particles may pass into body cells and begin to replicate. Other virus particles will be engulfed and broken up by macrophages. This is just the beginning of the immune response. The process your immune system uses to fight an invading virus is summarized in the figure below.

✔ **Reading Check** What are two things that can happen to virus particles when they enter the body?

Viral antigen

Viral antigen

Macrophage

Virus

1 Two Paths When virus particles invade the body, some of the particles are engulfed by macrophages. Other virus particles infect body cells. Macrophages that have engulfed virus particles, infected body cells, and virus particles all display viral antigens.

Body cell

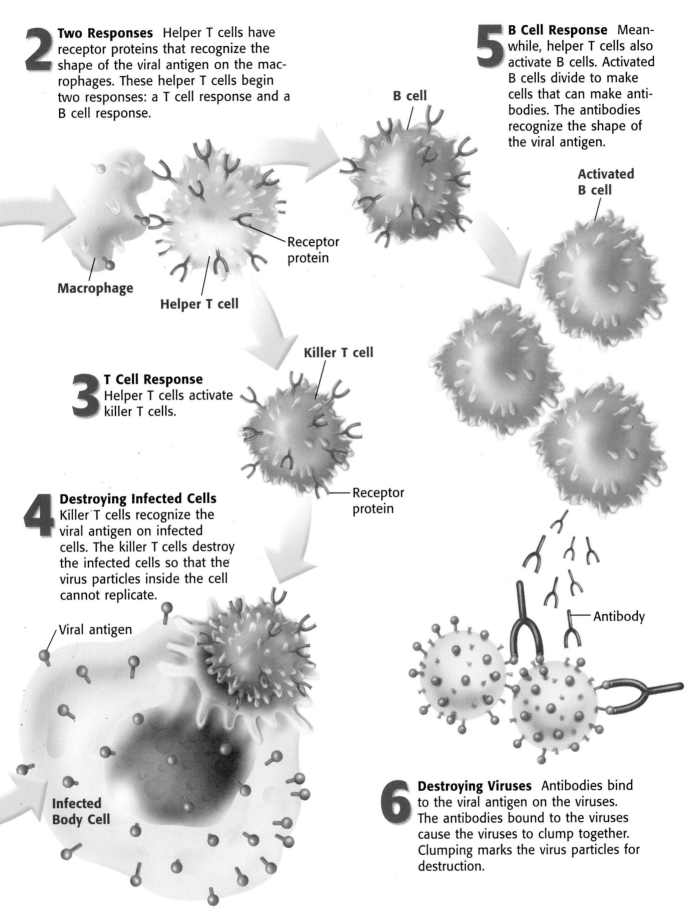

2 Two Responses Helper T cells have receptor proteins that recognize the shape of the viral antigen on the macrophages. These helper T cells begin two responses: a T cell response and a B cell response.

Macrophage

Helper T cell

Receptor protein

B cell

5 B Cell Response Meanwhile, helper T cells also activate B cells. Activated B cells divide to make cells that can make antibodies. The antibodies recognize the shape of the viral antigen.

Activated B cell

Killer T cell

3 T Cell Response Helper T cells activate killer T cells.

Receptor protein

4 Destroying Infected Cells Killer T cells recognize the viral antigen on infected cells. The killer T cells destroy the infected cells so that the virus particles inside the cell cannot replicate.

Viral antigen

Infected Body Cell

Antibody

6 Destroying Viruses Antibodies bind to the viral antigen on the viruses. The antibodies bound to the viruses cause the viruses to clump together. Clumping marks the virus particles for destruction.

Figure 3 *You may not feel well when you have a fever. But a fever is one way that your body fights infections.*

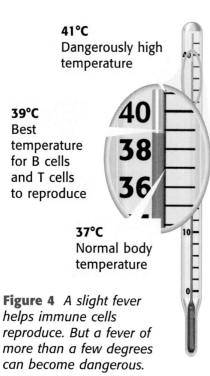

41°C
Dangerously high temperature

39°C
Best temperature for B cells and T cells to reproduce

37°C
Normal body temperature

Figure 4 *A slight fever helps immune cells reproduce. But a fever of more than a few degrees can become dangerous.*

memory B cell a B cell that responds to an antigen more strongly when the body is reinfected with an antigen than it does during its first encounter with the antigen

Fevers

The man in **Figure 3** is sick and has a fever. What is a fever? When macrophages activate the helper T cells, they send a chemical signal that tells your brain to turn up the thermostat. In a few minutes, your body's temperature can rise several degrees. A moderate fever of one or two degrees actually helps you get well faster because it slows the growth of some pathogens. As shown in **Figure 4,** a fever also helps B cells and T cells multiply faster.

Memory Cells

Your immune system can respond to a second encounter faster than it can respond the first time. B cells must have had previous contact with a pathogen before they can make the correct antibodies. During the first encounter with a new pathogen, specialized B cells make antibodies that are effective against that particular invader. This process takes about 2 weeks, which is far too long to prevent an infection. Therefore, the first time you are infected, you usually get sick.

A few of the B cells become memory B cells. **Memory B cells** are cells in your immune system that "remember" how to make an antibody for a particular pathogen. If the pathogen shows up again, the memory B cells produce B cells that make enough antibodies in just 3 or 4 days to protect you.

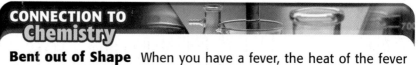

CONNECTION TO Chemistry

Bent out of Shape When you have a fever, the heat of the fever changes the shape of viral or bacterial proteins, slowing or preventing the reproduction of the pathogen. With an adult present, observe how an egg white changes as it cooks. What do you think happens to the protein in the egg white as it cooks?

ACTIVITY

Challenges to the Immune System

The immune system is a very effective body-defense system, but it is not perfect. The immune system is unable to deal with some diseases. There are also conditions in which the immune system does not work properly.

Allergies

Sometimes, the immune system overreacts to antigens that are not dangerous to the body. This inappropriate reaction is called an **allergy.** Allergies may be caused by many things, including certain foods and medicines. Many people have allergic reactions to pollen, shown in **Figure 5.** Symptoms of allergic reactions range from a runny nose and itchy eyes to more serious conditions, such as asthma.

Doctors are not sure why the immune system overreacts in some people. Scientists think allergies might be useful because the mucus draining from your nose carries away pollen, dust, and microorganisms.

Autoimmune Diseases

A disease in which the immune system attacks the body's own cells is called an **autoimmune disease.** In an autoimmune disease, immune-system cells mistake body cells for pathogens. One autoimmune disease is rheumatoid arthritis (ROO muh TOYD ahr THRIET IS), in which the immune system attacks the joints. A common location for rheumatoid arthritis is the joints of the hands, as shown in **Figure 6.** Other autoimmune diseases include type 1 diabetes, multiple sclerosis, and lupus.

✔ Reading Check Name four autoimmune diseases.

allergy a reaction to a harmless or common substance by the body's immune system

autoimmune disease a disease in which the immune system attacks the organism's own cells

Figure 5 *Pollen is one substance that can cause allergic reactions.*

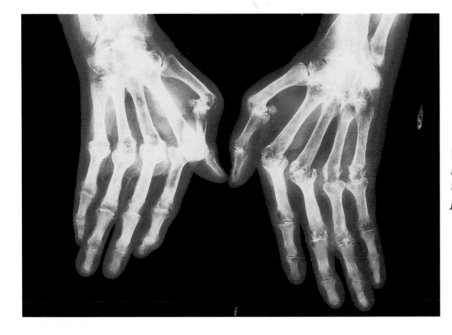

Figure 6 *In rheumatoid arthritis, immune-system cells cause joint-tissue swelling, which can lead to joint deformities.*

Figure 7 Immune Cells Fighting Cancer

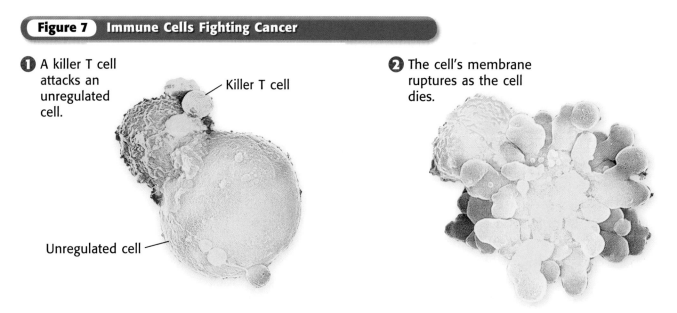

1 A killer T cell attacks an unregulated cell.

Killer T cell

Unregulated cell

2 The cell's membrane ruptures as the cell dies.

Cancer

Healthy cells divide at a carefully regulated rate. Occasionally, a cell doesn't respond to the body's regulation and begins dividing at an uncontrolled rate. As can be seen in **Figure 7,** killer T cells destroy this type of cell. Sometimes, the immune system cannot control the division of these cells. **Cancer** is the condition in which cells divide at an uncontrolled rate.

Many cancers will invade nearby tissues. They can also enter the cardiovascular system or lymphatic system. Cancers can then be transported to other places in the body. Cancers disrupt the normal activities of the organs they have invaded, sometimes leading to death. Today, though, there are many treatments for cancer. Surgery, radiation, and certain drugs can be used to remove or kill cancer cells or slow their division.

cancer a disease in which the cells begin dividing at an uncontrolled rate and become invasive

AIDS

The human immunodeficiency virus (HIV) causes acquired immune deficiency syndrome (AIDS). Most viruses infect cells in the nose, mouth, lungs, or intestines, but HIV is different. HIV infects the immune system itself, using helper T cells as factories to produce more viruses. You can see HIV particles in **Figure 8.** The helper T cells are destroyed in the process. Remember that the helper T cells put the B cells and killer T cells to work.

People with AIDS have very few helper T cells, so nothing activates the B cells and killer T cells. Therefore, the immune system cannot attack HIV or any other pathogen. People with AIDS don't usually die of AIDS itself. They die of other diseases that they are unable to fight off.

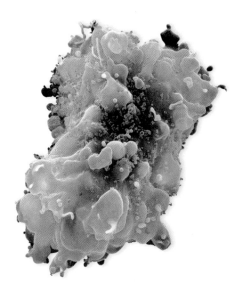

Figure 8 *The blue particles on this helper T cell are human immunodeficiency viruses. They replicated inside the T cell.*

✔ **Reading Check** What virus causes AIDS?

Summary

- Macrophages engulf pathogens, display antigens on their surface, and activate helper T cells. The helper T cells put the killer T cells and B cells to work.
- Killer T cells kill infected cells. B cells make antibodies.
- Fever helps speed immune-cell growth and slow pathogen growth.
- Memory B cells remember how to make an antibody for a pathogen that the body has previously fought.

- An allergy is the overreaction of the immune system to a harmless antigen.
- Autoimmune diseases are responses in which the immune system attacks healthy tissue.
- Cancer cells are cells that undergo uncontrolled division.
- AIDS is a disease that results when the human immunodeficiency virus kills helper T cells.

Using Key Terms

For each pair of terms, explain how the meanings of the terms differ.

1. *B cell* and *T cell*

2. *autoimmune disease* and *allergy*

Understanding Key Ideas

3. Your body's first line of defense against pathogens includes
   - a. skin.
   - b. macrophages.
   - c. T cells.
   - d. B cells.

4. List three ways your body defends itself against pathogens.

5. Name three different cells in the immune system, and describe how they respond to pathogens.

6. Describe four challenges to the immune system.

7. What characterizes a cancer cell?

Critical Thinking

8. **Identifying Relationships** Can your body make antibodies for pathogens that you have never been in contact with? Why or why not?

9. **Applying Concepts** If you had chickenpox at age 7, what might prevent you from getting chickenpox again at age 8?

Interpreting Graphics

10. Look at the graph below. Over time, people with AIDS become very sick and are unable to fight off infection. Use the information in the graph below to explain why this occurs.

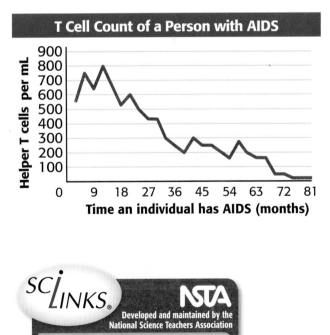

T Cell Count of a Person with AIDS

Helper T cells per mL (y-axis: 100–900)

Time an individual has AIDS (months) (x-axis: 0, 9, 18, 27, 36, 45, 54, 63, 72, 81)

SCiLINKS

NSTA
Developed and maintained by the
National Science Teachers Association

For a variety of links related to this chapter, go to www.scilinks.org

Topic: Body Defenses; Allergies
SciLinks code: HSM0181; HSM0048

Skills Practice Lab

OBJECTIVES

Investigate how diseases spread.

Analyze data about how diseases spread.

MATERIALS

- beaker or a cup, 200 mL
- eyedropper
- gloves, protective
- solution, unknown, 50 mL

SAFETY

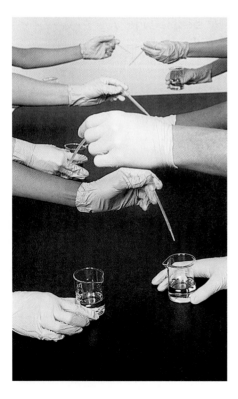

Passing the Cold

There are more than 100 viruses that cause the symptoms of the common cold. Any of the viruses can be passed from person to person—through the air or through direct contact. In this activity, you will track the progress of an outbreak in your class.

Ask a Question

1 With other members of your group, form a question about the spread of disease. For example "How are cold viruses passed from person to person?" or "How can the progress of an outbreak be modeled?"

Form a Hypothesis

2 Form a hypothesis based on the question you asked.

Test the Hypothesis

3 Obtain an empty cup or beaker, an eyedropper, and 50 mL of one of the solutions from your teacher. Only one student will have the "cold virus" solution. You will see a change in your solution when you have become "infected."

4 Your teacher will divide the class into two equal groups. If there is an extra student, that person will record data on the board. Otherwise, the teacher will act as the recorder.

5 The two groups should form straight lines, facing each other.

6 Each time your teacher says the word *mix,* fill your eyedropper with your solution, and place 10 drops of your solution in the beaker of the person in the line opposite you without touching your eyedropper to the other liquid.

7 Gently stir the liquid in your cup with your eyedropper. Do not put your eyedropper in anyone else's solution.

8 If your solution changes color, raise your hand so that the recorder can record the number of students who have been "infected."

9 Your teacher will instruct one line to move one person to the right. Then, the person at the end of the line without a partner should go to the other end of the line.

Results of Experiment			
Trial	Number of infected people	Total number of people	Percentage of infected people
1			
2			
3			
4			
5			
6			
7			
8			
9			
10			

DO NOT WRITE IN BOOK

10 Repeat steps 5–9 nine more times for a total of 10 trials.

11 Return to your desk, and create a data table in your notebook similar to the table above. The column with the title "Total number of people" will remain the same in every row. Enter the data from the board into your data table.

12 Find the percentage of infected people for the last column by dividing the number of infected people by the total number of people and multiplying by 100 in each line.

Analyze the Results

1 **Describing Events** Did you become infected? If so, during which trial did you become infected?

2 **Examining Data** Did everyone eventually become infected? If so, how many trials were necessary to infect everyone?

Draw Conclusions

3 **Interpreting Information** Explain at least one reason why this simulation may underestimate the number of people who might have been infected in real life.

4 **Applying Conclusions** Use your results to make a line graph showing the change in the infection percentage per trial.

Applying Your Data

Do research in the library or on the Internet to find out some of the factors that contribute to the spread of a cold virus. What is the best and easiest way to reduce your chances of catching a cold? Explain your answer.

Chapter Review

USING KEY TERMS

Complete each of the following sentences by choosing the correct term from the word bank.

antibody	cancer
infectious disease	B cell
noninfectious disease	T cell
pathogen	allergy

1 A(n) _____ is caused by a pathogen.

2 Antibiotics can be used to kill a(n) _____.

3 Macrophages attract helper _____.

4 A(n) _____ binds to an antigen.

5 An immune-system overreaction to a harmless substance is a(n) _____.

6 _____ is the unregulated growth of cells.

UNDERSTANDING KEY IDEAS

Multiple Choice

7 Pathogens are
   a. all viruses and microorganisms.
   b. viruses and microorganisms that cause disease.
   c. noninfectious organisms.
   d. all bacteria that live in water.

8 Which of the following is an infectious disease?
   a. allergies
   b. rheumatoid arthritis
   c. asthma
   d. a common cold

9 The skin keeps pathogens out by
   a. staying warm enough to kill pathogens.
   b. releasing killer T cells onto the surface.
   c. shedding dead cells and secreting oils.
   d. All of the above

10 Memory B cells
   a. kill pathogens.
   b. activate killer T cells.
   c. activate killer B cells.
   d. produce B cells that make antibodies.

11 A fever
   a. slows pathogen growth.
   b. helps B cells multiply faster.
   c. helps T cells multiply faster.
   d. All of the above

12 Macrophages
   a. make antibodies.
   b. release helper T cells.
   c. live in the gut.
   d. engulf pathogens.

Short Answer

13 Explain how macrophages start an immune response.

14 Describe the role of helper T cells in responding to an infection.

15 Name two ways that you come into contact with pathogens.

16 Concept Mapping Use the following terms to create a concept map: *macrophages, helper T cells, B cells, antibodies, antigens, killer T cells,* and *memory B cells.*

17 Identifying Relationships Why does the disappearance of helper T cells in AIDS patients damage the immune system?

18 Predicting Consequences Many people take fever-reducing drugs as soon as their temperature exceeds 37°C. Why might it not be a good idea to reduce a fever immediately with drugs?

19 Evaluating Data The risk of dying from a whooping cough vaccine is about one in 1 million. In contrast, the risk of dying from whooping cough is about one in 500. Discuss the pros and cons of this vaccination.

INTERPRETING GRAPHICS

The graph below compares the concentration of antibodies in the blood the first time you are exposed to a pathogen with the concentration of antibodies the next time you are exposed to the pathogen. Use the graph below to answer the questions that follow.

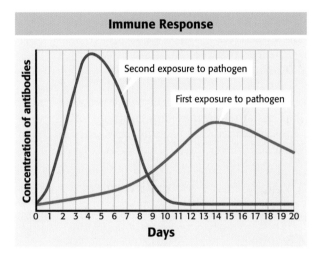

Immune Response

Concentration of antibodies

Second exposure to pathogen

First exposure to pathogen

0 1 2 3 4 5 6 7 8 9 10 11 12 13 14 15 16 17 18 19 20

Days

20 Are there more antibodies present during the first week of the first exposure or the first week of the second exposure? Why do you think this is so?

21 What is the difference in recovery time between the first exposure and second exposure? Why?

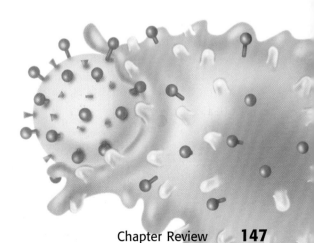

Standardized Test Preparation

Read each of the passages below. Then, answer the questions that follow each passage.

Passage 1 Bacteria are becoming resistant to many human-made antibiotics, which means that the drugs no longer affect the bacteria. Scientists now face the challenge of developing new antibiotics that can overcome the resistant strains of bacteria.

Antibiotics from animals are different from some human-made antibiotics. These antibiotics bore holes through the membranes that surround bacterial cells, causing the cells to disintegrate and die. Bacterial membranes don't <u>mutate</u> often, so they are less likely to become resistant to the animal antibiotics.

1. In this passage, what does *mutate* mean?

A to change

B to grow

C to form

D to degrade

2. Based on the passage, which of the following statements is a fact?

F Bacterial membranes are on the inside of the bacterial cell.

G Bacterial membranes are on the outside of the bacterial cell.

H All strains of bacteria mutate.

I Bacterial membranes never change.

3. Based on the passage, which of the following sentences is false?

A Antibiotics from animals are different from human-made antibiotics.

B Antibiotics from animals bore holes in bacterial membranes.

C Bacterial membranes don't change very often.

D Bacteria rarely develop resistance to human-made antibiotics.

Passage 2 Drinking water in the United States is generally safe, but water lines can break, or treatment plants can become flooded, allowing microorganisms to enter the public water supply. Bacteria growing in foods and beverages can cause illness, too. Refrigerating foods can slow the growth of many of these <u>pathogens</u>, but meat, fish, and eggs that are not cooked enough can still contain dangerous bacteria or parasites. Leaving food out at room temperature can give bacteria such as *salmonella* time to grow and produce toxins in the food. For these reasons, it is important to wash all used cooking tools.

1. Which of the following statements can you infer from this passage?

A Treatment plants help keep drinking water safe.

B Treatment plants never become flooded.

C Eliminating treatment plants would help keep water safe.

D New treatment plants are better than old ones.

2. Which of the following statements can you infer from the passage?

F Bacteria that live in food produce more toxins than molds produce.

G Cooking food thoroughly kills bacteria living in the food.

H Some bacteria are helpful to humans.

I Illnesses caused by bacteria living in food are seldom serious.

3. According to this passage, what do pathogens cause?

A disease

B flooding

C water-line breaks

D water supplies

The graph below shows the reported number of people living with HIV/AIDS. Use the graph to answer the questions that follow.

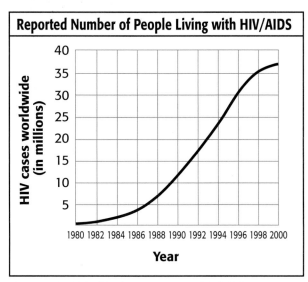

Reported Number of People Living with HIV/AIDS

HIV cases worldwide (in millions)

Year

Source: Joint United Nations Program on HIV/AIDS

1. When did the number of people living with HIV/AIDS reach 5 million?

  A 1985

  B 1986

  C 1987

  D 1988

2. When did the number of people living with HIV/AIDS reach 30 million?

  F 1996

  G 1997

  H 1998

  I 1999

3. When was the rate of increase of people with HIV/AIDS the **greatest**?

  A from 1980 to 1982

  B from 1984 to 1986

  C from 1988 to 1990

  D from 1998 to 2000

4. What percentage of the people who are infected with HIV do not yet have AIDS?

  F 10%

  G 24%

  H 75%

  I There is not enough information to determine the answer.

5. If the virus continued to spread as the graph indicates, in the year 2002, about how many people would be infected with HIV?

  A 30 million

  B 35 million

  C 39 million

  D 60 million

6. Which part of the graph indicates the rate of infection?

  F x-axis

  G y-axis

  H slope of the line being graphed

  I number of years in the sample

MATH

Read each question below, and choose the best answer.

1. Suppose you have 50,000 flu viruses on your fingers and you rub your eyes. Only 20,000 viruses enter your eyes, 10,000 dissolve in chemicals, and 10,000 are washed down into your nose. Of those, you sneeze out 2,000. How many viruses are left to wash down the back of your throat and possibly start an infection?

  A 50,000

  B 10,000

  C 8,000

  D 5,000

2. In which of the following lists are the numbers in order from smallest to greatest?

  F 0.027, 0.072, 0.270, 0.720

  G 0.270, 0.072, 0.720, 0.270

  H 0.072, 0.027, 0.270, 0.720

  I 0.720, 0.270, 0.072, 0.027

Science in Action

Weird Science

Frogs in the Medicine Cabinet?

Frog skin, mouse intestines, cow lungs, and shark stomachs are all being tested to make more effective medicines to combat harmful bacteria. In 1896, a biologist named Michael Zasloff was studying African clawed frogs. He noticed that cuts in the frogs' skin healed quickly and never became infected. Zasloff decided to investigate further. He found that when a frog was cut, its skin released a liquid antibiotic that killed invading bacteria. Furthermore, sand sharks, moths, pigs, mice, and cows also contain chemicals that kill bacteria and other microorganisms. These useful antibiotics are even found in the small intestines of humans!

Social Studies

Many medicines were discovered in plants or animals by people living near those plants or animals. Research the origin of one or two common medicines discovered this way. Make a poster showing a world map and the location of the medicines that you researched.

Scientific Discoveries

Medicine for Peanut Allergies

Scientists estimate that 1.5 million people in the United States suffer from peanut allergies. Every year 50 to 100 people in the United States die from an allergic reaction to peanuts. Peanuts and peanut oil are used to make many foods. People who have a peanut allergy sometimes mistakenly eat these foods and suffer severe reactions. A new drug has been discovered to help people control severe reactions. The drug is called TNX-901. The drug is actually an antibody that binds to the antibodies that the body makes during the allergic reaction to the peanuts. By binding these antibodies, the drug controls the allergic response.

Math ACTIVITY

During the testing of the new drug, 84 people were given four injections over the course of 4 months. One-fourth of the people participating received injections of a control that had no medicine in it. The rest of the people participating received different doses of the drug. How many people received the control? How many people received medicine? How many shots containing medicine were administered during the 4-month test?

Terrel Shepherd III

Nurse Terrel Shepherd III is a registered nurse (RN) at Texas Children's Hospital in Houston, Texas. RNs have many responsibilities. These responsibilities include giving patients their medications, assessing patients' health, and establishing intravenous access. Nurses also serve as a go-between for the patient and the doctor. Although most nurses work in hospitals or clinics, some nurses work for corporations. Pediatric nurses such as Shepherd work specifically with infants, children, and adolescents. The field of nursing offers a wide variety of job opportunities including home-care nurses, traveling nurses, and flight nurses. The hospital alone has many areas of expertise for nurses, including geriatrics (working with the elderly), intensive care, administration, and surgery. Traditionally, nursing has been considered to be a woman's career. However, since nursing began as a profession, men and women have practiced nursing. A career in nursing is possible for anyone who does well in science, enjoys people, and wants to make a difference in people's lives.

Language Arts ACTiViTY

WRITING SKILL Create a brochure that persuades people to consider a career in nursing. Describe nursing as a career, the benefits of becoming a nurse, and the education needed to be a nurse. Illustrate the brochure with pictures of nurses from the Internet or from magazines.

go.hrw.com

To learn more about these Science in Action topics, visit **go.hrw.com** and type in the keyword **HL5BD6F.**

Current Science

Check out Current Science® articles related to this chapter by visiting go.hrw.com. Just type in the keyword HL5CS27.

7

Staying Healthy

About the

What do you see in this photo? Sure, you can see five students facing the camera, but what else does the picture tell you? The bright eyes, happy smiles, and shiny hair show radiant health. Having a clear mind and a long, active life depend on having a healthy body. Keeping your body healthy depends on eating well; avoiding drugs, cigarettes, and alcohol; and staying safe.

PRE-READING ACTIVITY

FOLDNOTES **Booklet** Before you read the chapter, create the FoldNote entitled "Booklet" described in the **Study Skills** section of the Appendix. Label each page of the booklet with a main idea from the chapter. As you read the chapter, write what you learn about each main idea on the appropriate page of the booklet.

STARTUP ACTIVITY

Conduct a Survey

How healthy are the habits of your classmates? Find out for yourself.

Procedure

1. Copy and answer yes or no to each of the five questions at right. Do not put your name on the survey.

Analysis

1. As a class, record the data from the completed surveys in a chart. For each question, calculate the percentage of your class that answered yes.

2. What good and bad habits do your classmates have?

1. Do you exercise at least three times a week?

2. Do you wear a seat belt every time you ride in a car?

3. Do you eat five or more servings of fruits and vegetables every day?

4. Do you use sunscreen to protect your skin when you are outdoors?

5. Do you eat a lot of high-fat foods?

Good Nutrition

Does the saying "You are what you eat" mean that you are pizza? No, but substances in pizza help build your body.

Protein in the cheese may become part of your hair. Carbohydrates in the crust can give you energy for your next race.

Nutrients

Are you more likely to have potato chips or broccoli for a snack? If you eat many foods that are high in fat, such as potato chips, your food choices probably are not as healthy as they could be. Broccoli is a healthier food than potato chips. But eating only broccoli, as the person in **Figure 1** is doing, does not give you a balanced diet.

To stay healthy, you need to take in **nutrients,** or substances that provide the materials needed for life processes. Nutrients are grouped into six classes: *carbohydrates, proteins, fats, water, vitamins,* and *minerals.* Carbohydrates, proteins, and fats provide energy for the body in units called *Calories* (Cal).

Carbohydrates

Carbohydrates are your body's main source of energy. A **carbohydrate** is a chemical composed of simple sugars. There are two types of carbohydrates: simple and complex. *Simple carbohydrates* are sugars. They are easily digested and give you quick energy. *Complex carbohydrates* are made up of many sugar molecules linked together. They are digested slowly and give you long-lasting energy. Some complex carbohydrates are good sources of fiber. Fiber is a part of a healthy diet and is found in whole-grain foods, such as brown rice and whole-wheat bread. Many fruits and vegetables also contain fiber.

nutrient a substance in food that provides energy or helps form body tissues and that is necessary for life and growth

carbohydrate a class of energy-giving nutrients that includes sugars, starches, and fiber

Figure 1 *Eating only one food, even a healthy food, will not give you all the substances your body needs.*

Protein

Proteins are found in body fluids, muscle, bone, and skin. **Proteins** are nutrients used to build and repair your body. Your body makes the proteins it needs, but it must have the necessary building blocks, called *amino acids*. Your digestive system breaks down protein into individual amino acids that are then used to make new proteins. Some foods, such as poultry, fish, milk, and eggs, provide all of the amino acids your body needs. Foods that contain all of these essential amino acids are called *complete proteins. Incomplete proteins* contain only some of the essential amino acids. Most plant foods contain incomplete protein, but eating a variety of plant foods will provide all of the amino acids your body needs.

✓ **Reading Check** What is an incomplete protein? (*See the Appendix for answers to Reading Checks.*)

Figure 2 *This sample meal provides many of the nutrients a growing teenager needs.*

Fats

Another class of nutrients that is important to a healthy meal, such as the meal shown in **Figure 2,** is fat. **Fats** are energy-storage nutrients. Fats are needed to store and transport vitamins, produce hormones, keep skin healthy, and provide insulation. Fats also provide more energy than either proteins or carbohydrates. There are two types of fats: saturated and unsaturated. *Saturated fats* are found in meat, dairy products, coconut oil, and palm oil. Saturated fats raise blood cholesterol levels. Although *cholesterol* is a fat-like substance found naturally in the body, high levels can increase the risk of heart disease. *Unsaturated fats* and foods high in fiber may help reduce blood cholesterol levels. Your body cannot make unsaturated fats. They must come from vegetable oils and fish in your diet. The body needs both kinds of fats.

protein a molecule that is made up of amino acids and that is needed to build and repair body structures and to regulate processes in the body

fat an energy-storage nutrient that helps the body store some vitamins

Water

You cannot survive for more than a few days without water. Your body is about 70% water. Water is in every cell of your body. The main functions of water are to transport substances, regulate body temperature, and provide lubrication. Some scientists think you should drink at least eight glasses of water a day. When you exercise you need more water, as shown in **Figure 3.** You also get water from other liquids you drink and the foods you eat. Fresh fruits and vegetables, juices, soups, and milk are good sources of water.

Figure 3 *When you exercise, you need to drink more water.*

Table 1 Some Essential Vitamins

Vitamin	What it does	Where you get it
A	keeps skin and eyes healthy; builds strong bones and teeth	yellow and orange fruits and vegetables, leafy greens, meats, and milk
B (various forms)	helps body use carbohydrates; helps blood, nerves, and heart function	meats, whole grains, beans, peas, nuts, and seafood
C	strengthens tissues; helps the body absorb iron, fight disease	citrus fruits, leafy greens, broccoli, peppers, and cabbage
D	builds strong bones and teeth; helps the body use calcium and phosphorus	sunlight, enriched milk, eggs, and fish
E	protects red blood cells from destruction; keeps skin healthy	oils, fats, eggs, whole grains, wheat germ, liver, and leafy greens
K	assists with blood clotting	leafy greens, tomatoes, and potatoes

Minerals

If you eat a balanced diet, you should get all of the vitamins and minerals you need. **Minerals** are elements that are essential for good health. You need six minerals in large amounts: calcium, chloride, magnesium, phosphorus, potassium, and sodium. There are at least 12 minerals that are required in very small amounts. These include fluorine, iodine, iron, and zinc. Calcium is necessary for strong bones and teeth. Magnesium and sodium help the body use proteins. Potassium is needed to regulate your heartbeat and produce muscle movement, and iron is necessary for red blood cell production.

mineral a class of nutrients that are chemical elements that are needed for certain body processes

vitamin a class of nutrients that contain carbon and that are needed in small amounts to maintain health and allow growth

Vitamins

Vitamins are another class of nutrients. **Vitamins** are compounds that control many body functions. Only vitamin D can be made by the body, so you have to get most vitamins from food. **Table 1** provides information about six essential vitamins.

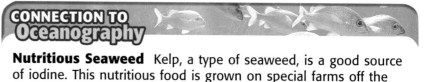

CONNECTION TO Oceanography

Nutritious Seaweed Kelp, a type of seaweed, is a good source of iodine. This nutritious food is grown on special farms off the coasts of China and Japan. What other nutritious foods come from the sea?

Eating for Good Health

Now you have learned which nutrients you need for good health. But how can you be sure to get all the important nutrients in the right amounts? To begin, keep in mind that most teenage girls need about 2,200 Cal per day, and most boys need about 2,800 Cal. Because different foods contain different nutrients, *where* you get your Calories is as important as *how many* you get. The Food Guide Pyramid, shown in **Figure 4,** can help you make good food choices.

Reading Check Using the Food Guide Pyramid below, design a healthy lunch that includes one food from each food group.

Brown Bag Test

1. Cut a **brown paper bag** into squares.
2. Gather a variety of **foods.** Place a piece of each food on a different square and leave overnight.
3. What do you see when you remove the food?
4. Which food had the most oil? Which food had the least?

Figure 4 **The Food Guide Pyramid**

The U.S. Department of Agriculture and the Department of Health and Human Services developed the Food Guide Pyramid to help Americans make healthy food choices. The Food Guide Pyramid divides foods into six groups. It shows how many servings you need daily from each group and gives examples of foods for each. This pyramid also provides sample serving sizes for each group. Within each group, the food choices are up to you.

Fats, oils, and sweets
Use sparingly.

Milk, yogurt, and cheese
2 to 3 servings
- 1 cup of milk or yogurt
- 1 1/2 oz of natural cheese
- 2 oz of processed cheese

Meat, poultry, fish, beans, eggs, and nuts 2 to 3 servings
- 2 to 3 oz of cooked poultry, fish, or lean meat
- 1/2 cup of cooked dried beans
- 1 egg

Vegetables 3 to 5 servings
- 1/2 cup of chopped vegetables
- 1 cup of raw, leafy vegetables
- 3/4 cup of cooked vegetables

Fruits 2 to 4 servings
- 1 medium apple, banana, or orange
- 1/2 cup of chopped, cooked, or canned fruit
- 3/4 cup of fruit juice

Bread, cereal, rice, and pasta 6 to 11 servings
- 1 slice of bread
- 1 oz of ready-to-eat cereal
- 1/2 cup of rice or pasta
- 1/2 cup of cooked cereal

Nutrition Facts

Serving Size 1/2 cup (120 ml) — **Serving information**
Servings per Container 2.5

Amount per Serving	Prepared
Calories	70 — **Number of Calories per serving**
Calories from Fat	25

	% Daily Value
Total Fat 2.5 g	4%
Saturated Fat 1 g	5%
Cholesterol 15 mg	5%
Sodium 960 mg	40%
Total Carbohydrate 8 g	3%
Dietary Fiber less than 1 g	4%
Sugars 1 g	
Protein 3 g	
Vitamin A	15%
Vitamin C — **Percentage of daily values**	0%
Calcium	0%
Iron	4%

*Percent Daily Values are based on a 2,000 Calorie diet. Your daily values may be higher or lower depending on your Calorie needs:

		Calories	2,000	2,500
Total Fat	Less than		65g	80g
Sat Fat	Less than		20g	25g
Cholesterol	Less than		300mg	300mg
Sodium	Less than		2,400mg	2,400mg
Total Carbohydrate			300g	375g
Dietary Fiber			25g	30g
Protein			50g	60g

Figure 5 *Nutrition Facts labels provide a lot of information.*

malnutrition a disorder of nutrition that results when a person does not consume enough of each of the nutrients that are needed by the human body

What Percentage?

Use the Nutrition Facts label above to answer the following question. The recommended daily value of fat is 72 g for teenage girls and 90 g for teenage boys. What percentage of the daily recommended fat value is provided in one cup of soup?

Reading Food Labels

Packaged foods must have Nutrition Facts labels. **Figure 5** shows a Nutrition Facts label for chicken noodle soup. Nutrition Facts labels show what amount of each nutrient is in one serving of the food. You can tell whether a food is high or low in a nutrient by looking at its daily value. Reading food labels can help you make healthy eating choices. The percentage of daily values shown is based on a diet that consists of 2,000 Cal per day. Most teenagers need more than 2,000 Cal per day. The number of Calories needed depends on factors such as height, weight, age, and level of activity. Playing sports and exercising use up Calories that need to be replaced for you to grow.

✓ Reading Check For what nutrients does chicken noodle soup provide more than 10% of the daily value?

Nutritional Disorders

Unhealthy eating habits can cause nutritional disorders. **Malnutrition** occurs when someone does not eat enough of the nutrients needed by the body. Malnutrition can result from eating too few or too many Calories or not taking in enough of the right nutrients. Malnutrition affects how one looks and how quickly one's body can repair damage and fight illness.

Anorexia Nervosa and Bulimia Nervosa

Anorexia nervosa (AN uh REKS ee uh nuhr VOH suh) is an eating disorder characterized by self-starvation and an intense fear of gaining weight. Anorexia nervosa can lead to severe malnutrition.

Bulimia nervosa (boo LEE mee uh nuhr VOH suh) is a disorder characterized by binge eating followed by induced vomiting. Sometimes, people suffering from bulimia nervosa use laxatives or diuretics to rid their bodies of food and water. Bulimia nervosa can damage teeth and the digestive system and can lead to kidney and heart failure.

Both anorexia and bulimia can cause weak bones, low blood pressure, and heart problems. These eating disorders can be fatal if not treated. If you are worried that you or someone you know may have an eating disorder, talk to an adult.

Obesity

Eating too much food that is high in fat and low in other nutrients, such as junk food and fast food, can lead to malnutrition. *Obesity* (oh BEE suh tee) is having an extremely high percentage of body fat. People suffering from obesity may not be eating a variety of foods that provide them with the correct balance of essential nutrients. Having an inactive lifestyle can also contribute to obesity.

Obesity increases the risk of high blood pressure, heart disease, and diabetes. Eating a more balanced diet and exercising regularly can help reduce obesity. Obesity may also be caused by other factors. Scientists are studying the links between obesity and heredity.

SECTION Review

Summary

- A healthy diet has a balance of carbohydrates, proteins, fats, water, vitamins, and minerals.
- The Food Guide Pyramid is a good guide for healthy eating.
- Nutrition Facts labels provide information needed to plan a healthy diet.
- Anorexia nervosa and bulimia nervosa cause malnutrition and damage to many body systems.
- Obesity can lead to heart disease and diabetes.

Using Key Terms

1. In your own words, write a definition for each of the following terms: *nutrient, mineral,* and *vitamin.*

Understanding Key Ideas

2. Malnutrition can be caused by
   a. obesity.
   b. bulimia nervosa.
   c. anorexia nervosa.
   d. All of the above

3. What information is found on a Nutrition Facts label?

4. Give an example of a carbohydrate, a protein, and a fat.

5. If vitamins and minerals do not supply energy, why are they important to a healthy diet?

6. How do anorexia nervosa and bulimia nervosa differ?

7. How can someone who is obese suffer from malnutrition?

Math Skills

8. If you eat 2,500 Cal per day and 20% are from fat, 30% are from protein, and 50% are from carbohydrates, how many Calories of each nutrient do you eat?

Critical Thinking

9. **Applying Concepts** Name some of the nutrients that can be found in a glass of milk.

10. **Identifying Relationships** Explain how eating a variety of foods can help ensure good nutrition.

11. **Predicting Consequences** How would your growth be affected if your diet consistently lacked important nutrients?

12. **Applying Concepts** Explain how you can use the Nutrition Facts label to choose food that is high in calcium.

SCiLINKS.

NSTA
Developed and maintained by the
National Science Teachers Association

For a variety of links related to this chapter, go to www.scilinks.org

Topic: Food Pyramids; Nutritional Disorders
SciLinks code: HSM0598; HSM1057

Risks of Alcohol and Other Drugs

You see them in movies and on television and read about them in magazines. But what are drugs?

You are exposed to information, and misinformation, about drugs every day. So, how can you make the best decisions?

What Is a Drug?

Any chemical substance that causes a physical or psychological change is called a **drug.** Drugs come in many forms, as shown in **Figure 1.** Some drugs enter the body through the skin. Other drugs are swallowed, inhaled, or injected. Drugs are classified by their effects. *Analgesics* (AN'l JEE ziks) relieve pain. *Antibiotics* (AN tie bie AHT iks) fight bacterial infections, and *antihistamines* (AN tie HIS tuh MEENZ) control cold and allergy symptoms. *Stimulants* speed up the central nervous system, and *depressants* slow it down. When used correctly, legal drugs can help your body heal. When used illegally or improperly, however, drugs can do great harm.

Dependence and Addiction

The body can develop *tolerance* to a drug. Tolerance means that larger and larger doses of the drug are needed to get the same effect. The body can also form a *physical dependence* or need for a drug. If the body doesn't receive a drug that it is physically dependent on, withdrawal symptoms occur. Withdrawal symptoms include nausea, vomiting, pain, and tremors.

      Addiction is the loss of control of drug-taking behavior. Once addicted, a person finds it very hard to stop taking a drug. Sometimes, the need for a drug is not due only to physical dependence. Some people also form *psychological dependence* on a drug, which means that they feel powerful cravings for the drug.

Figure 1 *All of these products contain drugs.*

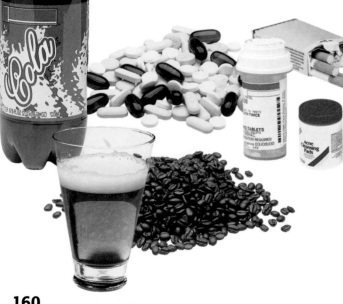

Types of Drugs

There are many kinds of drugs. Some drugs are made from plants, and some are made in a lab. You can buy some drugs at the grocery store, while others can be prescribed only by a doctor. Some drugs are illegal to buy, sell, or possess.

drug any substance that causes a change in a person's physical or psychological state

addiction a dependence on a substance, such as alcohol or another drug

Herbal Medicines

Information about herbal medicines has been handed down for centuries, and some herbs contain chemicals with important healing properties. The tea in **Figure 2** contains chamomile and is made from a plant. Chamomile has chemicals in it that can help you sleep. However, herbs are drugs and should be used carefully. The Federal Drug Administration does not regulate herbal medicines or teas and cannot guarantee their safety.

Figure 2 *Some herbs can be purchased in health-food stores. Medicinal herbs should always be used with care.*

Over-the-Counter and Prescription Drugs

Over-the-counter drugs can be bought without a prescription. A prescription is written by a doctor and describes the drug, directions for use, and the amount of the drug to be taken.

Many over-the-counter and prescription drugs are powerful healing agents. However, some drugs also produce unwanted side effects. *Side effects* are uncomfortable symptoms, such as nausea, headaches, drowsiness, or more serious problems.

Whether purchased with or without a prescription, all drugs must be used with care. Information on proper use can be found on the label. **Figure 3** shows some general drug safety tips.

✓ Reading Check What is the difference between an over-the-counter drug and a prescription drug? (*See the Appendix for answers to Reading Checks.*)

Figure 3 Drug Safety Tips

- *Never take another person's prescription medicine.*
- *Read the label before each use. Always follow the instructions on the label and those provided by your doctor or pharmacist.*
- *Do not take more or less medication than prescribed.*
- *Consult a doctor if you have any side effects.*
- *Throw away leftover and out-of-date medicines.*

Figure 4 Effects of Smoking

▼ Healthy lung tissue of a nonsmoker

▼ Damaged lung tissue of a smoker

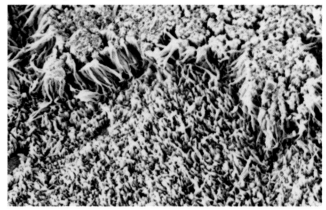

nicotine a toxic, addictive chemical that is found in tobacco and that is one of the major contributors to the harmful effects of smoking

alcoholism a disorder in which a person repeatedly drinks alcoholic beverages in an amount that interferes with the person's health and activities

Tobacco

Cigarettes are addictive, and smoking has serious health effects. **Nicotine** (NIK uh TEEN) is a chemical in tobacco that increases heart rate and blood pressure and is extremely addictive. Smokers experience a decrease in physical endurance. **Figure 4** shows the effects of smoking on the cilia of your lungs. Cilia clean the air you breathe and prevent debris from entering your lungs. Smoking increases the chances of lung cancer, and it has been linked to other cancers, emphysema, chronic bronchitis, and heart disease. Experts estimate that there are more than 430,000 deaths related to smoking each year in the United States. Secondhand smoke also poses significant health risks.

Like cigarettes, smokeless, or chewing, tobacco is addictive and can cause health problems. Nicotine is absorbed through the lining of the mouth. Smokeless tobacco increases the risk of several cancers, including mouth and throat cancer. It also causes gum disease and yellowing of the teeth.

Alcohol

It is illegal in most of the United States for people under the age of 21 to use alcohol. Alcohol slows down the central nervous system and can cause memory loss. Excessive use of alcohol can damage the liver, pancreas, brain, nerves, and cardiovascular system. In very large quantities, alcohol can cause death. Alcohol is a factor in more than half of all suicides, murders, and accidental deaths. **Figure 5** shows the results of one alcohol-related accident. Alcohol also affects decision making and can lead you to take unhealthy risks.

People can suffer from **alcoholism,** which means that they are physically and psychologically dependent on alcohol. Alcoholism is considered a disease, and genetic factors are thought to influence the development of alcoholism in some people.

Figure 5 *This car was in an accident involving a drunk driver.*

Figure 6 *Smoking marijuana can make your health and dreams go up in smoke.*

Marijuana

Marijuana is an illegal drug that comes from the Indian hemp plant. Marijuana affects different people in different ways. It may increase anxiety or cause feelings of paranoia. Marijuana slows reaction time, impairs thinking, and causes a loss of coordination. Regular use of marijuana can affect many areas of your life, as described in **Figure 6.**

narcotic a drug that is derived from opium and that relieves pain and induces sleep

Cocaine

Cocaine and its more purified form, crack, are made from the coca plant. Both drugs are illegal and highly addictive. Users can become addicted to them in a very short time. Cocaine can produce feelings of intense excitement followed by anxiety and depression. Both drugs increase heart rate and blood pressure and can cause heart attacks, even among first-time users.

✓ Reading Check What are two dangers to users of cocaine?

Narcotics and Designer Drugs

Drugs made from the opium plant are called **narcotics.** Some narcotics are used to treat severe pain. Narcotics are illegal unless prescribed by a doctor. Some narcotics are never legal. For example, heroin is one of the most addictive narcotics and is always illegal. Heroin is usually injected, and users often share needles. Therefore, heroin users have a high risk of becoming infected with diseases such as hepatitis and AIDS. Heroin users can also die of an overdose of the drug.

Other illegal drugs include inhalants, barbiturates (bahr BICH uhr itz), amphetamines (am FET uh MEENZ), and *designer drugs*. Designer drugs are made by making small changes to existing drugs. Ecstasy, or "X," is a designer drug that causes feelings of well-being. Over time, the drug causes lesions (LEE zhuhnz), or holes, in a user's brain, as shown in **Figure 7.** Ecstasy users are also more likely to develop depression.

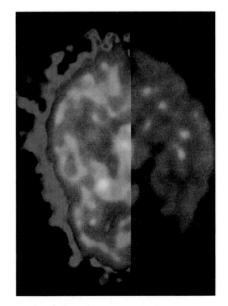

Figure 7 *The brain scan on the left shows a healthy brain. The scan on the right is from a teenager who has regularly used Ecstasy.*

Section 2 Risks of Alcohol and Other Drugs **163**

Figure 8 *Drug abuse can leave you depressed and feeling alone.*

Good Reasons

WRITING SKILL Discuss with your parent the possible effects of drug abuse on your family. Then, write yourself a letter giving reasons why you should stay drug-free. Put your letter in a safe place. If you ever find yourself thinking about using drugs, take out your letter and read it.

Hallucinogens

Hallucinogens (huh LOO si nuh juhnz) distort the senses and cause mood changes. Users have hallucinations, which means that they see and hear things that are not real. LSD and PCP are powerful, illegal hallucinogens. Sniffing glue or solvents can also cause hallucinations and serious brain damage.

Drug Abuse

A drug user takes a drug to prevent or improve a medical condition. The drug user obtains the drug legally and uses the drug properly. A drug abuser does not take a drug to relieve a medical condition. An abuser may take drugs for the temporary good feelings they produce, to escape from problems, or to belong to a group. The drug is often obtained illegally, and it is often taken without knowledge of the drug's dangers.

✓ **Reading Check** **What is the difference between drug use and drug abuse?**

How Drug Abuse Starts

Nicotine, alcohol, and marijuana are sometimes called *gateway drugs* because they are often the first drugs a person abuses. The abuse of other, more dangerous drugs may follow the abuse of gateway drugs. Peer pressure is often the reason that young people begin to use drugs. Teenagers may drink, smoke, or try marijuana to make friends or avoid being teased. Because drug abusers often stand out, it can sometimes be hard to see that many teenagers do not abuse drugs.

Many teenagers begin using illegal drugs to feel part of a group, but drug abuse has many serious consequences. Drug abuse can lead to problems with friends, family, school, and handling money. These problems often lead to depression and social isolation, as shown in **Figure 8.**

Many people who start using drugs do not recognize the dangers. Misinformation about drugs is everywhere. Several common drug myths are discussed in **Figure 9.**

Getting Off Drugs

People who abuse drugs undergo emotional and physical changes. Teenagers who had few problems often begin to have problems with school, family, and money when they start to use drugs.

The first step to quitting drugs is to admit to abusing drugs and to decide to stop. It is important for the addicted person to get the proper medical treatment. There are drug treatment centers, like the one shown in **Figure 10,** available to help. Getting off drugs can be extremely difficult. Withdrawal symptoms are often painful, and powerful cravings for a drug can continue long after a person quits. But people who stop abusing drugs lead happier and healthier lives.

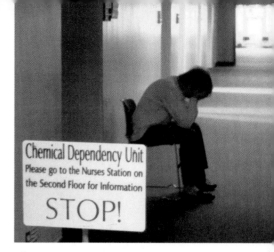

Figure 10 *Drug treatment centers help people get off drugs and back on track to healthier, happier lives.*

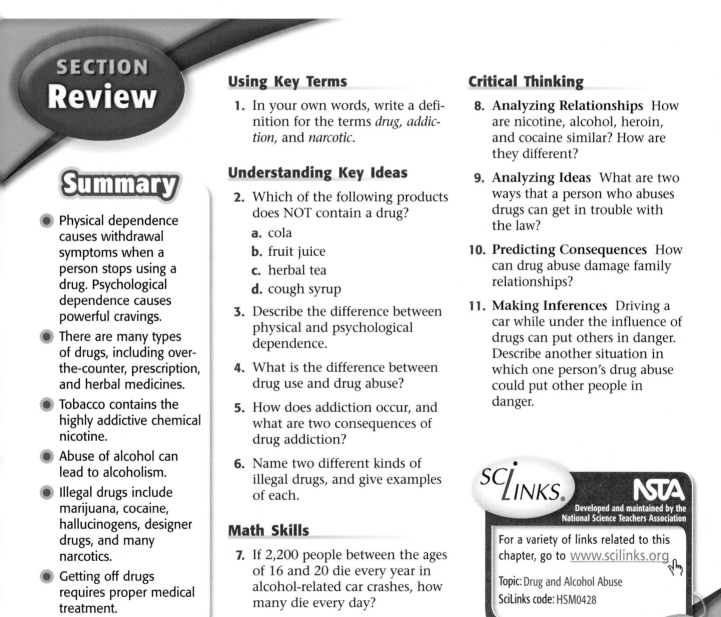

SECTION
Review

Summary

- Physical dependence causes withdrawal symptoms when a person stops using a drug. Psychological dependence causes powerful cravings.

- There are many types of drugs, including over-the-counter, prescription, and herbal medicines.

- Tobacco contains the highly addictive chemical nicotine.

- Abuse of alcohol can lead to alcoholism.

- Illegal drugs include marijuana, cocaine, hallucinogens, designer drugs, and many narcotics.

- Getting off drugs requires proper medical treatment.

Using Key Terms

1. In your own words, write a definition for the terms *drug, addiction,* and *narcotic.*

Understanding Key Ideas

2. Which of the following products does NOT contain a drug?
   a. cola
   b. fruit juice
   c. herbal tea
   d. cough syrup

3. Describe the difference between physical and psychological dependence.

4. What is the difference between drug use and drug abuse?

5. How does addiction occur, and what are two consequences of drug addiction?

6. Name two different kinds of illegal drugs, and give examples of each.

Math Skills

7. If 2,200 people between the ages of 16 and 20 die every year in alcohol-related car crashes, how many die every day?

Critical Thinking

8. **Analyzing Relationships** How are nicotine, alcohol, heroin, and cocaine similar? How are they different?

9. **Analyzing Ideas** What are two ways that a person who abuses drugs can get in trouble with the law?

10. **Predicting Consequences** How can drug abuse damage family relationships?

11. **Making Inferences** Driving a car while under the influence of drugs can put others in danger. Describe another situation in which one person's drug abuse could put other people in danger.

*SCI*LINKS.®

NSTA
Developed and maintained by the
National Science Teachers Association

For a variety of links related to this chapter, go to www.scilinks.org

Topic: Drug and Alcohol Abuse
SciLinks code: HSM0428

Healthy Habits

Do you like playing sports or acting in plays? How does your health affect your favorite activities?

Whatever you do, the better your health is, the better you can perform. Keeping yourself healthy is a daily responsibility.

Taking Care of Your Body

The science of preserving and protecting your health is known as **hygiene.** It sounds simple, but washing your hands is the best way to prevent the spread of disease and infection. You should always wash your hands after using the bathroom and before and after handling food. Taking care of your skin, hair, and teeth is important for good hygiene. Good hygiene includes regularly using sunscreen, shampooing your hair, and brushing and flossing your teeth daily.

Good Posture

Posture is also important to health. Good posture helps you look and feel your best. Bad posture strains your muscles and ligaments and makes breathing difficult. To have good posture, imagine a vertical line passing through your ear, shoulder, hip, knee, and ankle when you stand, as shown in **Figure 1.** When working at a desk, you should maintain good posture by pulling your chair forward and planting your feet firmly on the floor.

hygiene the science of health and ways to preserve health

Figure 1 *A slumped posture strains your lower back.*

When you have good posture, your ear, shoulder, hip, knee, and ankle are in a straight line.

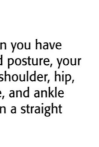

Bad posture strains your muscles and ligaments and can make breathing difficult.

Exercise

Aerobic exercise at least three times a week is essential to good health. **Aerobic exercise** is vigorous, constant exercise of the whole body for 20 minutes or more. Walking, running, swimming, and biking are all examples of aerobic exercise. **Figure 2** shows another popular aerobic exercise—basketball.

Aerobic exercise increases the heart rate. As a result, more oxygen is taken in and distributed throughout the body. Over time, aerobic exercise strengthens the heart, lungs, and bones. It burns Calories, helps your body conserve some nutrients, and aids digestion. It also gives you more energy and stamina. Aerobic exercise protects your physical and mental health.

Figure 2 *Aerobic exercise can be fun if you choose an activity you enjoy.*

Reading Check What are two benefits of regular exercise? (*See the Appendix for answers to Reading Checks.*)

Sleep

Believe it or not, teenagers actually need more sleep than younger children. Do you ever fall asleep in class, like the girl in **Figure 3,** or feel tired in the middle of the afternoon? If so, you may not be getting enough sleep. Scientists say that teenagers need about 9.5 hours of sleep each night.

At night, the body goes through several cycles of progressively deeper sleep, with periods of lighter sleep in between. If you do not sleep long enough, you will not enter the deepest, most restful period of sleep.

aerobic exercise physical exercise intended to increase the activity of the heart and lungs to promote the body's use of oxygen

Figure 3 *If you fall asleep easily during the day, you are probably not getting enough sleep.*

CONNECTION TO Language Arts

Dreamy Poetry

You are not wrong, who deem
That my days have been a dream;
Yet if hope has flown away
In a night, or in a day,
In a vision, or in none,
Is it therefore the less gone?
All that we see or seem
Is but a dream within a dream.

(Edgar Allan Poe,
"A Dream Within a Dream")

What do you think Poe means by "a dream within a dream?" Why do you think there are many poems written about dreams or sleep?

Coping with Stress

You have a big soccer game tomorrow. Are you excited and ready for action? You got a low grade on your English paper. Are you upset or angry? The game and the test are causing you stress. **Stress** is the physical and mental response to pressure.

Some stress is a normal part of life. Stress stimulates your body to prepare for difficult or dangerous situations. However, sometimes you may have no outlet for the stress, and it builds up. Many things are causing stress for the girl shown in **Figure 4.** Excess stress is harmful to your health and can decrease your ability to carry out your daily activities.

You may not even realize you are stressed until your body reacts. Perhaps you get a headache, have an upset stomach, or lie awake at night. You might feel tired all the time or begin an old nervous habit, such as nail-biting. You may become irritable or resentful. All of these things can be signs of too much stress.

Figure 4 *Can you identify all of the things in this picture that could cause stress?*

stress a physical or mental response to pressure

Dealing with Stress

Different people are stressed by different things. Once you identify the source of the stress, you can find ways to deal with it. If you cannot remove the cause of stress, here are some ideas for handling stress.

- Share your problems. Talk things over with someone you trust, such as a parent, friend, teacher, or school counselor.
- Make a list of all the things you would like to get done, and rank the things in order of importance. Do the most important things first.
- Exercise regularly, and get enough sleep.
- Pet a friendly animal.
- Spend some quiet time alone, or practice deep breathing or other relaxation techniques.

For another activity related to this chapter, go to **go.hrw.com** and type in the keyword **HL5BD7W.**

Injury Prevention

Have you ever fallen off your bike or sprained your ankle? Accidents happen, and they can cause injury and even death. It is impossible to prevent all accidents, but you can decrease your risk by using your common sense and following basic safety rules.

Safety Outdoors

Always dress appropriately for the weather and for the activity. Never hike or camp alone. Tell someone where you are going and when you expect to return. If you do not bring water from home, be sure to purify any water you drink in the wilderness.

Learn how to swim. It could save your life! Never swim alone, and do not dive into shallow water or water of unknown depth. When in a boat, wear a life jacket. If a storm threatens, get out of the water and seek shelter.

✓ **Reading Check** Name three safety tips for the outdoors.

Safety at Home

Many accidents can be avoided. **Figure 5** shows tips for safety around the house.

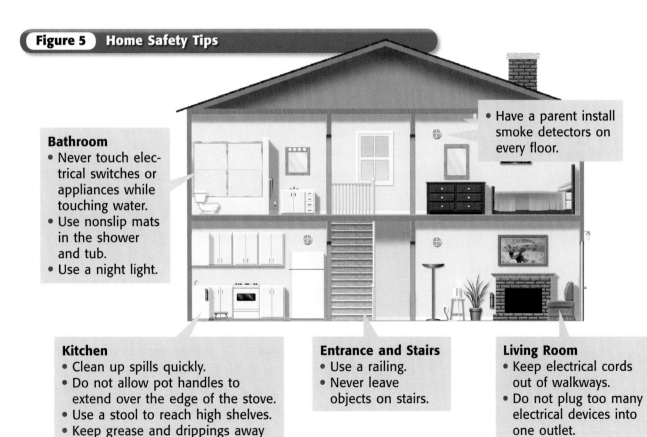

Figure 5 Home Safety Tips

• Have a parent install smoke detectors on every floor.

Bathroom
• Never touch electrical switches or appliances while touching water.
• Use nonslip mats in the shower and tub.
• Use a night light.

Kitchen
• Clean up spills quickly.
• Do not allow pot handles to extend over the edge of the stove.
• Use a stool to reach high shelves.
• Keep grease and drippings away from open flames.

Entrance and Stairs
• Use a railing.
• Never leave objects on stairs.

Living Room
• Keep electrical cords out of walkways.
• Do not plug too many electrical devices into one outlet.

Figure 6 *It is always important to use the appropriate safety equipment.*

Safety on the Road

In the car, always wear a seat belt, even if you are traveling only a short distance. Never ride in a car with someone who has been drinking. Safety equipment and common sense are your best defense against injury. When riding a bicycle, always wear a helmet like those shown in **Figure 6.** Ride with traffic, and obey all traffic rules. Be sure to signal when stopping or turning.

Safety in Class

Accidents can happen in school, especially in a lab class or during woodworking class. To avoid hurting yourself and others, always follow your teacher's instructions, and wear the proper safety equipment at all times.

When Accidents Happen

No matter how well you practice safety measures, accidents can still happen. What should you do if a friend chokes on food and cannot breathe? What if a friend is stung by a bee and has a violent allergic reaction?

Call for Help

Figure 7 *When calling 911, stay calm and listen carefully to what the dispatcher tells you.*

Once you've checked for other dangers, call for medical help immediately, as the person shown in **Figure 7** is doing. In most communities, you can dial 911. Speak slowly and clearly. Give the complete address and a description of the location. Describe the accident, the number of people injured, and the types of injuries. Ask what to do, and listen carefully to the instructions. Let the other person hang up first to be sure there are no more questions or instructions for you.

Learn First Aid

If you want to learn more about what to do in an emergency, you can take a first-aid or CPR course, such as the one shown in **Figure 8**. *CPR* can revive a person who is not breathing and has no heartbeat. If you are over 12 years old, you can become certified in both CPR and first aid. Some baby-sitting classes also provide information on first aid. The American Red Cross, community organizations, and local hospitals offer these classes. However, you should not attempt any lifesaving procedure unless you have been trained.

✓ **Reading Check** What is CPR, and how can you learn it?

Figure 8 *These teenagers are taking a CPR course to prepare themselves for emergency situations.*

SECTION Review

Summary

- Good hygiene includes taking care of your skin, hair, and teeth.
- Good posture is important to health.
- Exercise keeps your heart, lungs, and bones healthy.
- Teenagers need more than 9 hours of sleep to stay rested and healthy.
- Coping with stress is an important part of staying physically and emotionally healthy.
- It is important to be aware of the possible hazards around your home, outdoors, and at school. Using the appropriate safety equipment can also help keep you safe.

Using Key Terms

Complete each of the following sentences by choosing the correct term from the word bank.

hygiene	aerobic exercise
sleep	stress

1. The science of protecting your health is called ___.

2. ___ strengthens your heart, lungs, and bones.

3. ___ is the physical and mental response to pressure.

Understanding Key Ideas

4. Which of the following is important for good health?
   a. irregular exercise
   b. getting your hair cut
   c. taking care of your teeth
   d. getting plenty of sun

5. List two things you should do when calling for help in a medical emergency.

6. List three ways to stay safe when you are outside, and three ways to stay safe at home.

7. How do seat belts and safety equipment protect you?

Math Skills

8. It is estimated that only 65% of adults wear their seat belts. If there are 10,000 people driving in your area right now, how many of them are wearing their seat belts?

Critical Thinking

9. **Applying Concepts** What situations cause you stress? What can you do to help relieve the stress you are feeling?

10. **Making Inferences** According to the newspaper, the temperature outside is 61°F right now. Later, it will be 90°F outside. If you and your friends want to play soccer in the park, what should you wear? What should you bring with you?

SCiLINKS **NSTA**
Developed and maintained by the
National Science Teachers Association

For a variety of links related to this chapter, go to www.scilinks.org

Topic: Safety
SciLinks code: HSM1339

Skills Practice Lab

Keep It Clean

One of the best ways to prevent the spread of bacterial and viral infections is to frequently wash your hands with soap and water. Many companies advertise that their soap ingredients can destroy bacteria normally found on the body. In this activity, you will investigate how effective antibacterial soaps are at killing bacteria.

Procedure

1 Keeping the agar plates closed at all times, use the wax pencil to label the bottoms of three agar plates. Label one plate "Control," one plate "No soap," and one plate "Soap."

2 Without washing your hands, carefully press several surfaces of your hands on the agar plate marked "Control." Have your partner immediately put the cover back on the plate. After you touch the agar, do not touch anything with either hand.

3 Hold your right hand under running water for 2 min. Ask your partner to scrub all surfaces of your right hand with the scrub brush throughout these 2 min. Be sure that he or she scrubs under your fingernails. After scrubbing, your partner should turn off the water and open the plate marked "No soap." Touching only the agar, carefully press on the "No soap" plate with the same surfaces of your right hand that you used to press on the "Control" plate.

4 Repeat step 3, but use your left hand instead of your right. This time, ask your partner to scrub your left hand with liquid antibacterial soap and the scrub brush. Use the plate marked "Soap" instead of the plate marked "No soap."

5 Secure the lid of each plate to its bottom half with transparent tape. Place the plates upside down in the incubator. Incubate all three plates overnight at 37°C.

6 Remove the plates from the incubator, and turn them right side up. Check each plate for the presence of bacterial colonies, and count the number of colonies present on each plate. Record this information. **Caution:** Do not remove the lids on any of the plates.

Analyze the Results

1 **Examining Data** Compare the bacterial growth on the plates. Which plate contained the most growth? Which contained the least?

Draw Conclusions

2 **Drawing Conclusions** Does water alone effectively kill bacteria? Explain.

Applying Your Data

Repeat this experiment, but scrub with regular, not antibacterial, liquid soap. Describe how the results of the two experiments differ.

Chapter Review

USING KEY TERMS

Complete each of the following sentences by choosing the correct term from the word bank.

nutrients Food Guide
addiction Pyramid
malnutrition drug

1 Carbohydrates, proteins, fats, vitamins, minerals, and water are the six categories of ___.

2 The ___ divides foods into six groups and gives a recommended number of servings for each group.

3 Both bulimia nervosa and anorexia nervosa cause ___.

4 A physical or psychological dependence on a drug can lead to ___.

5 A(n) ___ is any substance that causes a change in a person's physical or psychological state.

UNDERSTANDING KEY IDEAS

Multiple Choice

6 Which of the following statements about drugs is true?

a. A child cannot become addicted to drugs.

b. Smoking just one or two cigarettes is safe for anyone.

c. Alcohol is not a drug.

d. Withdrawal symptoms may be painful.

7 What does alcohol do to the central nervous system (CNS)?

a. It speeds the CNS up.

b. It slows the CNS down.

c. It keeps the CNS regulated.

d. It has no effect on the CNS.

8 To keep your teeth healthy,

a. brush your teeth as hard as you can.

b. use a toothbrush until it is worn out.

c. brush at least twice a day.

d. floss at least once a week.

9 According to the Food Guide Pyramid, what foods should you eat most?

a. meats

b. milk, yogurt, and cheese

c. fruits and vegetables

d. bread, cereal, rice, and pasta

10 Which of the following can help you deal with stress?

a. ignoring your homework

b. drinking a caffeinated drink

c. talking to a friend

d. watching television

11 Tobacco use increases the risk of

a. lung cancer.

b. car accidents.

c. liver damage.

d. depression.

Short Answer

12 Are all narcotics illegal? Explain.

13 What are three dangers of tobacco and alcohol use?

14 What are the three types of nutrients that provide energy in Calories, and what is the main function of each type in the body?

15 Name two conditions that can lead to malnutrition.

16 Explain why you should always wear safety equipment when you ride your bicycle.

17 Concept Mapping Use the following terms to create a concept map: *carbohydrates, water, proteins, nutrients, fats, vitamins, minerals, saturated fats,* and *unsaturated fats.*

18 Applying Concepts You have recently become a vegetarian, and you worry that you are not getting enough protein. Name two foods that you could eat to get more protein.

19 Analyzing Ideas Your two-year-old cousin will be staying with your family. Name three things that you can do to make sure that the house is safe for a young child.

Look at the photos below. The people in the photos are not practicing safe habits. List the unsafe habits shown in these photos. For each unsafe habit, tell what the corresponding safe habit is.

20

21

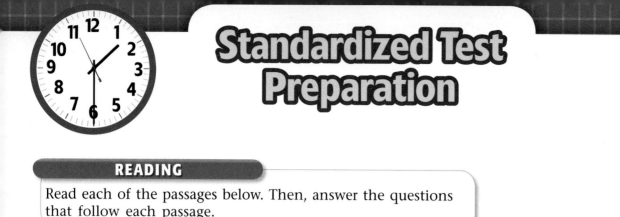
READING

Read each of the passages below. Then, answer the questions that follow each passage.

Passage 1 A <u>chronic</u> disease is a disease that, once developed, is always present and will not go away. Chronic bronchitis is a disease that causes the airways in the lungs to become swollen. This irritation causes a lot of mucus to form in the lungs. As a result, a person who has chronic bronchitis coughs a lot. Another chronic condition is emphysema. Emphysema destroys the tiny air sacs and the walls in the lungs. The holes in the air sacs cannot heal. Eventually, the lung tissue dies, and the lungs can no longer work. Cigarette smoking causes more than 80% of all cases of chronic bronchitis and emphysema.

1. In the passage, what does the word *chronic* mean?

A disappearing

B temporary

C always present

D mucus filled

2. According to the passage, what disease destroys the tiny air sacs and walls of the lungs?

F chronic bronchitis

G emphysema

H chronic cough

I cigarette smoking

3. Which of the following is a true statement according to the passage?

A Holes in the air sacs of lungs heal very quickly.

B Cigarette smoking causes more than 80% of all cases of chronic bronchitis and emphysema.

C Cigarette smoking does not cause chronic bronchitis or emphysema.

D Chronic bronchitis will go away after a person stops smoking cigarettes.

Passage 2 Each body reacts differently to alcohol. Several factors affect how a body reacts to alcohol. A person who has several drinks in a short time is likely to be affected more than a person who has a single drink in the same amount of time. Food in a drinker's stomach can also slow alcohol absorption into the blood. Finally, the way that women absorb and process alcohol differs from the way that men do. If a man and a woman drink the same amount of alcohol, the woman's blood alcohol content (BAC) will be higher than the man's. As BAC increases, mental and physical abilities decline. Muscle coordination, which is especially important for walking and driving, decreases. Vision becomes blurred. Speech and memory are impaired. A high BAC can cause a person to pass out or even die.

1. According to the passage, what does *BAC* stand for?

A blood alcohol content

B blood alcohol contaminant

C blurred alcohol capacity

D blood alcoholic coordination

2. According to the passage, which of the following factors can affect BAC?

F time of day

G food in the stomach

H age

I physical activity

3. Which of the following is a fact according to the passage?

A Alcohol does not affect mood or mental abilities.

B Men absorb alcohol in the same way that women do.

C Alcohol decreases muscle coordination.

D Everybody reacts to alcohol in the same way.

The figure below shows a sample prescription drug label. Use this figure to answer the questions that follow.

The People's Pharmacy
252 FIRST STREET
HOUSTON, TX 77077
(713) 242-2299
DEA# AS 3455

Rx 00674312C02/01/04   02/01/04

BAKER, RICHARD   CC

TAKE 1 TABLET BY MOUTH DAILY

TEQUIN   400MG TABS   (BMS)
DR. SANCHEZ, DAVID   QTY: 10   NO REFILL

CAUTION: FEDERAL LAW PROHIBITS THE TRANSFER OF THIS DRUG TO ANY OTHER PERSON THAN THE PATIENT TO WHOM IT WAS PRESCRIBED.

Keep out of reach of children.

Patient's name
Directions for taking the medicine
Name of drug
Doctor's name

1. According to the label, what is the patient's name?
- **A** Richard Baker
- **B** Baker Richard
- **C** David Sanchez
- **D** James Beard

2. According to the label, how often should the medication be taken?
- **F** once a day
- **G** twice a day
- **H** three times a day
- **I** once a week

3. According to the label, how many refills remain on the prescription?
- **A** 0
- **B** 1
- **C** 2
- **D** 3

4. If this patient follows the directions exactly, how long will he need to take this medicine?
- **F** 1 day
- **G** 5 days
- **H** 10 days
- **I** There is not enough data to determine the answer.

Read each question below, and choose the best answer.

1. Which of the following ratios is equal to 2/4?
- **A** 1/2
- **B** 17/18
- **C** 5/2
- **D** 7/2

2. If 1 gal = 3.79 L, how many liters are in 3 gal?
- **F** 3.79 L
- **G** 7.58 L
- **H** 11.37 L
- **I** 15.16 L

3. Approximately how many liters are in 5 gal?
- **A** 5 L
- **B** 10 L
- **C** 20 L
- **D** 30 L

4. Ada has just built a car for a Pinewood Derby. She wants to find the average speed of her new car. During her first test run, she goes 5 mi/h. During her second run, she goes 4 mi/h, and in her third run, she goes 6 mi/h. What is her average speed?
- **F** 4 mi/h
- **G** 5 mi/h
- **H** 6 mi/h
- **I** 7 mi/h

5. Which of the following numbers is largest?
- **A** 1×10^2
- **B** 1×10^5
- **C** 3×10^5
- **D** 5×10^4

6. On Saturday, Mae won a goldfish at the school carnival. On the way home, Mae and her mother bought a fishbowl for $10.25, a container of fish food for $3.75, and a plastic coral for $8.15. How much money did Mae and her mother spend?
- **F** $11.90
- **G** $18.40
- **H** $22.15
- **I** $30.30

Standardized Test Preparation

Science in Action

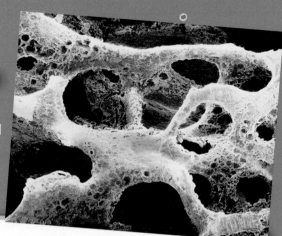

Bones can become severely weakened by the female athlete triad.

Science, Technology, and Society

Meatless Munching

Recent studies suggest that a vegetarian diet may reduce the risk of heart disease, adult-onset diabetes, and some forms of cancer. However, a vegetarian diet takes careful planning. Vegetarians must ensure that they get the proper balance of protein and vitamins in their diet. New foods that can help vegetarians remain healthy are being developed constantly. Meat substitutes are now made from soybeans, textured vegetable protein, and tofu. One new food, which is shown above, is made of a fungus that is a relative of mushrooms and truffles.

Scientific Discoveries

Female Athlete Triad

Getting enough exercise is an important part of staying healthy. But in 1992, doctors learned that too much exercise can be harmful for women. When a girl or woman exercises too much, three things can happen. She may lose too much weight. She may stop having her period. And her bones may become very weak. These three symptoms form the female athlete triad. To prevent this condition, female athletes need to take in enough Calories. Women who exercise heavily and try to lose weight may have a reduction in estrogen. Estrogen is the hormone that helps regulate the menstrual cycle. Low levels of estrogen and inadequate nutrition can cause bones to become weak and brittle. The photo above shows bone that has been weakened greatly.

Social Studies

WRITING SKILL Research a culture that has a mostly vegetarian diet, such as Hindu or Buddhist. What kinds of food do the people eat? Why don't they eat animals? Write a short report on your findings.

Math Activity

Some scientists recommend that teenagers get 1,200 to 1,500 mg of calcium every day. A cup of milk has 300 mg of calcium, and a serving of yogurt has 400 mg of calcium. Calculate two combinations of milk and yogurt that would give you the recommended 1,500 mg of calcium.

Russell Selger

Guidance Counselor Guidance counselors help students think about their future by helping them discover their interests. After focusing their interests, a guidance counselor helps students plan a good academic schedule. A guidance counselor might talk to you about taking an art or computer science class that may help you discover a hidden talent. Many skills are vital to being a good guidance counselor. The job requires empathy, which is the ability to understand and sympathize with another person's feelings. Counselors also need patience, good listening skills, and a love of helping young people. Russell Selger, a guidance counselor at Timberlane Middle School, has a great respect for middle school students. "The kids are just alive. They want to learn. There's something about the spark that they have, and it's so much fun to guide them through all of this stuff," he explains.

Language Arts ACTIVITY

WRITING SKILL Visit the guidance counselor's office at your school. What services does your guidance counselor offer? Conduct an interview with a guidance counselor. Ask why he or she became a counselor. Write an article for the school paper about your findings.

To learn more about these Science in Action topics, visit **go.hrw.com** and type in the keyword **HL5BD7F**.

Current Science

Check out Current Science® articles related to this chapter by visiting **go.hrw.com**. Just type in the keyword **HL5CS28**.

Inquiry Lab

Muscles at Work

Have you ever exercised outside on a cold fall day wearing only a thin warm-up suit or shorts? How did you stay warm? The answer is that your muscle cells contracted, and when contraction takes place, some energy is used to do work, and the rest is converted to thermal energy. This process helps your body maintain a constant temperature in cold conditions. In this activity, you will learn how the release of energy can cause a change in your body temperature.

MATERIALS

- clock (or watch) with a second hand
- thermometer, small, hand held
- other materials as approved by your teacher

Ask a Question

1 Write a question that you can test about how activity affects body temperature.

Form a Hypothesis

2 Form a group of four students. In your group, discuss several exercises that can produce a change in body temperature. Write a hypothesis that could answer the question you asked.

Test the Hypothesis

3 Develop an experimental procedure that includes the steps necessary to test your hypothesis. Be sure to get your teacher's approval before you begin.

4 Assign tasks to individuals in the group, such as note taking, data recording, and timing. What observations and data will you be recording? Design your data tables accordingly.

5 Perform your experiment as planned by your group. Be sure to record all observations in your data tables.

Analyze the Results

1 How did you determine if muscle contractions cause the release of thermal energy? Was your hypothesis supported by your data? Explain your results in a written report. Describe how you could improve your experimental method.

Applying Your Data

Why do humans shiver in the cold? Do all animals shiver? Find out why shivering is one of the first signs that your body is becoming too cold.

Model-Making Lab

Build a Lung

When you breathe, you actually pull air into your lungs because your diaphragm muscle causes your chest to expand. You can see this is true by placing your hands on your ribs and inhaling slowly. Did you feel your chest expand?

In this activity, you will build a model of a lung by using some common materials. You will see how the diaphragm muscle works to inflate your lungs. Refer to the diagrams at right as you construct your model.

MATERIALS

- bag, trash, small plastic
- balloon, small
- bottle, top half, 2 L
- clay, golf-ball-sized piece
- rubber bands (2)
- ruler, metric
- straw, plastic
- tape, transparent

Procedure

① Attach the balloon to the end of the straw with a rubber band. Make a hole through the clay, and insert the other end of the straw through the hole. Be sure at least 8 cm of the straw extends beyond the clay. Squeeze the ball of clay gently to seal the clay around the straw.

② Insert the balloon end of the straw into the neck of the bottle. Use the ball of clay to seal the straw and balloon into the bottle.

③ Turn the bottle gently on its side. Place the trash bag over the cut end of the bottle. Expand a rubber band around the bottom of the bottle to secure the bag. You may wish to reinforce the seal with tape. Before the plastic is completely sealed, gather the excess material of the bag into your hand, and press toward the inside of the bottle slightly. (You may need to tie a knot about halfway up from the bottom of the bag to take up excess material.) Use tape to finish sealing the bag to the bottle with the bag in this position. The excess air will be pushed out of the bottle.

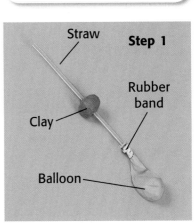

Step 1

Straw

Rubber band

Clay

Balloon

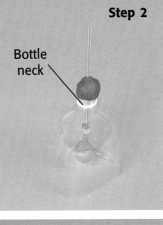

Step 2

Bottle neck

Analyze the Results

① What can you do with your model to make the "lung" inflate?

② What do the balloon, the plastic wrap, and the straw represent in your model?

③ Using your model, demonstrate to the class how air enters the lung and how air exits the lung.

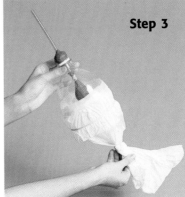

Step 3

Applying Your Data

Do some research to find out what an "iron lung" is and why it was used in the past. Research and write a report about what is used today to help people who have difficulty breathing.

Skills Practice Lab

Enzymes in Action

You know how important enzymes are in the process of digestion. This lab will help you see enzymes at work. Hydrogen peroxide is continuously produced by your cells. If it is not quickly broken down, hydrogen peroxide will kill your cells. Luckily, your cells contain an enzyme that converts hydrogen peroxide into two nonpoisonous substances. This enzyme is also present in the cells of beef liver. In this lab, you will observe the action of this enzyme on hydrogen peroxide.

Procedure

1. Draw a data table similar to the one below. Be sure to leave enough space to write your observations.

Data Table

Size and condition of liver	Experimental liquid	Observations
1 cm cube beef liver	2 mL water	
1 cm cube beef liver	2 mL hydrogen peroxide	DO NOT WRITE IN BOOK
1 cm cube beef liver (mashed)	2 mL hydrogen peroxide	

MATERIALS

- beef liver, 1 cm cubes (3)
- gloves, protective
- graduated cylinder, 10 mL
- hydrogen peroxide, fresh (4 mL)
- mortar and pestle (or fork and watch glass)
- plate, small
- spatula
- test tube (3)
- test-tube rack
- tweezers
- water

SAFETY

2 Get three equal-sized pieces of beef liver from your teacher, and use your forceps to place them on your plate.

3 Pour 2 mL of water into a test tube labeled "Water and liver."

4 Using the tweezers, carefully place one piece of liver in the test tube. Record your observations in your data table.

5 Pour 2 mL of hydrogen peroxide into a second test tube labeled "Liver and hydrogen peroxide."
Caution: Do not splash hydrogen peroxide on your skin. If you do get hydrogen peroxide on your skin, rinse the affected area with running water immediately, and tell your teacher.

6 Using the tweezers, carefully place one piece of liver in the test tube. Record your observations of the second test tube in your data table.

7 Pour another 2 mL of hydrogen peroxide into a third test tube labeled "Ground liver and hydrogen peroxide."

8 Using a mortar and pestle (or fork and watch glass), carefully grind the third piece of liver.

9 Using the spatula, scrape the ground liver into the third test tube. Record your observations of the third test tube in your data table.

Analyze the Results

1 What was the purpose of putting the first piece of liver in water? Why was this a necessary step?

2 Describe the difference you observed between the liver and the ground liver when each was placed in the hydrogen peroxide. How can you account for this difference?

Applying Your Data

Do plant cells contain enzymes that break down hydrogen peroxide? Try this experiment using potato cubes instead of liver to find out.

Skills Practice Lab

My, How You've Grown!

In humans, the process of development that takes place between fertilization and birth lasts about 266 days. In 4 weeks, the new individual grows from a single fertilized cell to an embryo whose heart is beating and pumping blood. All of the organ systems and body parts are completely formed by the end of the seventh month. During the last 2 months before birth, the baby grows, and its organ systems mature. At birth, the average mass of a baby is about 33,000 times as much as that of an embryo at 2 weeks of development! In this activity, you will discover just how fast a fetus grows.

MATERIALS

- paper, graph
- pencils, colored

Procedure

1. Using graph paper, make two graphs—one entitled "Length" and one entitled "Mass." On the length graph, use intervals of 25 mm on the y-axis. Extend the y-axis to 500 mm. On the mass graph, use intervals of 100 g on the y-axis. Extend this y-axis to 3,300 g. Use 2-week intervals for time on the x-axes for both graphs. Both x-axes should extend to 40 weeks.

2. Examine the data table at right. Plot the data in the table on your graphs. Use a colored pencil to draw the curved line that joins the points on each graph.

Analyze the Results

1. Describe the change in mass of a developing fetus. How can you explain this change?

2. Describe the change in length of a developing fetus. How does the change in mass compare to the change in length?

Increase of Mass and Length of Average Human Fetus		
Time (weeks)	Mass (g)	Length (mm)
2	0.1	1.5
3	0.3	2.3
4	0.5	5.0
5	0.6	10.0
6	0.8	15.0
8	1.0	30.0
13	15.0	90.0
17	115.0	140.0
21	300.0	250.0
26	950.0	320.0
30	1,500.0	400.0
35	2,300.0	450.0
40	3,300.0	500.0

Applying Your Data

Using the information in your graphs, estimate how tall a child would be at age 3 if he or she continued to grow at the same average rate that a fetus grows.

Model-Making Lab

Antibodies to the Rescue

Some cells of the immune system, called *B cells,* make antibodies that attack and kill invading viruses and microorganisms. These antibodies help make you immune to disease. Have you ever had chickenpox? If you have, your body has built up antibodies that can recognize that particular virus. Antibodies will attach themselves to the virus, tagging it for destruction. If you are exposed to the same disease again, the antibodies remember that virus. They will attack the virus even quicker and in greater number than they did the first time. This is the reason that you will probably never have chickenpox more than once.

In this activity, you will construct simple models of viruses and their antibodies. You will see how antibodies are specific for a particular virus.

MATERIALS

- craft materials, such as buttons, fabric scraps, pipe cleaners, and recycled materials
- paper, colored
- scissors
- tape (or glue)

Procedure

1. Draw the virus patterns shown on this page on a separate piece of paper, or design your own virus models from the craft supplies. Remember to design different receptors on each of your virus models.

2. Write a few sentences describing how your viruses are different.

3. Cut out the viruses, and attach them to a piece of colored paper with tape or glue.

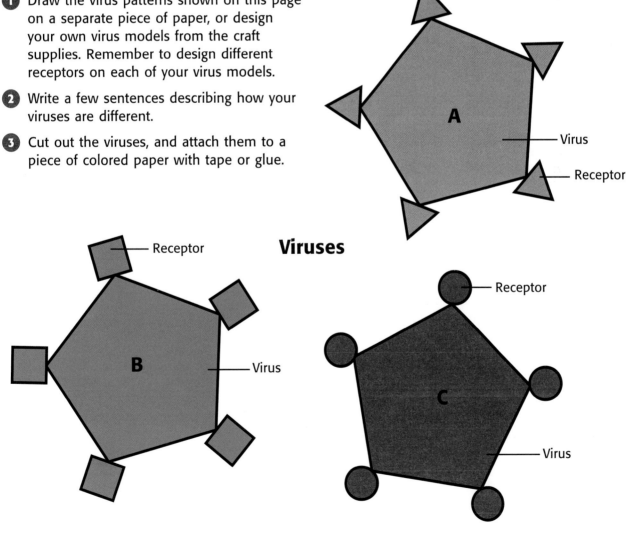

Viruses

4 Select the antibodies drawn below, or design your own antibodies that will exactly fit on the receptors on your virus models. Draw or create each antibody enough times to attach one to each receptor site on the virus.

Antibodies

5 Cut out the antibodies you have drawn. Arrange the antibodies so that they bind to the virus at the appropriate receptor. Attach them to the virus with tape or glue.

Analyze the Results

1 Explain how an antibody "recognizes" a particular virus.

2 After the attachment of antibodies to the receptors, what would be the next step in the immune response?

3 Many vaccines use weakened copies of the virus to protect the body. Use the model of a virus and its specific antibody to explain how vaccines work.

Draw Conclusions

4 Use your model of a virus to demonstrate to the class how a receptor might change or mutate so that a vaccine would no longer be effective.

Applying Your Data

Research in the library or on the Internet to find information about the discovery of the Salk vaccine for polio. Include information on how polio affects people today.

Research in the library or on the Internet to find information and write a report about filoviruses. What do they look like? What diseases do they cause? Why are they especially dangerous? Is there an effective vaccine against any filovirus? Explain.

Skills Practice Lab

To Diet or Not to Diet

There are six main classes of foods that we need in order to keep our bodies functioning properly: water, vitamins, minerals, carbohydrates, fats, and proteins. In this activity you will investigate the importance of a well-balanced diet in maintaining a healthy body. Then you will create a poster or picture that illustrates the importance of one of the three energy-producing nutrients—carbohydrates, fats, and proteins.

MATERIALS

- crayons (or markers), assorted colors
- diet books
- menus, fast-food (optional)
- nutrition reference books
- paper, white unlined

Procedure

1 Draw a table like the one below. Research in the library, on nutrition labels, in nutrition or diet books, or on the Internet to find the information you need to fill out the chart.

Nutrition Data Table			
	Fats	**Carbohydrates**	**Proteins**
Found in which foods			
Functions in the body		DO NOT WRITE IN BOOK	
Consequences of deficiency			

2 Choose one of the foods you have learned about in your research, and create a poster or picture that describes its importance in a well-balanced diet.

Analyze the Results

1 Based on what you have learned in this lab, how might you change your eating habits to have a well-balanced diet? Does the nutritional value of foods concern you? Why or why not? Write down your answers, and explain your reasoning.

Communicating Your Data

Write a paragraph explaining why water is a nutrient. Analyze a typical fast-food meal, and determine its overall nutritional value.

Contents

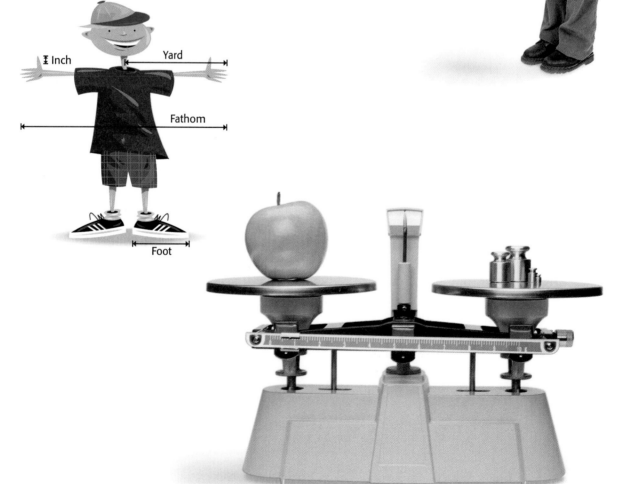

Appendix

✓ *Reading Check* Answers

Chapter 1 Body Organization and Structure

Section 1
Page 5: The stomach works with other organs, such as the small and large intestines, to digest food.

Page 6: Sample answer: The cardiovascular system includes the heart and blood vessels. These organs are also part of the circulatory system, which includes blood. Together, these systems deliver the materials cells need to survive.

Section 2
Page 9: Sample answer: As people grow, most of the cartilage that they start out with is replaced with bone.

Page 10: Sample answer: Joints are held together by ligaments. Cartilage cushions the area in a joint where bones meet.

Section 3
Page 13: Sample answer: One muscle, the flexor, bends part of the body. Another muscle, the extensor, straightens part of the body.

Page 15: Sample answer: Anabolic steroids can damage the heart, liver, and kidneys. They can also cause high blood pressure. Anabolic steroids can cause bones to stop growing.

Section 4
Page 17: The dermis is the layer of skin that lies beneath the epidermis. It is composed of a protein called *collagen,* while the epidermis contains keratin.

Page 18: Sample answer: A nail grows from living cells in the nail root at the base of the nail. As new cells form, the nail grows longer.

Chapter 2 Circulation and Respiration

Section 1
Page 30: The four main parts of the cardiovascular system are the heart and the arteries, capillaries, and veins.

Page 32: Arteries have thick, stretchy walls and carry blood away from the heart. Capillaries are tiny blood vessels that allow the exchange of oxygen, carbon dioxide, and nutrients between cells and blood. Veins are blood vessels that carry blood back to the heart.

Page 34: Atherosclerosis is dangerous because it can cause the buildup of material inside an artery. When the artery becomes blocked, blood can't flow and can't reach the cells. In some cases, a person can have a heart attack from a blocked artery.

Section 2
Page 36: plasma, red blood cells, white blood cells, and platelets

Page 37: White blood cells identify and attack pathogens that may make you sick.

Page 38: Systolic pressure is the pressure inside arteries when the ventricles contract. Diastolic pressure is the pressure inside the arteries when the ventricles are relaxed.

Page 39: The red blood cells of a person who has type O blood have no A or B antigens. The A or B antibodies in another person's blood will not react to the type O cells. It is safe for anyone to receive type O blood.

Section 3
Page 40: The lymphatic system is a secondary circulatory system in the body. The lymphatic system collects fluid and particles from between the cells and returns them to the cardiovascular system.

Page 42: The white pulp of the spleen is part of the lymphatic system. It helps fight infections by storing and producing lymphocytes. The red pulp of the spleen removes unwanted material, such as defective red blood cells, from the circulatory system.

Section 4
Page 45: nose, pharynx, larynx, trachea, bronchi, bronchioles, alveoli

Page 46: Cellular respiration is the process inside a cell in which oxygen is used to release energy stored in molecules of glucose. During the process, carbon dioxide (CO_2) and water are released.

Chapter 3 The Digestive and Urinary Systems

Section 1

Page 59: Enzymes cut proteins into amino acids that the body can use.

Page 61: Chyme is a soupy mixture of partially digested food in the stomach.

Page 63: Bile breaks large fat droplets into very small droplets. This process allows more fat molecules to be exposed to digestive enzymes.

Page 64: Fiber keeps the stool soft and keeps material moving through the large intestine.

Section 2

Page 67: Nephrons are microscopic filters inside the kidneys.

Page 68: Diuretics are chemicals that cause the kidneys to make more urine.

Chapter 4 Communication and Control

Section 1

Page 80: The CNS is the brain and the spinal cord. The PNS is all of the parts of the nervous system except the brain and the spinal cord.

Page 81: A neuron is a cell that has a cell body and a nucleus. A neuron also has dendrites that receive signals from other neurons and axons that send signals to other neurons.

Page 82: A nerve is a collection of nerve fibers, or axons, bundled together with blood vessels through which impulses travel between the central nervous system and other parts of the body.

Page 83: The PNS connects your CNS to the rest of your body, controls voluntary movements, and keeps your body's functions in balance.

Page 84: A voluntary action is an action over which you have conscious control. Voluntary activities include throwing a ball, playing a video game, talking to your friends, taking a bite of food, and raising your hand to answer a question in class. An involuntary action is an action that happens automatically. It is an action or process over which you do not have conscious control.

Page 85: The medulla is important because it controls your heart rate, blood pressure, and ordinary breathing.

Page 86: When someone touches your skin, an impulse that travels along a sensory neuron to your spinal cord and then to your brain is created. The response travels back from your brain to your spinal cord and then along a motor neuron to a muscle.

Section 2

Page 88: Skin can detect pressure, temperature, pain, and vibration.

Page 89: Reflexes are important because they can protect you from injury.

Page 90: Light strikes cells on the retina and triggers impulses in those cells. The impulses are carried to the brain, which interprets the impulses as images that you "see."

Page 91: In bright light, your iris contracts and reduces the amount of light entering the eye.

Page 92: Neurons in the cochlea convert waves into electrical impulses that the brain interprets as sound.

Section 3

Page 95: Sample answer: The thyroid gland increases the rate at which the body uses energy. The thymus gland regulates the immune system, which helps your body fight disease.

Page 96: Insulin helps regulate the amount of glucose in the blood.

Chapter 5   Reproduction and Development

Section 1

Page 109:   Sexual reproduction is reproduction in which the sex cells (egg and sperm) of two parents unite to form a new individual.

Page 110:   External fertilization happens when the sex cells unite outside of the female's body. Internal fertilization happens when the sex cells unite inside the female's body.

Page 111:   All mammals reproduce sexually and nurture their young with milk.

Section 2

Page 112:   testes, epididymis, vas deferens, urethra, penis

Page 114:   Twins happen about 30 times in every 1,000 births.

Section 3

Page 116:   Fertilization happens when the nucleus of a sperm unites with the nucleus of an egg. Implantation happens after the fertilized egg travels down the fallopian tube to the uterus and embeds itself in the wall of the uterus.

Page 117:   The placenta is important because it provides the embryo with oxygen and nutrients from the mother's blood. Wastes from the embryo also travel to the placenta, where they are carried to the mother so that she can excrete them.

Page 118:   The embryo is now called a *fetus.* The fetus's face begins to look more human, and the fetus can swallow, grows rapidly (triples in size), and begins to make movements that the mother can feel.

Page 120: A person's reproductive system becomes mature.

Chapter 6   Body Defenses and Disease

Section 1

Page 135:   Cooking kills dangerous bacteria or parasites living in meat, fish, and eggs.

Page 137:   Frank's doctor did not prescribe antibiotics because Frank had a cold. Colds are caused by viruses. Antibiotics can't stop viruses.

Section 2

Page 139:   Macrophages engulf, or eat, any microorganisms or viruses that enter your body.

Page 140:   If a virus particle enters the body, it may pass into body cells and begin to replicate. Or it may be engulfed and broken up by macrophages.

Page 143:   rheumatoid arthritis, diabetes, multiple sclerosis, and lupus

Page 144:   HIV causes AIDS.

Chapter 7   Staying Healthy

Section 1

Page 157:   An incomplete protein does not contain all of the essential amino acids.

Page 159:   Sample answer: a peanut butter sandwich, a glass of milk, and fresh fruit and vegetable slices

Page 160:   One serving of chicken noodle soup provides more than 10% of the daily recommended allowance of vitamin A and sodium.

Section 2

Page 163:   Over-the-counter drugs can be bought without a prescription. Prescription drugs can be bought only with a prescription from a doctor or other medical professional.

Page 165:   First-time use of cocaine can cause a heart attack or can cause a person to become addicted.

Page 166:   Drug use is the proper use of a legal drug. Drug abuse is either the use of an illegal drug or the improper use of a legal drug.

Section 3

Page 169:   Aerobic exercise strengthens the heart, lungs, and bones and reduces stress. Regular exercise also burns Calories and can give you more energy.

Page 171:   Sample answers: Never hike or camp alone, dress for the weather, learn how to swim, wear a life jacket, and never drink unpurified water.

Page 173:   CPR is a way to revive someone whose heart has stopped beating. CPR classes are available in many places in the community.

Appendix

Study Skills

FoldNote Instructions

Have you ever tried to study for a test or quiz but didn't know where to start? Or have you read a chapter and found that you can remember only a few ideas? Well, FoldNotes are a fun and exciting way to help you learn and remember the ideas you encounter as you learn science!

FoldNotes are tools that you can use to organize concepts. By focusing on a few main concepts, FoldNotes help you learn and remember how the concepts fit together. They can help you see the "big picture." Below you will find instructions for building 10 different FoldNotes.

Pyramid

1. Place a sheet of paper in front of you. Fold the lower left-hand corner of the paper diagonally to the opposite edge of the paper.

2. Cut off the tab of paper created by the fold (at the top).

3. Open the paper so that it is a square. Fold the lower right-hand corner of the paper diagonally to the opposite corner to form a triangle.

4. Open the paper. The creases of the two folds will have created an X.

5. Using scissors, cut along one of the creases. Start from any corner, and stop at the center point to create two flaps. Use tape or glue to attach one of the flaps on top of the other flap.

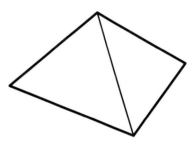

Double Door

1. Fold a sheet of paper in half from the top to the bottom. Then, unfold the paper.

2. Fold the top and bottom edges of the paper to the crease.

Booklet

1. Fold a sheet of paper in half from left to right. Then, unfold the paper.

2. Fold the sheet of paper in half again from the top to the bottom. Then, unfold the paper.

3. Refold the sheet of paper in half from left to right.

4. Fold the top and bottom edges to the center crease.

5. Completely unfold the paper.

6. Refold the paper from top to bottom.

7. Using scissors, cut a slit along the center crease of the sheet from the folded edge to the creases made in step 4. Do not cut the entire sheet in half.

8. Fold the sheet of paper in half from left to right. While holding the bottom and top edges of the paper, push the bottom and top edges together so that the center collapses at the center slit. Fold the four flaps to form a four-page book.

Layered Book

1. Lay one sheet of paper on top of another sheet. Slide the top sheet up so that 2 cm of the bottom sheet is showing.

2. Hold the two sheets together, fold down the top of the two sheets so that you see four 2 cm tabs along the bottom.

3. Using a stapler, staple the top of the FoldNote.

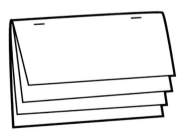

Key-Term Fold

1. Fold a sheet of lined notebook paper in half from left to right.

2. Using scissors, cut along every third line from the right edge of the paper to the center fold to make tabs.

Four-Corner Fold

1. Fold a sheet of paper in half from left to right. Then, unfold the paper.

2. Fold each side of the paper to the crease in the center of the paper.

3. Fold the paper in half from the top to the bottom. Then, unfold the paper.

4. Using scissors, cut the top flap creases made in step 3 to form four flaps.

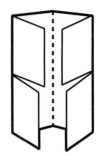

Three-Panel Flip Chart

1. Fold a piece of paper in half from the top to the bottom.

2. Fold the paper in thirds from side to side. Then, unfold the paper so that you can see the three sections.

3. From the top of the paper, cut along each of the vertical fold lines to the fold in the middle of the paper. You will now have three flaps.

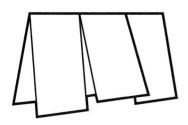

Table Fold

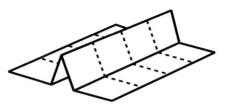

1. Fold a piece of paper in half from the top to the bottom. Then, fold the paper in half again.

2. Fold the paper in thirds from side to side.

3. Unfold the paper completely. Carefully trace the fold lines by using a pen or pencil.

Two-Panel Flip Chart

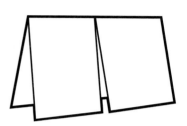

1. Fold a piece of paper in half from the top to the bottom.

2. Fold the paper in half from side to side. Then, unfold the paper so that you can see the two sections.

3. From the top of the paper, cut along the vertical fold line to the fold in the middle of the paper. You will now have two flaps.

Tri-Fold

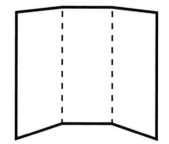

1. Fold a piece a paper in thirds from the top to the bottom.

2. Unfold the paper so that you can see the three sections. Then, turn the paper sideways so that the three sections form vertical columns.

3. Trace the fold lines by using a pen or pencil. Label the columns "Know," "Want," and "Learn."

Graphic Organizer Instructions

Graphic Organizer

Have you ever wished that you could "draw out" the many concepts you learn in your science class? Sometimes, being able to *see* how concepts are related really helps you remember what you've learned. Graphic Organizers do just that! They give you a way to draw or map out concepts.

All you need to make a Graphic Organizer is a piece of paper and a pencil. Below you will find instructions for four different Graphic Organizers designed to help you organize the concepts you'll learn in this book.

Spider Map

1. Draw a diagram like the one shown. In the circle, write the main topic.

2. From the circle, draw legs to represent different categories of the main topic. You can have as many categories as you want.

3. From the category legs, draw horizontal lines. As you read the chapter, write details about each category on the horizontal lines.

Comparison Table

1. Draw a chart like the one shown. Your chart can have as many columns and rows as you want.

2. In the top row, write the topics that you want to compare.

3. In the left column, write characteristics of the topics that you want to compare. As you read the chapter, fill in the characteristics for each topic in the appropriate boxes.

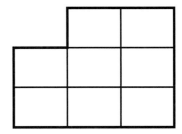

Chain-of-Events-Chart

1. Draw a box. In the box, write the first step of a process or the first event of a timeline.

2. Under the box, draw another box, and use an arrow to connect the two boxes. In the second box, write the next step of the process or the next event in the timeline.

3. Continue adding boxes until the process or timeline is finished.

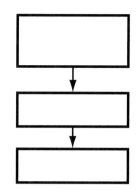

Concept Map

1. Draw a circle in the center of a piece of paper. Write the main idea of the chapter in the center of the circle.

2. From the circle, draw other circles. In those circles, write characteristics of the main idea. Draw arrows from the center circle to the circles that contain the characteristics.

3. From each circle that contains a characteristic, draw other circles. In those circles, write specific details about the characteristic. Draw arrows from each circle that contains a characteristic to the circles that contain specific details. You may draw as many circles as you want.

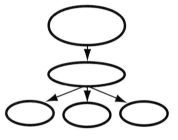

Appendix

SI Measurement

The International System of Units, or SI, is the standard system of measurement used by many scientists. Using the same standards of measurement makes it easier for scientists to communicate with one another.

SI works by combining prefixes and base units. Each base unit can be used with different prefixes to define smaller and larger quantities. The table below lists common SI prefixes.

SI Prefixes

Prefix	Symbol	Factor	Example
kilo-	k	1,000	kilogram, 1 kg = 1,000 g
hecto-	h	100	hectoliter, 1 hL = 100 L
deka-	da	10	dekameter, 1 dam = 10 m
		1	meter, liter, gram
deci-	d	0.1	decigram, 1 dg = 0.1 g
centi-	c	0.01	centimeter, 1 cm = 0.01 m
milli-	m	0.001	milliliter, 1 mL = 0.001 L
micro-	μ	0.000 001	micrometer, 1 μm = 0.000 001 m

SI Conversion Table

SI units	From SI to English	From English to SI
Length		
kilometer (km) = 1,000 m	1 km = 0.621 mi	1 mi = 1.609 km
meter (m) = 100 cm	1 m = 3.281 ft	1 ft = 0.305 m
centimeter (cm) = 0.01 m	1 cm = 0.394 in.	1 in. = 2.540 cm
millimeter (mm) = 0.001 m	1 mm = 0.039 in.	
micrometer (μm) = 0.000 001 m		
nanometer (nm) = 0.000 000 001 m		
Area		
square kilometer (km^2) = 100 hectares	1 km^2 = 0.386 mi^2	1 mi^2 = 2.590 km^2
hectare (ha) = 10,000 m^2	1 ha = 2.471 acres	1 acre = 0.405 ha
square meter (m^2) = 10,000 cm^2	1 m^2 = 10.764 ft^2	1 ft^2 = 0.093 m^2
square centimeter (cm^2) = 100 mm^2	1 cm^2 = 0.155 in.^{2}	1 in.^{2} = 6.452 cm^2
Volume		
liter (L) = 1,000 mL = 1 dm^3	1 L = 1.057 fl qt	1 fl qt = 0.946 L
milliliter (mL) = 0.001 L = 1 cm^3	1 mL = 0.034 fl oz	1 fl oz = 29.574 mL
microliter (μL) = 0.000 001 L		
Mass		
kilogram (kg) = 1,000 g	1 kg = 2.205 lb	1 lb = 0.454 kg
gram (g) = 1,000 mg	1 g = 0.035 oz	1 oz = 28.350 g
milligram (mg) = 0.001 g		
microgram (μg) = 0.000 001 g		

Appendix

Measuring Skills

Using a Graduated Cylinder

When using a graduated cylinder to measure volume, keep the following procedures in mind:

1. Place the cylinder on a flat, level surface before measuring liquid.

2. Move your head so that your eye is level with the surface of the liquid.

3. Read the mark closest to the liquid level. On glass graduated cylinders, read the mark closest to the center of the curve in the liquid's surface.

Using a Meterstick or Metric Ruler

When using a meterstick or metric ruler to measure length, keep the following procedures in mind:

1. Place the ruler firmly against the object that you are measuring.

2. Align one edge of the object exactly with the 0 end of the ruler.

3. Look at the other edge of the object to see which of the marks on the ruler is closest to that edge. (Note: Each small slash between the centimeters represents a millimeter, which is one-tenth of a centimeter.)

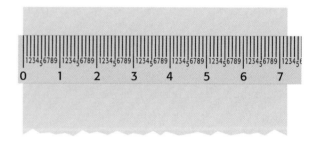

Using a Triple-Beam Balance

When using a triple-beam balance to measure mass, keep the following procedures in mind:

1. Make sure the balance is on a level surface.

2. Place all of the countermasses at 0. Adjust the balancing knob until the pointer rests at 0.

3. Place the object you wish to measure on the pan. **Caution:** Do not place hot objects or chemicals directly on the balance pan.

4. Move the largest countermass along the beam to the right until it is at the last notch that does not tip the balance. Follow the same procedure with the next-largest countermass. Then, move the smallest countermass until the pointer rests at 0.

5. Add the readings from the three beams together to determine the mass of the object.

6. When determining the mass of crystals or powders, first find the mass of a piece of filter paper. Then, add the crystals or powder to the paper, and remeasure. The actual mass of the crystals or powder is the total mass minus the mass of the paper. When finding the mass of liquids, first find the mass of the empty container. Then, find the combined mass of the liquid and container. The mass of the liquid is the total mass minus the mass of the container.

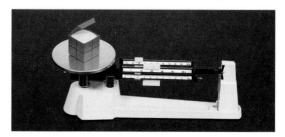

Scientific Methods

The ways in which scientists answer questions and solve problems are called **scientific methods.** The same steps are often used by scientists as they look for answers. However, there is more than one way to use these steps. Scientists may use all of the steps or just some of the steps during an investigation. They may even repeat some of the steps. The goal of using scientific methods is to come up with reliable answers and solutions.

Six Steps of Scientific Methods

1 Ask a Question

Good questions come from careful **observations.** You make observations by using your senses to gather information. Sometimes, you may use instruments, such as microscopes and telescopes, to extend the range of your senses. As you observe the natural world, you will discover that you have many more questions than answers. These questions drive investigations.

Questions beginning with *what, why, how,* and *when* are important in focusing an investigation. Here is an example of a question that could lead to an investigation.

Question: How does acid rain affect plant growth?

2 Form a Hypothesis

After you ask a question, you need to form a **hypothesis.** A hypothesis is a clear statement of what you expect the answer to your question to be. Your hypothesis will represent your best "educated guess" based on what you have observed and what you already know. A good hypothesis is testable. Otherwise, the investigation can go no further. Here is a hypothesis based on the question, "How does acid rain affect plant growth?"

Hypothesis: Acid rain slows plant growth.

The hypothesis can lead to predictions. A prediction is what you think the outcome of your experiment or data collection will be. Predictions are usually stated in an if-then format. Here is a sample prediction for the hypothesis that acid rain slows plant growth.

Prediction: If a plant is watered with only acid rain (which has a pH of 4), then the plant will grow at half its normal rate.

3 Test the Hypothesis

After you have formed a hypothesis and made a prediction, your hypothesis should be tested. One way to test a hypothesis is with a controlled experiment. A **controlled experiment** tests only one factor at a time. In an experiment to test the effect of acid rain on plant growth, the **control group** would be watered with normal rain water. The **experimental group** would be watered with acid rain. All of the plants should receive the same amount of sunlight and water each day. The air temperature should be the same for all groups. However, the acidity of the water will be a variable. In fact, any factor that is different from one group to another is a **variable.** If your hypothesis is correct, then the acidity of the water and plant growth are *dependant variables.* The amount a plant grows is dependent on the acidity of the water. However, the amount of water each plant receives and the amount of sunlight each plant receives are *independent variables.* Either of these factors could change without affecting the other factor.

Sometimes, the nature of an investigation makes a controlled experiment impossible. For example, the Earth's core is surrounded by thousands of meters of rock. Under such circumstances, a hypothesis may be tested by making detailed observations.

4 Analyze the Results

After you have completed your experiments, made your observations, and collected your data, you must analyze all the information you have gathered. Tables and graphs are often used in this step to organize the data.

5 Draw Conclusions

After analyzing your data, you can determine if your results support your hypothesis. If your hypothesis is supported, you (or others) might want to repeat the observations or experiments to verify your results. If your hypothesis is not supported by the data, you may have to check your procedure for errors. You may even have to reject your hypothesis and make a new one. If you cannot draw a conclusion from your results, you may have to try the investigation again or carry out further observations or experiments.

6 Communicate Results

After any scientific investigation, you should report your results. By preparing a written or oral report, you let others know what you have learned. They may repeat your investigation to see if they get the same results. Your report may even lead to another question and then to another investigation.

Scientific Methods in Action

Scientific methods contain loops in which several steps may be repeated over and over again. In some cases, certain steps are unnecessary. Thus, there is not a "straight line" of steps. For example, sometimes scientists find that testing one hypothesis raises new questions and new hypotheses to be tested. And sometimes, testing the hypothesis leads directly to a conclusion. Furthermore, the steps in scientific methods are not always used in the same order. Follow the steps in the diagram, and see how many different directions scientific methods can take you.

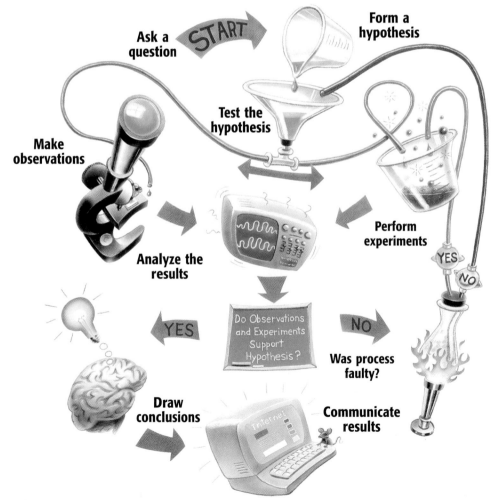

Making Charts and Graphs

Pie Charts

A pie chart shows how each group of data relates to all of the data. Each part of the circle forming the chart represents a category of the data. The entire circle represents all of the data. For example, a biologist studying a hardwood forest in Wisconsin found that there were five different types of trees. The data table at right summarizes the biologist's findings.

Wisconsin Hardwood Trees	
Type of tree	Number found
Oak	600
Maple	750
Beech	300
Birch	1,200
Hickory	150
Total	3,000

How to Make a Pie Chart

1 To make a pie chart of these data, first find the percentage of each type of tree. Divide the number of trees of each type by the total number of trees, and multiply by 100.

$$\frac{600 \text{ oak}}{3,000 \text{ trees}} \times 100 = 20\%$$

$$\frac{750 \text{ maple}}{3,000 \text{ trees}} \times 100 = 25\%$$

$$\frac{300 \text{ beech}}{3,000 \text{ trees}} \times 100 = 10\%$$

$$\frac{1,200 \text{ birch}}{3,000 \text{ trees}} \times 100 = 40\%$$

$$\frac{150 \text{ hickory}}{3,000 \text{ trees}} \times 100 = 5\%$$

2 Now, determine the size of the wedges that make up the pie chart. Multiply each percentage by 360°. Remember that a circle contains 360°.

20% × 360° = 72°   25% × 360° = 90°

10% × 360° = 36°   40% × 360° = 144°

5% × 360° = 18°

3 Check that the sum of the percentages is 100 and the sum of the degrees is 360.

20% + 25% + 10% + 40% + 5% = 100%

72° + 90° + 36° + 144° + 18° = 360°

4 Use a compass to draw a circle and mark the center of the circle.

5 Then, use a protractor to draw angles of 72°, 90°, 36°, 144°, and 18° in the circle.

6 Finally, label each part of the chart, and choose an appropriate title.

A Community of Wisconsin Hardwood Trees

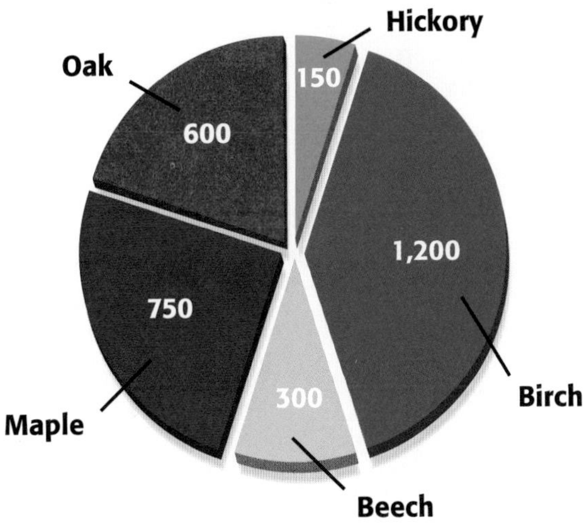

Line Graphs

Line graphs are most often used to demonstrate continuous change. For example, Mr. Smith's students analyzed the population records for their hometown, Appleton, between 1900 and 2000. Examine the data at right.

Because the year and the population change, they are the *variables*. The population is determined by, or dependent on, the year. Therefore, the population is called the **dependent variable,** and the year is called the **independent variable.** Each set of data is called a **data pair.** To prepare a line graph, you must first organize data pairs into a table like the one at right.

Population of Appleton, 1900–2000	
Year	Population
1900	1,800
1920	2,500
1940	3,200
1960	3,900
1980	4,600
2000	5,300

How to Make a Line Graph

1. Place the independent variable along the horizontal (*x*) axis. Place the dependent variable along the vertical (*y*) axis.

2. Label the *x*-axis "Year" and the *y*-axis "Population." Look at your largest and smallest values for the population. For the *y*-axis, determine a scale that will provide enough space to show these values. You must use the same scale for the entire length of the axis. Next, find an appropriate scale for the *x*-axis.

3. Choose reasonable starting points for each axis.

4. Plot the data pairs as accurately as possible.

5. Choose a title that accurately represents the data.

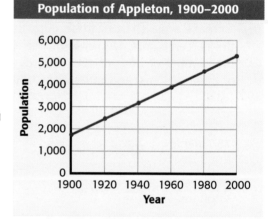

How to Determine Slope

Slope is the ratio of the change in the *y*-value to the change in the *x*-value, or "rise over run."

1. Choose two points on the line graph. For example, the population of Appleton in 2000 was 5,300 people. Therefore, you can define point *a* as (2000, 5,300). In 1900, the population was 1,800 people. You can define point *b* as (1900, 1,800).

2. Find the change in the *y*-value. (*y* at point *a*) − (*y* at point *b*) = 5,300 people − 1,800 people = 3,500 people

3. Find the change in the *x*-value. (*x* at point *a*) − (*x* at point *b*) = 2000 − 1900 = 100 years

4. Calculate the slope of the graph by dividing the change in *y* by the change in *x*.

$$slope = \frac{change\ in\ y}{change\ in\ x}$$

$$slope = \frac{3{,}500\ people}{100\ years}$$

$$slope = 35\ people\ per\ year$$

In this example, the population in Appleton increased by a fixed amount each year. The graph of these data is a straight line. Therefore, the relationship is **linear.** When the graph of a set of data is not a straight line, the relationship is **nonlinear.**

Using Algebra to Determine Slope

The equation in step 4 may also be arranged to be

$$y = kx$$

where y represents the change in the y-value, k represents the slope, and x represents the change in the x-value.

$$slope = \frac{change\ in\ y}{change\ in\ x}$$

$$k = \frac{y}{x}$$

$$k \times x = \frac{y \times x}{x}$$

$$kx = y$$

Bar Graphs

Bar graphs are used to demonstrate change that is not continuous. These graphs can be used to indicate trends when the data cover a long period of time. A meteorologist gathered the precipitation data shown here for Hartford, Connecticut, for April 1–15, 1996, and used a bar graph to represent the data.

Precipitation in Hartford, Connecticut April 1–15, 1996			
Date	Precipitation (cm)	Date	Precipitation (cm)
April 1	0.5	April 9	0.25
April 2	1.25	April 10	0.0
April 3	0.0	April 11	1.0
April 4	0.0	April 12	0.0
April 5	0.0	April 13	0.25
April 6	0.0	April 14	0.0
April 7	0.0	April 15	6.50
April 8	1.75		

How to Make a Bar Graph

1 Use an appropriate scale and a reasonable starting point for each axis.

2 Label the axes, and plot the data.

3 Choose a title that accurately represents the data.

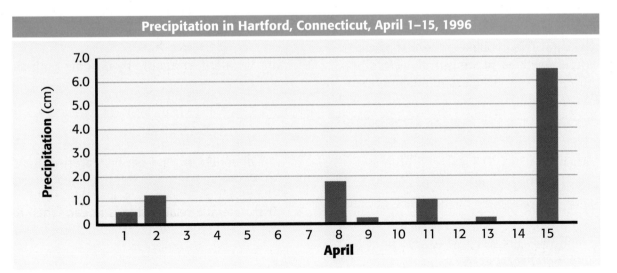

Math Refresher

Science requires an understanding of many math concepts. The following pages will help you review some important math skills.

Averages

An **average,** or **mean,** simplifies a set of numbers into a single number that *approximates* the value of the set.

Example: Find the average of the following set of numbers: 5, 4, 7, and 8.

Step 1: Find the sum.
$$5 + 4 + 7 + 8 = 24$$

Step 2: Divide the sum by the number of numbers in your set. Because there are four numbers in this example, divide the sum by 4.

$$\frac{24}{4} = 6$$

The average, or mean, is **6.**

Ratios

A **ratio** is a comparison between numbers, and it is usually written as a fraction.

Example: Find the ratio of thermometers to students if you have 36 thermometers and 48 students in your class.

Step 1: Make the ratio.
$$\frac{36 \text{ thermometers}}{48 \text{ students}}$$

Step 2: Reduce the fraction to its simplest form.
$$\frac{36}{48} = \frac{36 \div 12}{48 \div 12} = \frac{3}{4}$$

The ratio of thermometers to students is **3 to 4,** or $\frac{3}{4}$. The ratio may also be written in the form 3:4.

Proportions

A **proportion** is an equation that states that two ratios are equal.

$$\frac{3}{1} = \frac{12}{4}$$

To solve a proportion, first multiply across the equal sign. This is called *cross-multiplication.* If you know three of the quantities in a proportion, you can use cross-multiplication to find the fourth.

Example: Imagine that you are making a scale model of the solar system for your science project. The diameter of Jupiter is 11.2 times the diameter of the Earth. If you are using a plastic-foam ball that has a diameter of 2 cm to represent the Earth, what must the diameter of the ball representing Jupiter be?

$$\frac{11.2}{1} = \frac{x}{2 \text{ cm}}$$

Step 1: Cross-multiply.
$$\frac{11.2}{1} \diagup\!\!\!\!\diagdown \frac{x}{2}$$
$$11.2 \times 2 = x \times 1$$

Step 2: Multiply.
$$22.4 = x \times 1$$

Step 3: Isolate the variable by dividing both sides by 1.
$$x = \frac{22.4}{1}$$
$$x = 22.4 \text{ cm}$$

You will need to use a ball that has a diameter of **22.4** cm to represent Jupiter.

Percentages

A **percentage** is a ratio of a given number to 100.

> **Example:** What is 85% of 40?

Step 1: Rewrite the percentage by moving the decimal point two places to the left.

$$0.85$$

Step 2: Multiply the decimal by the number that you are calculating the percentage of.

$$0.85 \times 40 = 34$$

85% of 40 is **34**.

Decimals

To **add** or **subtract decimals,** line up the digits vertically so that the decimal points line up. Then, add or subtract the columns from right to left. Carry or borrow numbers as necessary.

> **Example:** Add the following numbers: 3.1415 and 2.96.

Step 1: Line up the digits vertically so that the decimal points line up.

$$\begin{array}{r} 3.1415 \\ + 2.96 \\ \hline \end{array}$$

Step 2: Add the columns from right to left, and carry when necessary.

$$\begin{array}{r} {}^{1}\ {}^{1} \\ 3.1415 \\ + 2.96 \\ \hline 6.1015 \end{array}$$

The sum is **6.1015.**

Fractions

Numbers tell you how many; **fractions** tell you *how much of a whole*.

> **Example:** Your class has 24 plants. Your teacher instructs you to put 5 plants in a shady spot. What fraction of the plants in your class will you put in a shady spot?

Step 1: In the denominator, write the total number of parts in the whole.

$$\frac{?}{24}$$

Step 2: In the numerator, write the number of parts of the whole that are being considered.

$$\frac{5}{24}$$

So, $\frac{5}{24}$ of the plants will be in the shade.

Reducing Fractions

It is usually best to express a fraction in its simplest form. Expressing a fraction in its simplest form is called *reducing* a fraction.

> **Example:** Reduce the fraction $\frac{30}{45}$ to its simplest form.

Step 1: Find the largest whole number that will divide evenly into both the numerator and denominator. This number is called the *greatest common factor* (GCF).

Factors of the numerator 30:

> 1, 2, 3, 5, 6, 10, **15,** 30

Factors of the denominator 45:

> 1, 3, 5, 9, **15,** 45

Step 2: Divide both the numerator and the denominator by the GCF, which in this case is 15.

$$\frac{30}{45} = \frac{30 \div 15}{45 \div 15} = \frac{2}{3}$$

Thus, $\frac{30}{45}$ reduced to its simplest form is $\frac{2}{3}$.

Adding and Subtracting Fractions

To **add** or **subtract fractions** that have the **same denominator,** simply add or subtract the numerators.

Examples:

$$\frac{3}{5} + \frac{1}{5} = ? \text{ and } \frac{3}{4} - \frac{1}{4} = ?$$

Step 1: Add or subtract the numerators.

$$\frac{3}{5} + \frac{1}{5} = \frac{4}{} \text{ and } \frac{3}{4} - \frac{1}{4} = \frac{2}{}$$

Step 2: Write the sum or difference over the denominator.

$$\frac{3}{5} + \frac{1}{5} = \frac{4}{5} \text{ and } \frac{3}{4} - \frac{1}{4} = \frac{2}{4}$$

Step 3: If necessary, reduce the fraction to its simplest form.

$\frac{4}{5}$ cannot be reduced, and $\frac{2}{4} = \frac{1}{2}$.

To **add** or **subtract fractions** that have **different denominators,** first find the least common denominator (LCD).

Examples:

$$\frac{1}{2} + \frac{1}{6} = ? \text{ and } \frac{3}{4} - \frac{2}{3} = ?$$

Step 1: Write the equivalent fractions that have a common denominator.

$$\frac{3}{6} + \frac{1}{6} = ? \text{ and } \frac{9}{12} - \frac{8}{12} = ?$$

Step 2: Add or subtract the fractions.

$$\frac{3}{6} + \frac{1}{6} = \frac{4}{6} \text{ and } \frac{9}{12} - \frac{8}{12} = \frac{1}{12}$$

Step 3: If necessary, reduce the fraction to its simplest form.

The fraction $\frac{4}{6} = \frac{2}{3}$, and $\frac{1}{12}$ cannot be reduced.

Multiplying Fractions

To **multiply fractions,** multiply the numerators and the denominators together, and then reduce the fraction to its simplest form.

Example:

$$\frac{5}{9} \times \frac{7}{10} = ?$$

Step 1: Multiply the numerators and denominators.

$$\frac{5}{9} \times \frac{7}{10} = \frac{5 \times 7}{9 \times 10} = \frac{35}{90}$$

Step 2: Reduce the fraction.

$$\frac{35}{90} = \frac{35 \div 5}{90 \div 5} = \frac{7}{18}$$

Dividing Fractions

To **divide fractions,** first rewrite the divisor (the number you divide by) upside down. This number is called the *reciprocal* of the divisor. Then multiply and reduce if necessary.

Example:

$$\frac{5}{8} \div \frac{3}{2} = ?$$

Step 1: Rewrite the divisor as its reciprocal.

$$\frac{3}{2} \rightarrow \frac{2}{3}$$

Step 2: Multiply the fractions.

$$\frac{5}{8} \times \frac{2}{3} = \frac{5 \times 2}{8 \times 3} = \frac{10}{24}$$

Step 3: Reduce the fraction.

$$\frac{10}{24} = \frac{10 \div 2}{24 \div 2} = \frac{5}{12}$$

Scientific Notation

Scientific notation is a short way of representing very large and very small numbers without writing all of the place-holding zeros.

Example: Write 653,000,000 in scientific notation.

Step 1: Write the number without the place-holding zeros.

653

Step 2: Place the decimal point after the first digit.

6.53

Step 3: Find the exponent by counting the number of places that you moved the decimal point.

6.53000000

The decimal point was moved eight places to the left. Therefore, the exponent of 10 is positive 8. If you had moved the decimal point to the right, the exponent would be negative.

Step 4: Write the number in scientific notation.

$$6.53 \times 10^8$$

Area

Area is the number of square units needed to cover the surface of an object.

Formulas:

area of a square = side × side
area of a rectangle = length × width
area of a triangle = $\frac{1}{2}$ × base × height

Examples: Find the areas.

Triangle

area = $\frac{1}{2}$ × base × height
area = $\frac{1}{2}$ × 3 cm × 4 cm
area = **6 cm²**

4 cm

3 cm

Rectangle
area = length × width
area = 6 cm × 3 cm
area = **18 cm²**

3 cm

6 cm

Square
area = side × side
area = 3 cm × 3 cm
area = **9 cm²**

3 cm

3 cm

Volume

Volume is the amount of space that something occupies.

Formulas:

volume of a cube =
side × side × side

volume of a prism =
area of base × height

Examples:

Find the volume of the solids.

Cube
volume = side × side × side
volume = 4 cm × 4 cm × 4 cm
volume = **64 cm³**

4 cm

4 cm

4 cm

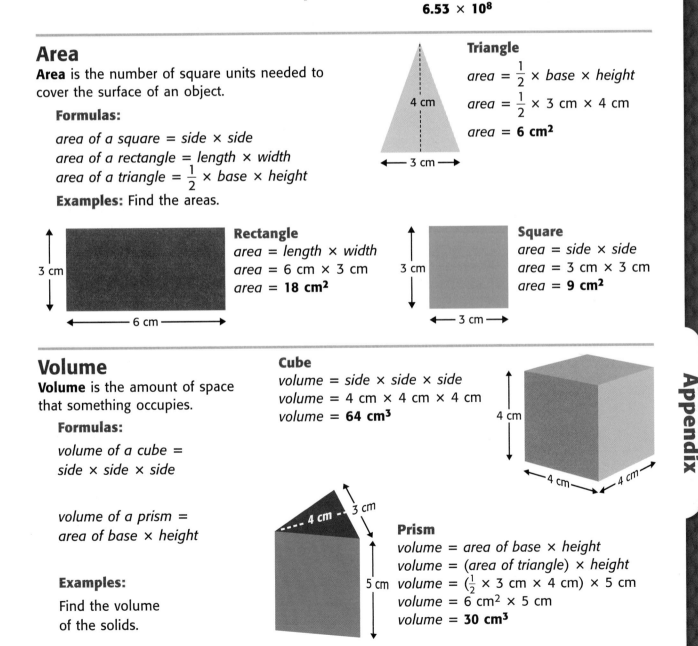

4 cm

3 cm

5 cm

Prism
volume = area of base × height
volume = (area of triangle) × height
volume = ($\frac{1}{2}$ × 3 cm × 4 cm) × 5 cm
volume = 6 cm² × 5 cm
volume = **30 cm³**

Temperature Scales

Temperature can be expressed by using three different scales: Fahrenheit, Celsius, and Kelvin. The SI unit for temperature is the kelvin (K).

Although 0 K is much colder than 0°C, a change of 1 K is equal to a change of 1°C.

Three Temperature Scales

	Fahrenheit	Celsius	Kelvin
Water boils	212°	100°	373
Body temperature	98.6°	37°	310
Room temperature	68°	20°	293
Water freezes	32°	0°	273

Temperature Conversions Table

To convert	Use this equation:	Example
Celsius to Fahrenheit °C → °F	$°F = \left(\dfrac{9}{5} \times °C\right) + 32$	Convert 45°C to °F. $°F = \left(\dfrac{9}{5} \times 45°C\right) + 32 = 113°F$
Fahrenheit to Celsius °F → °C	$°C = \dfrac{5}{9} \times (°F - 32)$	Convert 68°F to °C. $°C = \dfrac{5}{9} \times (68°F - 32) = 20°C$
Celsius to Kelvin °C → K	$K = °C + 273$	Convert 45°C to K. $K = 45°C + 273 = 318\ K$
Kelvin to Celsius K → °C	$°C = K - 273$	Convert 32 K to °C. $°C = 32K - 273 = -241°C$

Using the Microscope

Parts of the Compound Light Microscope

- The **ocular lens** magnifies the image 10×.
- The **low-power objective** magnifies the image 10×.
- The **high-power objective** magnifies the image either 40× or 43×.
- The **revolving nosepiece** holds the objectives and can be turned to change from one magnification to the other.
- The **body tube** maintains the correct distance between the ocular lens and objectives.
- The **coarse-adjustment knob** moves the body tube up and down to allow focusing of the image.
- The **fine-adjustment knob** moves the body tube slightly to bring the image into sharper focus.
- The **stage** supports a slide.
- **Stage clips** hold the slide in place for viewing.
- The **diaphragm** controls the amount of light coming through the stage.
- The light source provides a **light** for viewing the slide.
- The **arm** supports the body tube.
- The **base** supports the microscope.

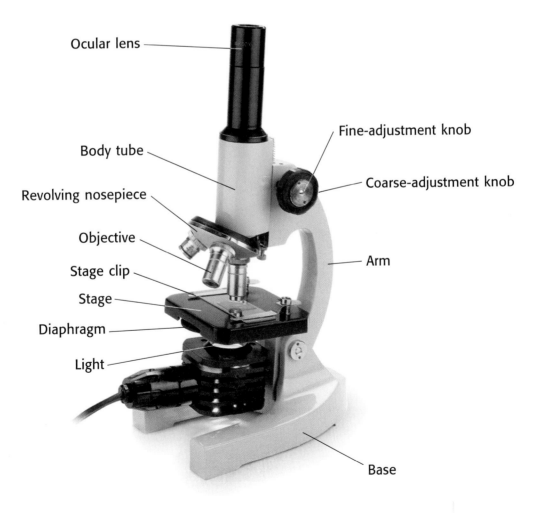

Ocular lens

Fine-adjustment knob

Body tube

Coarse-adjustment knob

Revolving nosepiece

Objective

Arm

Stage clip

Stage

Diaphragm

Light

Base

Proper Use of the Compound Light Microscope

1. Use both hands to carry the microscope to your lab table. Place one hand beneath the base, and use the other hand to hold the arm of the microscope. Hold the microscope close to your body while carrying it to your lab table.

2. Place the microscope on the lab table at least 5 cm from the edge of the table.

3. Check to see what type of light source is used by your microscope. If the microscope has a lamp, plug it in and make sure that the cord is out of the way. If the microscope has a mirror, adjust the mirror to reflect light through the hole in the stage. **Caution:** If your microscope has a mirror, do not use direct sunlight as a light source. Direct sunlight can damage your eyes.

4. Always begin work with the low-power objective in line with the body tube. Adjust the revolving nosepiece.

5. Place a prepared slide over the hole in the stage. Secure the slide with the stage clips.

6. Look through the ocular lens. Move the diaphragm to adjust the amount of light coming through the stage.

7. Look at the stage from eye level. Slowly turn the coarse adjustment to lower the objective until the objective almost touches the slide. Do not allow the objective to touch the slide.

8. Look through the ocular lens. Turn the coarse adjustment to raise the low-power objective until the image is in focus. Always focus by raising the objective away from the slide. Never focus the objective downward. Use the fine adjustment to sharpen the focus. Keep both eyes open while viewing a slide.

9. Make sure that the image is exactly in the center of your field of vision. Then, switch to the high-power objective. Focus the image by using only the fine adjustment. Never use the coarse adjustment at high power.

10. When you are finished using the microscope, remove the slide. Clean the ocular lens and objectives with lens paper. Return the microscope to its storage area. Remember to use both hands when carrying the microscope.

Making a Wet Mount

1. Use lens paper to clean a glass slide and a coverslip.

2. Place the specimen that you wish to observe in the center of the slide.

3. Using a medicine dropper, place one drop of water on the specimen.

4. Hold the coverslip at the edge of the water and at a 45° angle to the slide. Make sure that the water runs along the edge of the coverslip.

5. Lower the coverslip slowly to avoid trapping air bubbles.

6. Water might evaporate from the slide as you work. Add more water to keep the specimen fresh. Place the tip of the medicine dropper next to the edge of the coverslip. Add a drop of water. (You can also use this method to add stain or solutions to a wet mount.) Remove excess water from the slide by using the corner of a paper towel as a blotter. Do not lift the coverslip to add or remove water.

Glossary

A

addiction a dependence on a substance, such as alcohol or another drug (161)

aerobic exercise physical exercise intended to increase the activity of the heart and lungs to promote the body's use of oxygen (167)

alcoholism a disorder in which a person repeatedly drinks alcoholic beverages in an amount that interferes with the person's health and activities (162)

allergy a reaction to a harmless or common substance by the body's immune system (141)

alveoli (al VEE uh LIE) any of the tiny air sacs of the lungs where oxygen and carbon dioxide are exchanged (45)

antibody a protein made by B cells that binds to a specific antigen (137)

artery a blood vessel that carries blood away from the heart to the body's organs (32)

asexual reproduction reproduction that does not involve the union of sex cells and in which one parent produces offspring that are genetically identical to the parent (108)

autoimmune disease a disease in which the immune system attacks the organism's own cells (141)

B

B cell a white blood cell that makes antibodies (137)

blood the fluid that carries gases, nutrients, and wastes through the body and that is made up of platelets, white blood cells, red blood cells, and plasma (36)

blood pressure the force that blood exerts on the walls of the arteries (38)

brain the mass of nerve tissue that is the main control center of the nervous system (84)

bronchus (BRAHNG kuhs) one of the two tubes that connect the lungs with the trachea (45)

C

cancer a tumor in which the cells begin dividing at an uncontrolled rate and become invasive (142)

capillary a tiny blood vessel that allows an exchange between blood and cells in tissue (32)

carbohydrate a class of energy-giving nutrients that includes sugars, starches, and fiber; contains carbon, hydrogen, and oxygen (154)

cardiovascular system a collection of organs that transport blood throughout the body (30)

central nervous system the brain and the spinal cord; its main function is to control the flow of information in the body (80)

cochlea (KAHK lee uh) a coiled tube that is found in the inner ear and that is essential to hearing (92)

D

dermis the layer of skin below the epidermis (17)

digestive system the organs that break down food so that it can be used by the body (58)

drug any substance that causes a change in a person's physical or psychological state (160)

E

egg a sex cell produced by a female (109)

embryo (EM bree OH) a plant or an animal in an early stage of development; a developing human, from fertilization through the first 8 weeks of development (the 10th week of pregnancy) (116)

endocrine system a collection of glands and groups of cells that secrete hormones that regulate growth, development, and homeostasis; includes the pituitary, thyroid, parathyroid, and adrenal glands, the hypothalamus, the pineal body, and the gonads (94)

epidermis (EP uh DUHR mis) the surface layer of cells on a plant or animal (17)

esophagus (i SAHF uh guhs) a long, straight tube that connects the pharynx to the stomach (60)

external fertilization the union of sex cells outside the bodies of the parents (110)

F

fat an energy-storage nutrient that helps the body store some vitamins (155)

feedback mechanism a cycle of events in which information from one step controls or affects a previous step (89)

fetus (FEET uhs) a developing human from seven or eight weeks after fertilization until birth (118)

G

gallbladder a sac-shaped organ that stores bile produced by the liver (63)

gland a group of cells that make special chemicals for the body (94)

H

homeostasis (HOH mee OH STAY sis) the maintenance of a constant internal state in a changing environment (4)

hormone a substance that is made in one cell or tissue and that causes a change in another cell or tissue in a different part of the body (94)

hygiene the science of health and ways to preserve health (166)

I

immune system the cells and tissues that recognize and attack foreign substances in the body (137)

immunity the ability to resist or recover from an infectious disease (134)

infectious disease a disease that is caused by a pathogen and that can be spread from one individual to another (132)

integumentary system (in TEG yoo MEN tuhr ee SIS tuhm) the organ system that forms a protective covering on the outside of the body (16, 88)

internal fertilization fertilization of an egg by sperm that occurs inside the body of a female (110)

J

joint a place where two or more bones meet (10)

K

kidney one of the pair of organs that filter water and wastes from the blood and that excrete products as urine (67)

L

large intestine the wider and shorter portion of the intestine that removes water from mostly digested food and that turns the waste into semisolid feces, or stool (64)

larynx (LAR ingks) the area of the throat that contains the vocal cords and produces vocal sounds (45)

liver the largest organ in the body; it makes bile, stores and filters blood, and stores excess sugars as glycogen (63)

lymph the fluid that is collected by the lymphatic vessels and nodes (40)

lymphatic system (lim FAT ik SIS tuhm) a collection of organs whose primary function is to collect extracellular fluid and return it to the blood; the organs in this system include the lymph nodes and the lymphatic vessels (40)

lymph nodes oval masses of lymphatic tissue found in the lymphatic vessels that filter lymph (41)

M

macrophage (MAK roh FAYJ) an immune system cell that engulfs pathogens and other materials (137)

malnutrition a disorder of nutrition that results when a person does not consume enough of each of the nutrients that are needed by the human body (158)

memory B cell a B cell that responds to an antigen more strongly when the body is reinfected with an antigen than it does during its first encounter with the antigen (140)

mineral a class of nutrients that are chemical elements that are needed for certain body processes (156)

muscular system the organ system whose primary function is movement and flexibility (12)

N

narcotic a drug that is derived from opium and that relieves pain and induces sleep; examples include heroine, morphine, and codeine (163)

nephron the unit in the kidney that filters blood (67)

nerve a collection of nerve fibers through which impulses travel between the central nervous system and other parts of the body (82)

neuron (NOO RAHN) a nerve cell that is specialized to receive and conduct electrical impulses (81)

nicotine (NIK uh TEEN) a toxic, addictive chemical that is found in tobacco and that is one of the major contributors to the harmful effects of smoking (162)

noninfectious disease a disease that cannot spread from one individual to another (132)

nutrient a substance in food that provides energy or helps form body tissues and that is necessary for life and growth (154)

O

organ a collection of tissues that carry out a specialized function of the body (5)

ovary in flowering plants, the lower part of a pistil that produces eggs in ovules (320); in the female reproductive system of animals, an organ that produces eggs (113)

P

pancreas the organ that lies behind the stomach and that makes digestive enzymes and hormones that regulate sugar levels (62)

pathogen a virus, microorganism, or other organism that causes disease (132)

penis the male organ that transfers sperm to a female and that carries urine out of the body (112)

peripheral nervous system (puh RIF uhr uhl NUHR vuhs SIS tuhm) all of the parts of the nervous system except for the brain and the spinal cord (80)

pharynx (FAR ingks) in flatworms, the muscular tube that leads from the mouth to the gastrovascular cavity; in animals with a digestive tract, the passage from the mouth to the larynx and esophagus (45)

placenta (pluh SEN tuh) the structure that attaches a developing fetus to the uterus and that enables the exchange of nutrients, wastes, and gases between the mother and the fetus (116)

protein a molecule that is made up of amino acids and that is needed to build and repair body structures and to regulate processes in the body (155)

pulmonary circulation (PUL muh NER ee SUHR kyoo LAY shuhn) the flow of blood from the heart to the lungs and back to the heart through the pulmonary arteries, capillaries, and veins (33)

R

reflex an involuntary and almost immediate movement in response to a stimulus (89)

respiration in biology, the exchange of oxygen and carbon dioxide between living cells and their environment; includes breathing and cellular respiration (44)

respiratory system a collection of organs whose primary function is to take in oxygen and expel carbon dioxide; the organs of this system include the lungs, the throat, and the passageways that lead to the lungs (44)

retina the light-sensitive inner layer of the eye, which receives images formed by the lens and transmits them through the optic nerve to the brain (90)

S

sexual reproduction reproduction in which the sex cells from two parents unite to produce offspring that share traits from both parents (109)

skeletal system the organ system whose primary function is to support and protect the body and to allow the body to move (8)

small intestine the organ between the stomach and the large intestine where most of the breakdown of food happens and most of the nutrients from food are absorbed (62)

sperm the male sex cell (109)

spleen the largest lymphatic organ in the body; serves as a blood reservoir, disintegrates old red blood cells, and produces lymphocytes and plasmids (42)

stomach the saclike, digestive organ between the esophagus and the small intestine that breaks down food by the action of muscles, enzymes, and acids (61)

stress a physical or mental response to pressure (168)

systemic circulation (sis TEM ik SUHR kyoo LAY shuhn) the flow of blood from the heart to all parts of the body and back to the heart (33)

T

T cell an immune system cell that coordinates the immune system and attacks many infected cells (137)

testes the primary male reproductive organs, which produce sperm cells and testosterone (singular, *testis*) (112)

thymus the main gland of the lymphatic system; it releases mature T lymphocytes (41)

tissue a group of similar cells that perform a common function (4)

tonsils small, rounded masses of lymphatic tissue located in the pharynx and in the passage from the mouth to the pharynx (43)

trachea (TRAY kee uh) in insects, myriapods, and spiders, one of a network of air tubes; in vertebrates, the tube that connects the larynx to the lungs (45)

U

umbilical cord (uhm BIL i kuhl KAWRD) the structure that connects an embryo and then the fetus to the placenta and through which blood vessels pass (117)

urinary system the organs that make, store, and eliminate urine (66)

uterus in female mammals, the hollow, muscular organ in which a fertilized egg is embedded and in which the embryo and fetus develop (113)

V

vagina the female reproductive organ that connects the outside of the body to the uterus (113)

vein in biology, a vessel that carries blood to the heart (32)

vitamin a class of nutrients that contain carbon and that are needed in small amounts to maintain health and allow growth (156)

Glossary

Spanish Glossary

A

addiction/adicción una dependencia de substancia, tal como el alcohol u otra droga (161)

aerobic exercise/ejercicio aeróbico ejercicio físico cuyo objetivo es aumentar la actividad del corazón y los pulmones para hacer que el cuerpo use más oxígeno (167)

alcoholism/alcoholismo un trastorno en el cual una persona consume bebidas alcohólicas repetidamente en una cantidad tal que interfiere con su salud y sus actividades (162)

allergy/alergia una reacción del sistema inmunológico del cuerpo a una substancia inofensiva o común (141)

alveoli/alveolo cualquiera de las diminutas bolsas de aire de los pulmones, en donde ocurre el intercambio de oxígeno y dióxido de carbono (45)

antibody/anticuerpo una proteína producida por las células B que se une a un antígeno específico (137)

artery/arteria un vaso sanguíneo que transporta sangre del corazón a los órganos del cuerpo (32)

asexual reproduction/reproducción asexual reproducción que no involucra la unión de células sexuales, en la que un solo progenitor produce descendencia que es genéticamente igual al progenitor (108)

autoimmune disease/enfermedad autoinmune una enfermedad en la que el sistema inmunológico ataca las células del propio organismo (141)

B

B cell/célula B un glóbulo blanco de la sangre que fabrica anticuerpos (137)

blood/sangre el líquido que lleva gases, nutrientes y desechos por el cuerpo y que está formado por plaquetas, glóbulos blancos, glóbulos rojos y plasma (36)

blood pressure/presión sanguínea la fuerza que la sangre ejerce en las paredes de las arterias (38)

brain/encéfalo la masa de tejido nervioso que es el centro principal de control del sistema nervioso (84)

bronchus/bronquio uno de los dos tubos que conectan los pulmones con la tráquea (45)

C

cancer/cáncer un tumor en el cual las células comienzan a dividirse a una tasa incontrolable y se vuelven invasivas (142)

capillary/capilar diminuto vaso sanguíneo que permite el intercambio entre la sangre y las células de los tejidos (32)

carbohydrate/carbohidrato una clase de nutrientes que proporcionan energía; incluye los azúcares, los almidones y las fibras; contiene carbono, hidrógeno y oxígeno (154)

cardiovascular system/aparato cardiovascular un conjunto de órganos que transportan la sangre a través del cuerpo (30)

central nervous system/sistema nervioso central el cerebro y la médula espinal; su principal función es controlar el flujo de información en el cuerpo (80)

cochlea/cóclea un tubo enrollado que se encuentra en el oído interno y es esencial para poder oír (92)

D

dermis/dermis la capa de piel que está debajo de la epidermis (17)

digestive system/aparato digestivo los órganos que descomponen la comida de modo que el cuerpo la pueda usar (58)

drug/droga cualquier substancia que produce un cambio en el estado físico o psicológico de una persona (160)

E

egg/óvulo una célula sexual producida por una hembra (109)

embryo/embrión una planta o un animal en una de las primeras etapas de su desarrollo; un ser humano desde la fecundación hasta las primeras 8 semanas de desarrollo (décima semana del embarazo) (116)

endocrine system/sistema endocrino un conjunto de glándulas y grupos de células que secretan hormonas que regulan el crecimiento, el desarrollo y la homeostasis; incluye las glándulas pituitaria, tiroides, paratiroides y suprarrenal, el hipotálamo, el cuerpo pineal y las gónadas (94)

epidermis/epidermis la superficie externa de las células de una planta o animal (17)

esophagus/esófago un conducto largo y recto que conecta la faringe con el estómago (60)

external fertilization/fecundación externa la unión de células sexuales fuera del cuerpo de los progenitores (110)

F

fat/grasa un nutriente que almacena energía y ayuda al cuerpo a almacenar algunas vitaminas (155)

feedback mechanism/mecanismo de retroalimentación un ciclo de sucesos en el que la información de una etapa controla o afecta a una etapa anterior (89)

fetus/feto un ser humano en desarrollo de las semanas siete a ocho después de la fecundación hasta el nacimiento (118)

G

gallbladder/vesícula biliar un órgano que tiene la forma de una bolsa y que almacena la bilis producida por el hígado (63)

gland/glándula un grupo de células que elaboran ciertas substancias químicas para el cuerpo (94)

H

homeostasis/homeostasis la capacidad de mantener un estado interno constante en un ambiente en cambio (4)

hormone/hormona una substancia que es producida en una célula o tejido, la cual causa un cambio en otra célula o tejido ubicado en una parte diferente del cuerpo (94)

hygiene/higiene la ciencia de la salud y las formas de preservar la salud (166)

I

immune system/sistema inmunológico las células y tejidos que reconocen y atacan substancias extrañas en el cuerpo (137)

immunity/inmunidad la capacidad de resistir una enfermedad infecciosa o recuperarse de ella (134)

infectious disease/enfermedad infecciosa una enfermedad que es causada por un patógeno y que puede transmitirse de un individuo a otro (132)

integumentary system/sistema integumentario el sistema de órganos que forma una cubierta de protección en la parte exterior del cuerpo (16, 88)

internal fertilization/fecundación interna fecundación de un óvulo por un espermatozoide, la cual ocurre dentro del cuerpo de la hembra (110)

J

joint/articulación un lugar donde se unen dos o más huesos (10)

K

kidney/riñón uno de los dos órganos que filtran el agua y los desechos de la sangre y excretan productos en fomra de orina (67)

L

large intestine/intestino grueso la porción más ancha y más corta del intestino, que elimina el agua de los alimentos casi totalmente digeridos y convierte los desechos en heces semisólidas o excremento (64)

larynx/laringe el área de la garganta que contiene las cuerdas vocales y que produce sonidos vocales (45)

liver/hígado el órgano más grande del cuerpo; produce bilis, almacena y filtra la sangre, y almacena el exceso de azúcares en forma de glucógeno (63)

lymph/linfa el fluido que es recolectado por los vasos y nodos linfáticos (40)

lymphatic system/sistema linfático un conjunto de órganos cuya función principal es recolectar el fluido extracelular y regresarlo a la sangre; los órganos de este sistema incluyen los nodos linfáticos y los vasos linfáticos (40)

lymph nodes/nodos linfáticos masas ovaladas de tejido linfático que se encuentran en los vasos linfáticos y filtran la linfa (41)

M

macrophage/macrófago una célula del sistema inmunológico que envuelve a los patógenos y otros materiales (137)

malnutrition/desnutrición un trastorno de nutrición que resulta cuando una persona no consume una cantidad suficiente de cada nutriente que el cuerpo humano necesita (158)

memory B cell/célula B de memoria una célula B que responde con mayor eficacia a un antígeno cuando el cuerpo vuelve a infectarse con él que cuando lo encuentra por primera vez (140)

mineral/mineral una clase de nutrientes que son elementos químicos necesarios para ciertos procesos del cuerpo (156)

muscular system/sistema muscular el sistema de órganos cuya función principal es permitir el movimiento y la flexibilidad (12)

N

narcotic/narcótico una droga que proviene del opio, la cual alivia el dolor e induce el sueño; entre los ejemplos se encuentran la heroína, morfina y codeína (163)

nephron/nefrona la unidad del riñón que filtra la sangre (67)

nerve/nervio un conjunto de fibras nerviosas a través de las cuales se desplazan los impulsos entre el sistema nervioso central y otras partes del cuerpo (82)

neuron/neurona una célula nerviosa que está especializada en recibir y transmitir impulsos eléctricos (81)

nicotine/nicotina una substancia química tóxica y adictiva que se encuentra en el tabaco y que es una de las principales causas de los efectos dañinos de fumar (162)

noninfectious disease/enfermedad no infecciosa una enfermedad que no se contagia de una persona a otra (132)

nutrient/nutriente una substancia de los alimentos que proporciona energía o ayuda a formar tejidos corporales y que es necesaria para la vida y el crecimiento (154)

O

organ/órgano un conjunto de tejidos que desempeñan una función especializada en el cuerpo (5)

ovary/ovario en las plantas con flores, la parte inferior del pistilo que produce óvulos (320); en el aparato reproductor femenino de los animales, un órgano que produce óvulos (113)

P

pancreas/páncreas el órgano que se encuentra detrás del estómago y que produce las enzimas digestivas y las hormonas que regulan los niveles de azúcar (62)

pathogen/patógeno un virus, microorganismo u otra substancia que causa enfermedades (132)

penis/pene el órgano masculino que transfiere espermatozoides a una hembra y que lleva la orina hacia el exterior del cuerpo (112)

peripheral nervous system/sistema nervioso periférico todas las partes del sistema nervioso, excepto el encéfalo y la médula espinal (80)

pharynx/faringe en los gusanos planos, el tubo muscular que va de la boca a la cavidad gastrovascular; en los animales que tienen tracto digestivo, el conducto que va de la boca a la laringe y al esófago (45)

placenta/placenta la estructura que une al feto en desarrollo con el útero y que permite el intercambio de nutrientes, desechos y gases entre la madre y el feto (116)

protein/proteína una molécula formada por aminoácidos que es necesaria para construir y reparar estructuras corporales y para regular procesos del cuerpo (155)

pulmonary circulation/circulación pulmonar el flujo de sangre del corazón a los pulmones y de vuelta al corazón a través de las arterias, los capilares y las venas pulmonares (33)

R

reflex/reflejo un movimiento involuntario y prácticamente inmediato en respuesta a un estímulo (89)

respiration/respiración en biología, el intercambio de oxígeno y dióxido de carbono entre células vivas y su ambiente; incluye la respiración y la respiración celular (44)

respiratory system/aparato respiratorio un conjunto de órganos cuya función principal es tomar oxígeno y expulsar dióxido de carbono; los órganos de este aparato incluyen a los pulmones, la garganta y las vías que llevan a los pulmones (44)

retina/retina la capa interna del ojo, sensible a la luz, que recibe imágenes formadas por el lente ocular y las transmite al cerebro por medio del nervio óptico (90)

S

sexual reproduction/reproducción sexual reproducción en la que se unen las células sexuales de los dos progenitores para producir descendencia que comparte caracteres de ambos progenitores (109)

skeletal system/sistema esquelético el sistema de órganos cuya función principal es sostener y proteger el cuerpo y permitir que se mueva (8)

small intestine/intestino delgado el órgano que se encuentra entre el estómago y el intestino grueso en el cual se produce la mayor parte de la descomposición de los alimentos y se absorben la mayoría de los nutrientes (62)

sperm/espermatozoide la célula sexual masculina (109)

spleen/bazo el órgano linfático más grande del cuerpo; funciona como depósito para la sangre, desintegra los glóbulos rojos viejos y produce linfocitos y plásmidos (42)

stomach/estómago el órgano digestivo con forma de bolsa ubicado entre el esófago y el intestino delgado, que descompone los alimentos por la acción de músculos, enzimas y ácidos (61)

stress/estrés una respuesta física o mental a la presión (168)

systemic circulation/circulación sistémica el flujo de sangre del corazón a todas las partes del cuerpo y de vuelta al corazón (33)

T

T cell/célula T una célula del sistema inmunológico que coordina el sistema inmunológico y ataca a muchas células infectadas (137)

testes/testículos los principales órganos reproductores masculinos, los cuales producen espermatozoides y testosterona (112)

thymus/timo la glándula principal del sistema linfático; libera linfocitos T maduros (41)

tissue/tejido un grupo de células similares que llevan a cabo una función común (4)

tonsils/amígdalas masas pequeñas y redondas de tejido linfático, ubicadas en la faringe y en el paso de la boca a la faringe (43)

trachea/tráquea en los insectos, miriápodos y arañas, uno de los conductos de una red de conductos de aire; en los vertebrados, el conducto que une la laringe con los pulmones (45)

U

umbilical cord/cordón umbilical la estructura que une al embrión y después al feto con la placenta, a través de la cual pasan vasos sanguíneos (117)

urinary system/sistema urinario los órganos que producen, almacenan y eliminan la orina (66)

uterus/útero en los mamíferos hembras, el órgano hueco y muscular en el que se incrusta el óvulo fecundado y en el que se desarrollan el embrión y el feto (113)

V

vagina/vagina el órgano reproductivo femenino que conecta la parte exterior del cuerpo con el útero (113)

vein/vena en biología, un vaso que lleva sangre al corazón (32)

vitamin/vitamina una clase de nutrientes que contiene carbono y que es necesaria en pequeñas cantidades para mantener la salud y permitir el crecimiento (156)

Index

Boldface page numbers refer to illustrative material, such as figures, tables, margin elements, photographs, and illustrations.

Index

Index

Index

Credits

Abbreviations used: (t) top, (c) center, (b) bottom, (l) left, (r) right, (bkgd) background

PHOTOGRAPHY

Front Cover Mehau Kulyk/Photo Researchers, Inc.

Skills Practice Lab Teens Sam Dudgeon/HRW

Connection to Astrology Corbis Images; **Connection to Biology** David M. Phillips/Visuals Unlimited; **Connection to Chemistry** Digital Image copyright © 2005 PhotoDisc; **Connection to Environment** Digital Image copyright © 2005 PhotoDisc; **Connection to Geology** Letraset Phototone; **Connection to Language Arts** Digital Image copyright © 2005 PhotoDisc; **Connection to Meteorology** Digital Image copyright © 2005 PhotoDisc; **Connection to Oceanography** © ICONOTEC; **Connection to Physics** Digital Image copyright © 2005 PhotoDisc

Table of Contents iv (tl), Sam Dudgeon/HRW; iv–v (t), © Nih / Science Source/Photo Researchers, Inc.; v (bl), © Rob Van Petten/Getty Images/The Image Bank; x (bl), Sam Dudgeon/HRW; xi (tl), John Langford/HRW; xi (b), Sam Dudgeon/HRW; xii (tl), Victoria Smith/HRW; xii (bl), Stephanie Morris/HRW; xii (br), Sam Dudgeon/HRW; xiii (tl), Patti Murray/Animals, Animals; xiii (tr), Jana Birchum/HRW; xiii (b), Peter Van Steen/HRW

Chapter One 2–3 AFP/CORBIS; 4–5 (b–bkgd), © David Madison/Getty Images/Stone; 6 Sam Dudgeon/HRW; 8 Sam Dudgeon/HRW; 10 (c), HRW Photo by Sergio Purtell/FOCA; 10 (r), HRW Photo by Sergio Purtell/FOCA; 10 (l), SP/FOCA/HRW Photo; 11 Scott Camazine/Photo Researchers, Inc.; 12 (bkgd), © Bob Torrez/Getty Images/Stone; 12 (bl–inset), Dr. E.R. Degginger; 12 (r–inset), Manfred Kage/Peter Arnold, Inc. ; 12 (tl–inset), © G.W. Willis/Biological Photo Service; 14 (r), Sam Dudgeon/HRW; 14 (l), Chris Hamilton; 16 Sam Dudgeon/HRW; 18 (bkgd), Peter Van Steen/HRW; 18 (l), Dr. Robert Becker/Custom Medical Stock Photo; 18 (r), Peter Van Steen/HRW; 21 Sam Dudgeon/HRW; 22 Sam Dudgeon/HRW; 23 (t), Sam Dudgeon/HRW; 23 (b), Peter Van Steen/HRW; 26 (l), © Dan McCoy/Rainbow; 26 (r), Reuters/David Gray/NewsCom; 27 (t), Photo courtesy of Dr. Zahra Beheshti; 27 (b), Creatas/PictureQuest

Chapter Two 28–29 © Nih/Science Source/Photo Researchers, Inc.; 32 (l), O. Meckes/Nicole Ottawa/Photo Researchers; 32 (r), O. Meckes/Nicole Ottawa/Photo Researchers; 34 © John Bavosi/Photo Researchers, Inc.; 36 Susumu Nishinaga/Science Photo Library/Photo Researchers, Inc.; 37 (b), Don Fawcett/Photo Researchers; 39 © Getty Images/The Image Bank; 42 © Collection CNRI/Phototake Inc./Alamy Photos; 47 (l), Matt Meadows/Peter Arnold, Inc.; 47 (r), Matt Meadows/Peter Arnold, Inc.; 48 (b), Sam Dudgeon/HRW; 54 (l), Richard T. Nowitz/Phototake; 54 (r), © Paul A. Souders/CORBIS; 55 Courtesy of the Boggy Creek Gang Camp

Chapter Three 56–57 © ISM/Phototake; 65 (t), Victoria Smith/HRW; 68 Getty Images/The Image Bank; 69 Stephen J. Krasemann/DRK Photo; 70 (b), Sam Dudgeon/HRW; 76 (l), J.H. Robinson/Photo Researchers; 76 (r), REUTERS/David Gray/NewsCom; 77 (t), Peter Van Steen/HRW

Chapter Four 78–79 Omikron/Photo Researchers, Inc.; 85 (t), Sam Dudgeon/HRW; 89 Sam Dudgeon/HRW; 96 (c), Sam Dudgeon/HRW; 97 Will & Deni McIntyre/Photo Researchers; 98 (r), Sam Dudgeon/HRW; 98 (l), Sam Dudgeon/HRW; 99 Sam Dudgeon/HRW; 101 (t), Sam Dudgeon/HRW; 104 (l), Victoria Smith/HRW; 104 (r), Mike Derer/AP/Wide World Photos; 105 (t), Photo courtesy of Dr. Bertha Madras; 105 (b), SPL/Photo Researchers, Inc.

Chapter Five 106–107 Lennart Nilsson/Albert Bonniers Forlag AB, A Child Is Born, Dell Publishing Company; 108 (r), Visuals Unlimited/Cabisco; 108 (l), Innerspace Visions; 110 (b), Photo Researchers; 110 (t), Digital Image copyright © 2005 PhotoDisc Green; 111 © Charles Phillip/CORBIS; 114 Chip Henderson; 119 (tl), Petit Format/Nestle/Science Source/Photo Researchers, Inc.; 119 (cl), Photo Lennart Nilsson/Albert Bonniers Forlag AB, A Child Is Born, Dell Publishing Company; 119 (cr), Photo Lennart Nilsson/Albert Bonniers Forlag AB, A Child Is Born, Dell Publishing Company; 119 (br), Keith/Custom Medical Stock Photo; 119 (tr), David M. Phillips/Photo Researchers, Inc.; 120 (l), Peter Van Steen/HRW; 120 (cl), Peter Van Steen/HRW; 120 (c), Peter Van Steen/HRW; 120 (cr), Peter Van Steen/HRW; 120 (r), Peter Van Steen/HRW; 121 © Mark Harmel/Getty Images/FPG International; 123 Digital Image copyright © 2005 PhotoDisc; 124 Peter Van Steen/HRW; 125 Photo Lennart Nilsson/Albert Bonniers Forlag AB, A Child Is Born, Dell Publishing Company; 128 (r), Jim Tunell/Zuma Press/NewsCom; 128 (l), © Michael Clancy; 129 (l), ZEPHYR/Science Photo Library/Photo Researchers, Inc.; 129 (r), Salem Community College

Chapter Six 130–131 (t), © K. Kjeldsen/Photo Researchers, Inc.; 132 (br), CNRI/Science Photo Library/Photo Researchers; 132 (bl), Tektoff–RM/CNRI/Science Photo Library/Photo Researchers, 133 (t), Kent Wood/Photo Researchers; 134 (b), Peter Van Steen/HRW ; 136 (b), Peter Van Steen/HRW; 140 (t), John Langford/HRW Photo; 141 (b), Clinical Radiology Dept., Salisbury District Hospital/Science Photo Library/Photo Researchers; 141 (t), SuperStock; 142 (b), Photo Lennart Nilsson/Albert Bonniers Forlag AB; 142 (tl), Dr. A. Liepins/Science Photo Library/Photo Researchers; 142 (tr), Dr. A. Liepins/Science Photo Library/Photo Researchers; 144 Sam Dudgeon/HRW; 147 (t), Peter Van Steen/HRW ; 150 (l), E. R. Degginger/Bruce Coleman; 150 (r), Chris Rogers/Index Stock Imagery, Inc.; 151 (t), Peter Van Steen/HRW; 151 (b), Corbis

Chapter Seven 152–153 © Arthur Tilley/Getty Images/Taxi; 154 Peter Van Steen/HRW; 155 (b), Peter Van Steen/HRW; 155 (t), Sam Dudgeon/HRW; 156 (c), Image Copyright ©2004 PhotoDisc, Inc./HRW; 156 (t), Image Copyright ©2004 PhotoDisc, Inc./HRW; 156 (bl), CORBIS Images/HRW; 156 (br), CORBIS Images/HRW; 157 © John Kelly/Getty Images/Stone; 158 John Burwell/FoodPix; 159 Peter Van Steen/HRW; 160 Peter Van Steen/HRW; 161 (b), Peter Van Steen/HRW; 161 (t), ©1999 Steven Foster; 162 (tl), E. Dirksen/Photo Researchers; 162 (b), Spencer Grant/Photo Researchers, Inc.; 162 (tr), Dr. Andrew P. Evans/Indiana University; 164 Jeff Greenberg/PhotoEdit; 165 Mike Siluk/The Image Works; 166 Sam Dudgeon/HRW; 167 (t), © Rob Van Petten/Getty Images/The Image Bank; 167 (b), Peter Van Steen/HRW; 168 Sam Dudgeon/HRW; 170 (b), Peter Van Steen/HRW; 170 (t), © Mug Shots/CORBIS; 171 Peter Van Steen/HRW; 172 Digital Image copyright © 2005 PhotoDisc; 174 (t), © John Kelly/Getty Images/Stone; 174 (b), Peter Van Steen/HRW; 175 (t), Peter Van Steen/HRW; 175 (b), Peter Van Steen/HRW; 178 (l), Brian Hagiwara/FoodPix; 179 (r), Courtesy Russell Selger; 179 (l), © Eyebyte/Alamy Photos

Lab Book/Appendix "LabBook Header", "L", Corbis Images; "a", Letraset Phototone; "b", and "B", HRW; "o", and "k", images ©2006 PhotoDisc/HRW; 183 Peter Van Steen/HRW; 184 (t), Sam Dudgeon/HRW; 184 (b), Sam Dudgeon/HRW; 194 Sam Dudgeon/HRW; 195 Sam Dudgeon/HRW; 200 (t), Peter Van Steen/HRW; 200 (b), Sam Dudgeon/HRW; 211 CENCO

Credits